Steve Giddins

The French Winawer

move by move

EVERYMAN CHESS

www.everymanchess.com

First published in 2013 by Gloucester Publishers Limited, Northburgh House,
10 Northburgh Street, London EC1V 0AT

British Library Cataloguing-in-Publication Data
A catalogue record for this book is available from the British Library.

ISBN: 978 1 85744 992 1

Distributed in North America by The Globe Pequot Press, P.O Box 480,
246 Goose Lane, Guilford, CT 06437-0480.

All other sales enquiries should be directed to Everyman Chess, Northburgh House,
10 Northburgh Street, London EC1V 0AT
tel: 020 7253 7887 fax: 020 7490 3708
email: info@everymanchess.com; website: www.everymanchess.com

Everyman Chess Series
Chief advisor: Byron Jacobs
Commissioning editor: John Emms
Assistant editor: Richard Palliser

Typeset and edited by First Rank Publishing, Brighton.
Cover design by Horatio Monteverde.

About the Author

Steve Giddins is a FIDE Master and a former editor of *British Chess Magazine*. He spent a number of years of his professional life based in Moscow, where he learnt Russian and acquired an extensive familiarity with Russian chess literature and the training methods of the Russian/Soviet chess school. He's the author of several outstanding books and is well known for his clarity and no-nonsense advice. He has also translated over 20 books, for various publishers, and has contributed regularly to chess magazines and websites.

Other Everyman Chess books by the author:
The Greatest Ever Chess Endgames
The English: Move by Move

Contents

Series Foreword

Move by Move is a series of opening books which uses a question-and-answer format. One of our main aims of the series is to replicate - as much as possible - lessons between chess teachers and students.

All the way through, readers will be challenged to answer searching questions, to test their skills in chess openings and indeed in other key aspects of the game. It's our firm belief that practising your skills like this is an excellent way to study chess openings, and to study chess in general.

Many thanks go to all those who have been kind enough to offer inspiration, advice and assistance in the creation of *Move by Move*. We're really excited by this series and hope that readers will share our enthusiasm.

John Emms
Everyman Chess

Bibliography

Dangerous Weapons: The French, J.Watson (Everyman Chess 2007)

Ein Leben lang Französische Verteidigung – richtig gespielt!, W.Uhmann (Thomas Beyer Verlags Gmbh 1991) – also available in English as *Winning with the French* (Batsford 1995)

Play the French, vols 1-4, J.Watson (Pergamon/Everyman Chess, 1986-2012)

The Complete French, L.Psakhis (Batsford 1992)

The Flexible French, V.Moskalenko (New in Chess 2008)

The French Defence Main Line Winawer, J.Moles (Batsford 1975)

The Winawer: Modern and Auxiliary Lines, J.Moles & K.Wicker (Batsford 1979)

The Wonderful Winawer, V.Moskalenko (New in Chess 2010)

Introduction

The Winawer French is one of the great black openings, and is characterized by the initial moves:

1 e4 e6 2 d4 d5 3 ♘c3 ♗b4

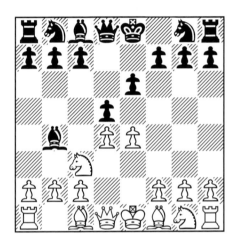

Black brings out his bishop to pin the white knight, thereby attacking the e4-pawn, and also threatening to capture on c3, thus damaging the white pawn structure. The result is usually an unbalanced middlegame, in which Black concedes the two bishops and takes on weakened dark squares, but where he has the superior pawn structure.

The variation is named (at least, in English-speaking countries) after Simon Winawer (1838-1919), a Polish player, although, as so often with chess openings, his right to be identified with the line is less than wholly convincing. He played it against Steinitz in his first international appearance at Paris 1867, losing a miniature, but it had already appeared before that in other games, including a Steinitz-Blackburne match game in 1863. Despite this, it is Winawer's name that has stuck.

These early efforts notwithstanding, the man who initially put the Winawer on the map was Aron Nimzowitsch, and indeed, on the Continent, the variation is sometimes referred to as the Nimzowitsch Variation. In the post-Steinitz era, the two bishops were regarded as a great strength, and the Winawer was consequently frowned upon. However, Nimzo-

Nimzowitsch was always a great 'knights man', and it is therefore not surprising that he should have been attracted to the Winawer, especially when one considers the similarity with his eponymous defence to the queen's pawn 1 d4 ♘f6 2 c4 e6 3 ♘c3 ♗b4.

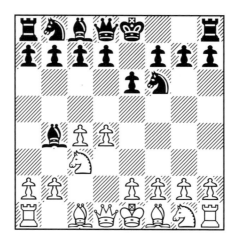

Here too, Black frequently surrenders the bishop-pair, in order to double the white pawns, and the affinity between the two openings is clear for all to see.

Most of Nimzowitsch's opponents played 4 exd5, which Tarrasch had argued was a good response against the Winawer, on the basis that the bishop was slightly misplaced on b4. Capablanca also used this continuation as White, most famously in the opening game of his 1927 World Championship match against Alekhine. His defeat in that game did much to make white players turn to 4 e5 as the main line.

That leads us on to the next great Winawer pioneer, who was Mikhail Botvinnik. He used the variation as his principal defence against 1 e4, from the early 1930s right up until the end of the 1950s, and if anyone's name should be associated with the opening, it should be his. After initially preferring 5...♗xc3+ in the main line, he also subsequently researched 5...♗a5, nowadays generally referred to as the Armenian Variation, but used by Botvinnik as far back as the 1946 radio match between the USSR and the USA, where he employed the line to beat Reshevsky in a famous game. Botvinnik's successes resulted in the popularity of the Winawer growing markedly at all levels, and by the 1960s it had clearly supplanted 3...♘f6 as the most popular third move.

The third of the great trio of Winawer practitioners was the East German Grandmaster, Wolfgang Uhlmann, who emerged in the international arena in the late 1950s. He has used the Winawer almost exclusively for over 50 years, still employing it to this day, in the veterans events and Bundesliga games that he still plays.

Two other names without whom the pantheon of great Winawer players is not complete are perennial arch-rivals Tigran Petrosian and Viktor Korchnoi. The former's practice tended to concentrate more on the closed lines with 4...b6, whilst Korchnoi was for much of his career the most successful player of the main lines. Both have left us a wealth of instructive games in this opening.

In more recent years, double Soviet Champion Lev Psakhis has probably been the leading Winawer player, with the Armenians Vaganian and Lputian also being important figures, especially in relation to the 5...♗a5 lines. The Winawer has lost ground in the popularity stakes at top GM level over the past 15 years, but the Spanish-resident Ukrainian Grandmaster, Viktor Moskalenko, remains a faithful practitioner, and his books on the opening are highly recommended (see the Bibliography).

I have myself played the Winawer for some 25 years, with great success. The unbalanced nature of the positions, and their clear strategical outlines, make it an opening that can be learned relatively easily by the average player, in my opinion. With one or two exceptions, it is an opening where memorisation of detailed tactical lines is much less important than understanding the plans and ideas, which makes it ideal for the amateur player. It is also a surprisingly flexible opening, where Black has many different move orders, which enable him to avoid specific preparation by the opponent, and also to choose the set-up he likes best.

I can heartily recommend the Winawer to players at all levels, and I hope this book will contribute to helping them understand the key ideas and typical plans behind this inexhaustibly rich and fascinating opening.

Acknowledgements

Thanks go to John Emms and Byron Jacobs of Everyman, for their usual highly professional and supportive job, and to the staff of the La Torretta café in Rochester, whose friendly atmosphere and superb coffee provided such welcome relaxation between sessions working on this book.

This book is dedicated to GM Neil McDonald and IM John Watson, which will doubtless come as a shock to both! It was watching Neil's successes with the French, whilst I was playing alongside him on the Gravesend team in the mid-1980s, that inspired me to take up the French myself. Once I decided to do so, the first volume of John Watson's *Play the French*, which appeared in 1986, provided the basis of my repertoire and continued to do so for the next 25 years. Between them, these two gentlemen changed my chess career, and brought me both great practical success and enormous enjoyment. I am deeply grateful to both.

Steve Giddins
Rochester, Kent
October 2012

Game 1
V.Smyslov-M.Botvinnik
USSR Championship, Moscow 1944

1 e4 e6 2 d4 d5 3 ♘c3 ♗b4

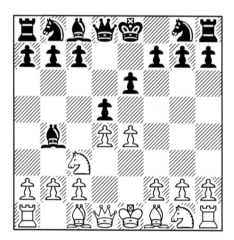

This is the move which characterises the Winawer Variation. Black brings out his bishop to an active position, pinning the white knight, and thus threatening to capture on e4. The main point is to try to force White to clarify the position in the centre.

Question: Isn't it true that Fischer once condemned the Winawer as bad?

Answer: It is indeed. Annotating his game against Darga in *My 60 Memorable Games*, he wrote: "I may yet be forced to admit the Winawer is sound. But I doubt it! It is anti-positional and weakens the kingside".

Question: What exactly did he mean?

Answer: Well, there are several points. Firstly, the old adage says one should develop knights before bishops in the opening, and the Winawer breaks that rule. However, that is a minor point. More importantly, in the French Defence, Black establishes his central pawns on light squares. With a light-square pawn structure, Black would usually need to retain his dark-squared bishop to cover the black squares, yet in most lines of the Winawer, he exchanges his king's bishop for the white knight on c3. That risks leaving his dark squares very weak, and also his kingside is vulnerable to the queen raid ♕g4, attacking the undefended g7-pawn. That can be hard to defend, because the move ...g6 would weaken the dark squares very severely.

> **Question:** Sounds like Fischer had a point!
> So why are you advocating the Winawer for Black?

Answer: Fischer was right up to a point, in that the Winawer has these drawbacks. But it also has some advantages. The exchange on c3 doubles the white pawns, and with White having been induced to close the position with e5, he frequently finds it hard to get his dark-squared bishop into active play – after all, most of White's pawns are on dark squares, obstructing that bishop. Black therefore argues that his own dark-square weaknesses are not as important as they may seem, because they are hard to attack. At the end of the day, a weakness is only a weakness if it can be effectively attacked. Black hopes that White's own weaknesses, notably his doubled c-pawns and isolated a-pawn, will prove at least as vulnerable as the dark squares in Black's camp.

> **Question:** So what you are saying is that
> the Winawer produces an unbalanced game?

Answer: Exactly, and that is one of its great attractions.

4 e5

Certainly the main move, although White has no fewer than five alternatives, of varying degrees of respectability. These fourth move alternatives are examined in Games 23-25.

4...c5

Similarly, Black has several alternatives here, which are considered in Game 22. However, the text is the most logical response. Black attacks the enemy pawn centre in the classic French Defence manner. He also allows his queen to come out to a5, from where it attacks the split white queenside pawns.

5 a3

Once again, not the only move, but the main line. White's fifth move alternatives are examined in Game 21.

5...♗xc3+ 6 bxc3 ♘e7

Black can also play 6...♕c7 (Game 19) and 6...♕a5 (Game 13), as well as even 6...♘c6, but the text is again the main line, and brings about something of a *tabiya* for the Winawer.

What can we say about this position? From White's side, he has the two bishops, and, as we have already noted, he can hope to make especially good use of his dark-squared bishop. It is clear that if this bishop can occupy the a3-square, for example, it could cut through the black position most effectively. White also has more space on the kingside, and if the black king castles kingside, White has ideas such as ♕g4, ♗d3, etc, with threats against the king.

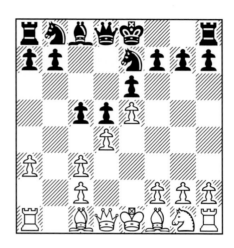

Question: So what has Black obtained in return?

Answer: He has damaged the white pawn structure on the queenside, and has also forced White to close the position to a significant degree, by the advance e4-e5. This means that White's bishop-pair may not find it so easy to become active, whereas Black's knights can jump around within the closed structure. Black has ideas such as ...♘bc6, ...♛a5, maybe ...♘f5, etc. He can also close the position even more, by advancing ...c5-c4. This will further block things, and also drive White's king's bishop from an active post on d3.

Question: What about the black king? Isn't it vulnerable on the kingside?

Answer: Maybe, although often it proves less easy to attack than one might think. In addition, Black is by no means committed to short castling. Frequently, he castles on the other side, especially if he has closed the position with ...c5-c4.

Question: And what about Black's traditional 'bad bishop' on c8?

Answer: That has a few options. One plan is ...b6 and ...♗a6, but that is only possible in relatively rare cases. More often, it comes to d7, and then either looks to take up a post on a4, harassing White's queenside, or else to emerge on the other wing, by means of ...♗e8, ...f6 and ...♗g6/h5.

Question: That looks rather slow!

Answer: Yes, and it often comes about only later in the middlegame, but if the bishop does manage to emerge over that side of the board, it can be a very good piece. With the position being relatively closed, slow manoeuvring is frequently the order of the day anyway.

7 a4

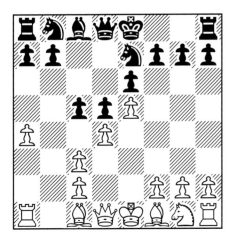

Question: What is the idea of this move? Shouldn't White be developing his pieces?

Answer: Actually, this is one of the two main approaches for White, in this position. As we noted above, a key element in White's strategy is to activate his unopposed dark-squared bishop, and the most obvious place to put it is a3, from where it will bear down the a3-f8 diagonal, cutting through the heart of Black's position. The text immediately sets about trying to do that.

Question: So is this good for White?

Answer: Not necessarily. There is one big drawback to the move, namely that the pawn on a4 can actually be quite vulnerable. Once the bishop goes to a3, the a4-pawn will be undefended, and Black can attack it with ...♕a5, and also maybe ...♗d7. In fact, if Black is determined to take the a-pawn, it is quite hard for White to defend it in the long run.

Question: So 7 a4 is a gambit?

Answer: Of sorts, yes. It is not a traditional gambit, seeking rapid development and a quick attack; rather, White is prepared to make a long-term positional sacrifice of the pawn, in order to get his bishop on to a good diagonal.

White can also adopt the same positional approach with 7 ♘f3 which often transposes. However, he also has a radically different approach to the position, with the sharp move 7 ♕g4, immediately attacking the g7-pawn. This move is examined in Games 16-18.

7...♘bc6

A natural developing move, bringing the knight to a good square, and exerting pressure against the d4-pawn.

8 ♘f3 ♕a5

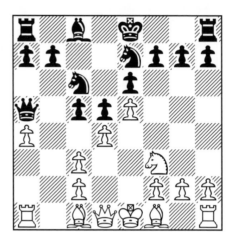

Once again, the most natural move. Black brings his queen to an active post, attacking White's vulnerable queenside pawns. The c3-pawn, in particular, is threatened with check, so must be defended.

9 ♗d2

Question: Wait a minute – I thought this bishop was aiming at the square a3?

Answer: Indeed it was, and Black will claim that he has scored a small success, by inducing it to settle for the more passive square d2.

Question: So why doesn't White defend the pawn with 9 ♕d2?
Is he afraid of the queen exchange after 9...cxd4?

Answer: As we will see later, White is not really afraid of the immediate queen exchange, but it is one problem with the move 8 ♕d2. In fact, the latter is a perfectly respectable option, that has been preferred by many white players in the Winawer (including both Fischer and Smyslov, as we will see). We will examine it in Games 8-12.

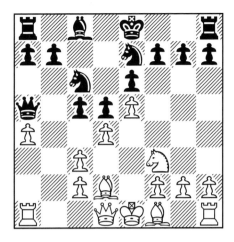

9...c4!?

> *Question:* Not sure why you mark this with '!?'. Isn't it almost forced,
> in view of the threat of 10 c4, attacking the queen?

Answer: That was certainly what most people thought, for decades, and ...c5-c4 became almost a reflex action in such positions. However, the modern preference is to retain the tension as long as possible in such positions, here with the move 9...♗d7.

> *Question:* So you are not afraid of 10 c4 then?

Answer: No. We will discuss these issues more fully in Game 3, but the bottom line is that this advance often leaves the white centre too weak and his position undeveloped.

> *Question:* Going back to the position after 9...c4, what is going on?
> I thought you said this was part of Black's plans anyway?

Answer: It is to some extent. For years, the move was seen almost as a *sine qua non* of Black's play in such positions. It was assumed that he has to close the position, to prevent the white bishops becoming too active. Botvinnik won quite a few games in such positions, usually by annexing the a4-pawn and eventually triumphing, but gradually white players learnt how to coordinate their forces more effectively, and the downsides of the advance ...c5-c4 began to emerge more clearly.

> *Question:* And these are?

Answer: By releasing the pressure on d4, Black gives White a free hand to reorganise his position and start building pressure on the kingside. He also weakens his dark squares further, by fixing another pawn on a white square; for example, the a3-f8 diagonal is now more inviting than ever for the white queen's bishop, should he ever succeed in freeing himself from the need to defend c3.

> **Question:** And what about the loss of the a4-pawn?

Answer: This is an irritant for White, certainly, but if he organises his counterplay with sufficient energy, practice suggests that he can exploit the time taken by Black to win that pawn. Even after winning it, it is very hard for Black to exploit his material advantage on the queenside.

10 ♘g5

A standard reaction to the early closing of the centre by ...c5-c4. Now there is no pressure against d4, White redeploys his knight, freeing his f-pawn to advance, and also looking to provoke weaknesses in the black kingside. However, with the white bishop not yet having left f1, there is also a case for the move 10 g3 with the idea of ♗h3, 0-0, ♘h4 and f4-f5. White would have good chances of developing an initiative in such a fashion.

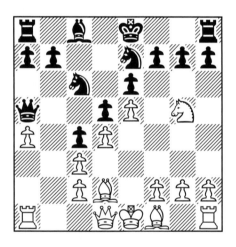

10...h6

> **Question:** Is this necessary? After all, you said White wanted to
> provoke some kingside weaknesses, so why oblige him?

Answer: That is a good point. On g5, the knight annoys Black, perhaps, but it is not clear how much real effect it has. The attack on f7 stops long castling, and moves such as ♕h5 may be in the air, but it is still not clear whether Black could not just play a move such as 10...♗d7, although then after, say, 11 g3, he still has to decide what to do about his king. It is probably hard to avoid the move ...h6 for too long.

11 ♘h3

Question: So the threat now is f4-f5?

Answer: Actually, the bigger threat is probably 12 ♘f4, followed by ♘h5. It is quite awkward to defend g7, and Black is reluctant to play ...g6 himself, because of the drastic further weakening of his dark squares.

11...♘g6

See the last note. Black stops 12 ♘f4.

12 ♕f3?

Question: Why is this bad?

Answer: It is just too slow. White intends to exchange knights on f4, recapturing with the queen, but, as we will see, his plan is too slow and Black can meanwhile take the a4-pawn with relative impunity. Keres recommended 12 ♗e2 ♗d7 13 ♗h5, another typical manoeuvre in such positions. After 13...♘ce7 14 0-0 we transpose into the game Planinc-Timman, analysed in the notes to Game 3.

12...♗d7 13 ♘f4 ♘xf4 14 ♕xf4 ♘e7!

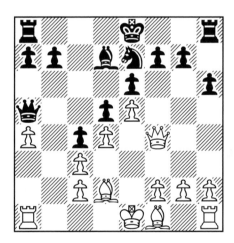

An excellent move, which underlines the inadequacy of White's approach. The knight move does two things: firstly, it transfers the knight to the kingside, where it can fulfil a defensive role (for example, ♕g4 can now be met by ...♘f5, defending g7), and secondly, it unmasks the bishop on d7, which simply intends to capture on a4. As we have emphasised above, taking the a-pawn is certainly something Black is very happy to do if he can get away with it, and White needs to react energetically on the kingside in response. Here, he has no real kingside initiative by way of compensation for the impending material deficit.

15 h4 ♗xa4 16 h5

White sets up the basis for a kingside pawn storm, with g4-g5 to follow, but this proves too little, too late.

16...♕b5

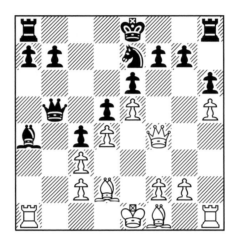

By unpinning the bishop, Black threatens another pawn on c2. The effectiveness of a bishop on a4 in such structures is something we will see elsewhere in this book.

17 ♔d1

Question: Eh? Surely this is not forced?

Answer: No, but White reasons that he needs to get his king away from the kingside anyway, so he can pursue his ambitions there with g4-g5, and he reckons his king is relatively safe on d1.

Question: Hmm. It all looks a bit desperate to me!

Answer: Indeed it is. Things have gone seriously wrong for White, and he knows it.

17...♖c8 18 ♗c1 ♖c6

The rook is on its way to a6.

19 ♗e2 ♖a6

Threatening 20...♗xc2+, hence White's next.

20 ♔d2

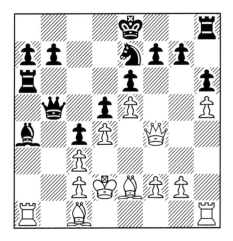

20...0-0!

Resolutely refusing to be frightened of ghosts. Botvinnik judges that the coming White pawn storm with g4 is nothing to be frightened of.

21 g4 f6!

The point of Black's play. Far from going passive on the kingside, he hits back, opening the f-file and including his rook in the defence along the sixth rank.

22 exf6 ♖xf6 23 ♕c7 ♖f7 24 ♕d8+ ♔h7 25 f4 ♕a5 26 ♕b8 ♘c6

The computer points out that the move 26...e5! is very strong here, with the point that 27 fxe5 (if 27 ♕xe5 ♘c6 28 ♕e3 ♖e7 29 ♕f2 ♖e4 and d4 drops) 27...♖f4 unexpectedly leaves White unable to defend the d4-pawn. Botvinnik's move is less incisive, although he has similar ideas.

27 ♕e8 ♖e7 28 ♕g6+

28 ♕f8 ♕d8 29 ♕xd8 ♘xd8 would enable White to put up tougher resistance, but it is quite understandable that Smyslov was reluctant to trade queens into a pawn-down end-game.

28...♔g8 29 ♗a3

29 g5 may look threatening, but in fact, after 29...♘xd4 30 gxh6 ♘xe2 31 ♔xe2 ♕xc3 White has no real threats against the black king.

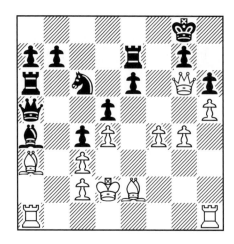

29...e5

Unmasking the rook on a6.

30 fxe5

30 dxe5 is slightly more tenacious, but even so, after 30...♞d4! (30...♞xe5 31 ♕f5 is much less convincing) 31 ♗b4 ♕b5 32 ♗xe7 ♖xg6 Black should win.

30...♞xd4 31 ♗b4 ♕d8

31...♕b5 is even better.

32 ♕xa6

32 ♗xe7 ♕xe7 33 cxd4 ♖xg6 34 hxg6 ♕b4+ 35 ♔c1 (35 ♔e3 ♗xc2 is no better) 35...c3 is decisive.

32...bxa6 33 cxd4 ♖b7 34 ♖xa4

Momentarily, White has a winning material advantage, but his scattered forces and exposed king soon suffer ruinous losses.

34...♕g5+ 35 ♔d1 a5

Good enough, but the computer points out that 35...c3 is mate in seven!

36 ♗f3 ♖xb4 37 ♗xd5+ ♔f8 38 ♖f1+ ♔e8 39 ♗c6+ ♔e7 40 ♖xb4 ♕xg4+ 0-1

Game 2
A.Tolush-M.Botvinnik
USSR Championship, Moscow 1945

1 e4 e6 2 d4 d5 3 ♘c3 ♗b4 4 e5 c5 5 a3 ♗xc3+ 6 bxc3 ♘e7 7 ♘f3

In the previous game, White chose 7 a4. The text is the other main positional attempt, and frequently transposes into 7 a4. However, as we will see, sometimes White can try to dispense with the move a3-a4 and exploit the tempo thus saved for more vigorous play on the kingside.

7...♕a5

7...♘bc6 is perhaps the more common move order nowadays, although the text can transpose.

8 ♗d2

Question: Is 8 ♕d2 possible here?

Answer: It certainly is, and we will look at such ♕d2 plans in Games 8-12. However, one could argue that with the white pawn not yet having advanced to a4, the move ♗d2 makes more sense, since he can dispense with the pawn advance altogether and play on the other wing.

8...c4!?

Once again, we see this thematic black idea, but also in a somewhat premature form. As we pointed out in the notes to Game 1, the threat of an early c3-c4 by White is less serious than it looks, whilst the white bishop has not yet committed itself to e2 or d3, so Black probably does better to remain flexible and develop with 8...♘bc6. This would transpose into more normal lines.

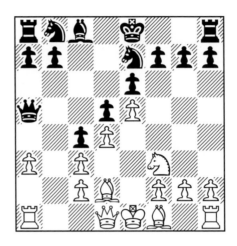

9 a4?!

Question: You don't like this typical move?

Answer: I don't greatly like it in this specific position, no. As we have discussed already, when Black closes the position with an early ...c5-c4, White needs to react vigorously on the kingside, else he is in danger of failing to develop any initiative on that wing, and just ending up watching while Black helps himself to the a4-pawn. That is what happened in Game 1, and we will see much the same scenario unfold in the present game.

As we pointed out in the last note, the white bishop being committed to d2 does not fit terribly well with the move a3-a4. I therefore think that, in this position, White should dispense with the advance of the a-pawn and get on with purposeful play on the other flank. There are two main ways of doing so:

a) The first is 9 g3, taking advantage of the fact that the bishop is still on f1. We pointed out such a possibility in Game 1 also. Play might continue 9...♘bc6 10 ♗h3 ♗d7 11 0-0 0-0-0 12 ♘g5 (12 ♘h4 is also possible) 12...♖df8 13 f4 with unclear play.

b) 9 ♘g5! is probably better still. White adopts the standard idea of provoking kingside weaknesses, whilst freeing his f-pawn to advance. After 9...h6 10 ♘h3 Black has:

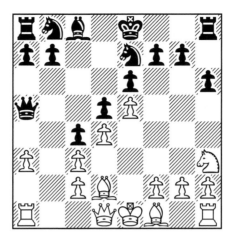

b1) 10...♘bc6 11 ♘f4 g6 (11...♗d7 12 ♘h5 and Black is forced into contortions to protect the g7-pawn) 12 g4!? ♗d7 13 ♗e2 0-0-0 14 0-0 and White will follow up with ♘g2 and f4, eventually preparing the break f4-f5. Once again, he must be rather better, albeit in a tough position.

b2) 10...♘g6 11 ♗e2 ♘c6 12 ♗h5 ♘ce7 13 0-0 with a similar position to that considered in Game 1, but with White having gained a tempo by omitting a3-a4. In addition, his a-pawn is much less vulnerable to capture on a3. The position is a tough one to play (Black is always very solid in such positions), but White must be somewhat better here.

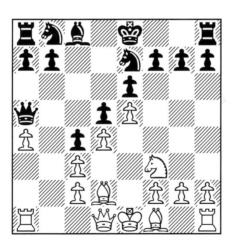

9...♘d7!?

> **Question:** This looks a bit unusual. Doesn't the knight usually go to c6?

Answer: Yes, but in this particular position, the text makes some sense. Black intends to win the white a4-pawn with the knight, by means of ...♘b6xa4. In Game 1, we saw him do this with the bishop, after ...♗d7xa4, but the knight is more active on a4 than the bishop. It attacks c3, and can be supported by ...b7-b5. *Ceteris paribus*, Black would rather take with the knight on a4, than the bishop.

> **Question:** So why doesn't this get played more often?

Answer: Well, as we have already discussed, Black cannot really force this position. If he wants to play the plan with ...c4 and ...♘d7, he needs to close the centre very early (as he did in the present game), but then White will usually have the option to dispense with the move a3-a4 and play for a more vigorous set-up on the other wing.

10 ♗e2?!

Once again, White plays too slowly and routinely, and allows Black to reach a good position. The move 10 ♘g5 was still best, although the tempo spent on a3-a4 makes it less effective here than in the previous note. A game D.Bronstein-V.Saigin, Moscow 1945, continued 10...h6 11 ♘h3 ♘b6 12 ♘f4 g6 13 h4 ♗d7 14 h5 with the initiative. However, even this is not so clear. In the game, Black played the terrible move 14...g5? and after 15 ♘e2 0-0-0 16 g4 ♖dg8 17 ♗h3 ♘xa4 18 f4 gxf4 19 0-0 his kingside was collapsing. But the Irish theoretician John Moles, in his classic 1975 treatise on the Winawer, pointed out that Black's structure is still very hard to crack after 14...0-0-0!: for example, 15 ♗e2 ♘xa4 16 hxg6 fxg6! 17 ♗g4 ♕a6! and it is not easy for White to step up the pressure. This line is a good illustration of the solidity of Black's position in such lines, even when White manages to work up a decent initiative.

10...♘b6 11 0-0 ♘xa4 12 ♘h4?

Another mistake, this time more serious. Thanks to Black's reply, the prospects of White ever getting in the break f4-f5 are reduced virtually to zero. Once again, White should try 12 ♘g5 h6 13 ♘h3.

12...♘g6!

When the white knight cannot retreat to g2, this move is highly effective against ♘h4. The exchange on g6 is virtually forced.

13 ♘xg6 hxg6

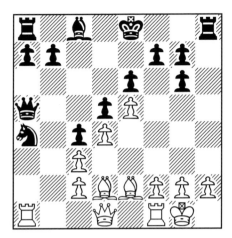

Now Black has an excellent position. The transfer of the pawn to g6 leaves White with no real prospects on the kingside, and he has no compensation at all for his pawn minus.
14 ♖e1 ♗d7 15 ♗f1 b5 16 ♕f3 ♖b8

> **Question:** What is the idea of this?

Answer: We saw a similar manoeuvre in Game 1. The rook is coming to b6, from where it will patrol the sixth rank. In this case, there is also a deeper purpose. Botvinnik sees that White is preparing to bring his bishop to a3, and he prepares a counter-measure against this.
17 ♖eb1 ♕c7 18 ♗c1 a5 19 ♗a3 ♖b6 20 ♕g3 ♕d8
Preparing ...♕h4, exchanging queens.
21 ♗d6

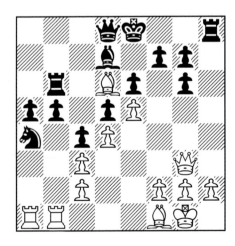

21...♖xd6!

Answer: It is a key idea for such French positions generally, and Winawer positions in particular. This positional exchange sacrifice eliminates White's best minor piece. Black already has a pawn for the exchange, and he will be able to round up the one on d6 as well. Materially, he will have enough for the exchange, but positionally, his knight will be worth a rook anyway.

Answer: The essential point is that the position is blocked. To be effective, rooks need open files. Here, they have none. This is why exchange sacrifices so frequently occur in the French, and we will see some further examples in this book.

22 exd6 ♗c6

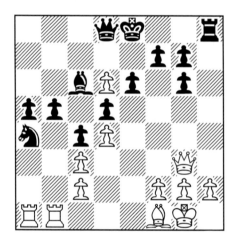

23 h3

White wants to be able to keep the queens on after Black's ...♕h4, hence he ensures the h2-pawn will not be attacked.

23...♔d7

Answer: It is a nice move, but is actually perfectly logical. Once again, it is all a consequence of the blocked nature of the position. The king is as safe as houses on d7, as White has no effective way to open the central files and get at it with his heavy pieces.

24 ♖e1 ♕h4 25 ♕e5

White desperately tries to keep the queens on, in order to complicate Black's task. If he acquiesces in the exchange, Black will just take on d6 and then set his central pawns in motion with ...f6 and ...e5. The latter is ultimately his key winning plan, and the only hope of preventing it is to keep the queens on, so that the central pawn advance will always result in some exposure of the black king.

25...♕f6 26 ♕g3

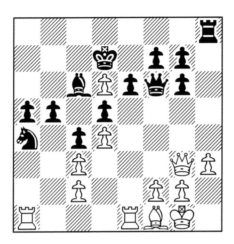

26...♖h4!

The start of another nice regrouping. Botvinnik intends to bring the rook to f4 and his queen to h4. Once he achieves that, the break ...b5-b4 will undermine the support of the d4-pawn. White's problem is that he has no counterplay.

27 ♖e3 ♖f4 28 ♗e2 ♕h4

Now White cannot avoid the exchange of queens.

29 ♗f3 b4

Not only is ...b3-b2 a threat, but the d4-pawn is now liable to drop off at any moment.

30 ♕xh4 ♖xh4 31 g3 ♖h8

31...♖xh3?! 32 cxb4 axb4 33 ♖b1 would give White much more hope. Instead, Botvinnik brings his rook back to defend the b4-pawn.

32 cxb4 axb4 33 ♖b1 ♖b8 34 h4 ♖b7 35 ♔h2 ♔xd6

White is defenceless.

36 g4 ♘c3 37 ♖a1 ♘b5 38 ♖d1 ♖a7 39 h5 g5 40 ♔g2 ♖a2 41 ♗e2 0-1

Here, the game was adjourned and White resigned without resuming. After Black takes on c2, his queenside pawns cost White a lot of material.

A classic Winawer game. It shows once again the need for White to react with vigour to Black's plan involving ...c5-c4 and the win of the a4-pawn. The other instructive aspect of the game is the power of Black's positional exchange sacrifice, and such sacrifices are very typical of the opening.

Game 3
J.Timman-V.Korchnoi
3rd matchgame, Leeuwarden 1976

1 e4 e6 2 d4 d5 3 ♘c3 ♗b4 4 e5 c5 5 a3 ♗xc3+ 6 bxc3 ♘e7 7 a4 ♘bc6 8 ♘f3 ♕a5 9 ♗d2 ♗d7

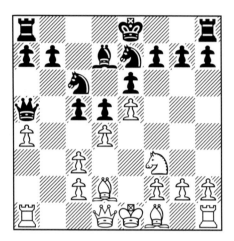

This is nowadays the main line of the ♘f3/a4 treatment in this variation. Both sides develop according to their desired scheme, and Black refrains from an early commitment to closing the position with ...c5-c4.

10 ♗e2

Question: This looks rather modest. Is it best?

Answer: For a long time, it was the main line. The problem is that the superficially natural-looking 10 ♗d3? simply encourages Black to play 10...c4 with tempo. However, White does have a major alternative in 10 ♗b5 and this move has actually become the most popular in this position, largely thanks to the variation seen in the present game, which White players have been unable to crack. The move 10 ♗b5 will be examined in Game 7.

10...f6

This is the key idea, which revitalised Black's position in this variation, when it was first introduced in the late 1970s. Black still avoids closing the centre, and instead attacks it again, creating the maximum tension in the centre of the board.

Question: But once again, Black ignores the threat of
a discovered attack on his queen, after 11 c4?

Answer: Yes, and this game will show what happens if White carries out that threat.

Before the discovery of 10...f6, Black almost always played 10...c4 here.

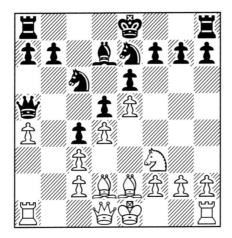

Answer: Probably not, but Black did experience a few reverses in this line during the 1970s, and these served to put black players off the position a bit.

Question: In Games 1 and 2, Black seemed to do very well in these blocked structures. So what changed?

Answer: Basically, white players learned how to handle them better. As we mentioned in the notes to the first two games, White needs to play dynamically. Botvinnik's opponents in the 1930s and 40s were still feeling their way in these lines, which were newly-developed at that time, and even players of the class of Smyslov took some time to work out exactly how they should handle their pieces in such positions. As an illustration of the modern understanding of the white structure, we will examine in full one of the key 1970s games, where White got things just right. The game in question is A.Planinec-J.Timman, Wijk aan Zee 1974. After 10...c4 (I have changed the move order somewhat to fit the present game), play continued:

11 ♘g5!

We have pointed out this standard idea several times in the notes to Game 1 and 2.

11...h6 12 ♘h3 ♘g6

Stopping the unpleasant ♘f4-h5, which ties Black down to the defence of g7.

13 0-0 0-0-0

Black almost always castles long in this variation, but John Watson suggests that 13...0-0!? followed by ...f7-f6, may be perfectly playable.

14 ♗h5 ♘ce7 15 f4

The same year, against the same opponent, Planinec varied his move order slightly with 15 ♕e1. However, his basic strategy was unchanged, and he won even more crushingly: 15...♔b8 16 ♗c1 ♖c8 17 ♗a3 ♕d8 18 a5 ♖g8 19 ♕c1 ♖c6 20 a6 b6 21 f4 f5 22 exf6 gxf6

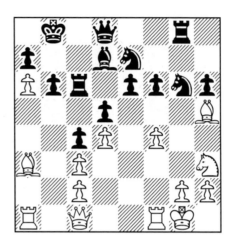

23 f5 ♘xf5 24 ♖xf5 exf5 25 ♕xh6 f4 (incredibly, the computer actually claims Black is okay after 25...♕e8 but even if true, this does not detract from the instructional value of Planinec's handling of the whole variation) 26 ♗xg6 ♗xh3 27 ♕xh3 ♖xg6 28 ♕h7 1-0 A.Planinec-J.Timman, Amsterdam 1974.

15...♖hg8 16 ♘f2 ♔b8

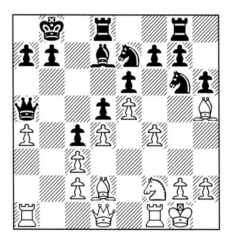

17 ♕e1!

Question: That looks a funny move!

Answer: Maybe, but it is very logical. Planinec wants to re-route his queen's bishop to the a3-f8 diagonal, so first he simply defends the c3-pawn.

17...♖c8

Answer: He could, and maybe even objectively should, just so as to have something for which to suffer. But whether he takes with bishop or knight (the latter after ...♘c8-b6xa4), he removes a guard from the key square f5, thus facilitating White's plan of preparing f4-f5. Black will also be tied up on the queenside, quite probably being forced into a subsequent ...b7-b5, which exposes his king. Note that in both Games 1 and 2, Botvinnik did not castle queenside!

18 ♗c1 ♕d8 19 ♘d1!

Another nice regrouping move. The knight is coming to e3, to support the advance f4-f5.

19...f5

Black has to find some play from somewhere, so he tries a kingside advance of his own, but this comes unstuck. However, it is hard to know what to recommend. If he sits tight, he is terribly passive and White can strengthen his position on both wings, with a free hand.

20 ♘e3 ♘h8 21 ♗a3 g5 22 a5

Another thematic idea in these lines. The despised a-pawn becomes a battering-ram against the black king position.

22...♗e8 23 ♗xe8 ♕xe8 24 ♕b1 gxf4 25 ♖xf4 ♘eg6 26 ♖f1 h5 27 ♔h1 f4

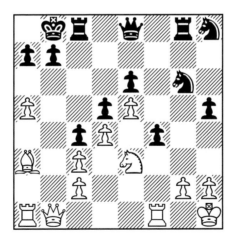

28 ♘d1!

This knight has already got through a lot of work in this game, and there is more to come. White is looking at playing ♘b2-a4, and then something with ♗d6+ and ♘b6+.

28...♘h4 29 ♗d6+ ♔a8 30 ♘b2

So strong is that threat that White does not even pause to defend g2.

30...♘f7 31 ♘a4 ♘xd6 32 exd6 ♕g6 33 ♖f2 ♘xg2 34 d7 ♖cd8 35 ♘c5 ♖b8

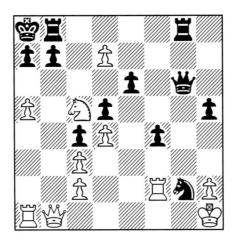

36 d8♕!

The final touch. White simply wins a piece.

36...♖gxd8 37 ♖xg2 ♕f7 38 ♕b6!

A very nice way of attacking the e6-pawn!

38...f3 39 ♖f2 ♕f4 40 ♘xe6 1-0

An extremely impressive performance by White. This game, and others like it, served to put Black off the standard plan with an early ...c5-c4, and sent him in search of the more dynamic approach with 10...f6, to which we now return.

11 c4

Not forced, but the critical move. The quiet 11 0-0 is seen in Game 4.

11...♕c7

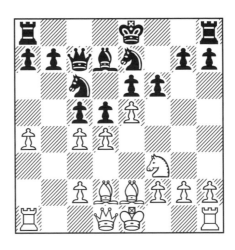

Answer: The main point is that we are heading for a much more open game than the sort of closed struggles we have seen hitherto in this book.

Answer: One might think so, but other factors are also relevant here. The main one is that White's centre has lost its stability. It is under attack from all sides, and cannot be maintained as a pawn unit. In particular, White cannot avoid the exchange on f6, which not only devalues his centre, but also opens the g-file. The safety of the white king frequently becomes an issue in such positions.

12 cxd5

Another Korchnoi game, played two years later, saw White hold back his second c-pawn, to try to keep his centre more stable, but he lost drastically: 12 exf6 gxf6 13 cxd5 ♘xd5 14 dxc5 0-0-0 15 0-0 e5 16 c3 (by comparison with the main game, White covers the d4-square, keeping the enemy knights out, but Black is very active nonetheless) 16...♖hg8 17 ♔h1 ♘f4 18 ♗c4?.

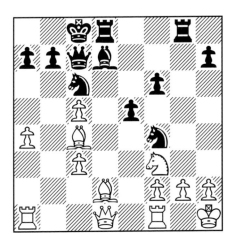

Answer: 18...♖xg2! 19 ♗xf4 ♖g4! (this is the move White had missed; his position is now falling apart) 20 ♕e2 ♖xf4 21 ♘d2 ♘a5 22 f3 ♘xc4 23 ♘xc4 ♕xc5 24 ♘d2 ♗f5 25 ♘e4 ♕c6 26 ♖ae1 ♗e6 27 ♖g1 f5 28 ♘g5 ♗d5 29 ♖g3 h6 0-1 L.Lederman-V.Korchnoi, Beersheba 1978.

Returning to move 14, a line which has been seen a number of times is 14 c3 0-0-0 15 0-0 ♖hg8 16 ♖e1 e5 17 c4 ♗h3 18 ♗f1 ♘b6 19 d5...

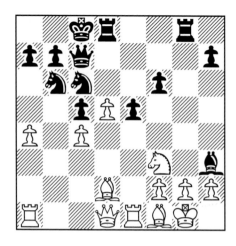

...and now 19...♘xc4! with the largely forced sequence 20 dxc6 ♕xc6 21 g3 ♗xf1 22 ♖xf1 e4 23 ♕b3 (or 23 ♕c2 ♕d5 24 ♗f4 exf3 when 25 ♖ac1! ♘e5 26 ♕xc5+ ♕xc5 27 ♖xc5+ ♘c6 28 ♖f5 is equal, but I.Mazi-I.Farago, Bled 1992, continued 25 ♖fc1?! when 25...♖ge8! with the idea 26 ♕xc4?? ♖e1+! favours Black) 23...♕d5 24 ♖ac1 (24 ♖fc1 ♘xd2 25 ♘xd2 ♕xd2 was E.Sharapov-K.Piorun, Grodzisk Mazowiecki 2007, and now 26 ♖xc5+ is equal) 24...♘xd2 25 ♘xd2 ♕xd2 26 ♖xc5+ ♔b8 27 ♖b5 ♖g7 28 ♖b1 ♖dd7 29 ♕e6 e3 30 fxe3 ♖ge7 31 ♕g8+ ♖d8 32 ♕b3 ♖dd7 33 ♕g8+ ♖d8 34 ♕b3 ♖dd7 ½-½ B.Spassky-V.Korchnoi, 4th matchgame, Belgrade 1977.

Returning to the immediate exchange on d5:

12...♘xd5 13 c4

John Watson considers this the most accurate move order. If instead 13 exf6 gxf6 14 c4 Black has the attractive option of 14...♘f4!.

13...♘de7 14 exf6 gxf6 15 dxc5 0-0-0

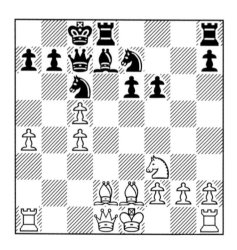

> **_Question:_** Wow! The position has changed rather drastically
> over the past few moves! What is going on?

Answer: The centre has cleared completely, and White has even won a pawn, at least temporarily. His bishops have full scope, particularly the dark-squared bishop.

> **_Question:_** So why isn't he better?

Answer: Several things. Firstly, his queenside pawns are quite weak. Secondly, although his bishops look active, the same can be said for the black knights. In the middlegame, knights may be inferior to bishops, when they lack secure central outposts, but if they have such outposts, they can be a match for bishops, even in an open position. Here, Black can play ...e6-e5, securing the d4-square, and then ...♘f5, when d4 offers a great central outpost for the knights. A further factor is that White's king will have to castle short, into the open g-file, which should offer Black good counterplay. All in all, the position seems dynamically balanced, but Black's practical results have been good.

16 ♗c3 e5 17 ♕d6

Timman decides that his king could be the more vulnerable in the middlegame, and therefore goes for a queen exchange. However, Black still has good, active play in the resulting ending, and Black has no real problems here.

17...♘f5 18 ♕xc7+

18 ♕xf6? is far too risky after 18...♖hf8 19 ♕g5 e4, with a virtually winning attack.

18...♔xc7 19 0-0 ♘fd4 20 ♘xd4 ♘xd4 21 ♗d1 ♔c6

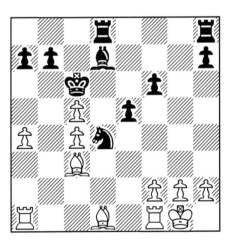

22 ♗xd4?

This is the real start of White's problems. The exchange gives Black a powerful passed pawn, which in the end, costs White the game. He could maintain the balance with 22 f4.

22...exd4 23 ♗f3+ ♔xc5 24 ♗xb7 ♗f5

With his strong passed pawn, and much the more active king, Black is simply better here.

25 ♗f3 ♖he8 26 ♖a2 ♖b8 27 ♖d2 ♖b1

27...♖b4 and even 27...♖b3 are more natural, but Korchnoi wishes to prevent any chance of White ganging up on the passed d-pawn and winning it.

28 g4 ♖ee1 29 ♖xe1 ♖xe1+ 30 ♔g2 ♗e4 31 ♗xe4 ♖xe4 32 ♔f3 ♖e5

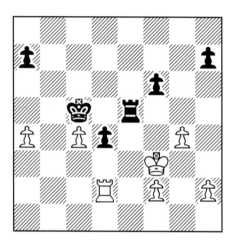

With his king cut off on the kingside, White is helpless against the enemy king and passed d-pawn.

33 h4

33 ♖d1 ♔xc4 34 ♖c1+ ♔b3 35 ♖d1 ♔c3 36 ♖c1+ ♔d2 37 ♖c7 d3 is no better. The king and pawn ending after 33 ♖e2! is also hopeless: for example, 33...♔xc4 34 ♖xe5 fxe5 35 ♔e2 ♔c3 36 ♔d1 ♔d3 37 h4 ♔e4 38 h5 ♔f4 39 f3 e4 and White loses his kingside pawns.

33...♔xc4 34 ♖c2+ ♔b3 35 ♖c7 d3 36 ♖xh7 ♖d5

Now the d-pawn is unstoppable.

37 ♖b7+ ♔c2 38 ♖c7+ ♔b1 39 ♖b7+ ♔a1 40 ♖b5 ♖d8 0-1

This game, and those quoted in the notes, is a good illustration of how Black's dynamic play enables him at least to hold the balance in the open positions resulting from 10...f6 11 c4 ♕c7. Although White's bishops gain more scope, his crumbling pawn centre and potentially exposed king give Black enough compensation. The realisation that Black does not need to close the position with ...c5-c4 was a major development in the understanding of this variation.

Game 4
F.Van Seters-V.Korchnoi
Skopje Olympiad 1972

1 e4 e6 2 d4 d5 3 ♘c3 ♗b4 4 e5 c5 5 a3 ♗xc3+ 6 bxc3 ♘e7 7 ♘f3 ♗d7 8 a4 ♕a5 9 ♗d2 ♘bc6 10 ♗e2 f6

For the sake of clarity in presenting the lines, I have changed the move order here. In the game, play in fact proceeded 10...c4 11 0-0 f6, transposing.

11 0-0

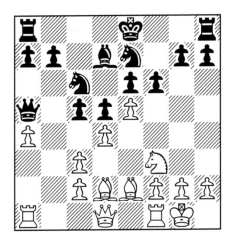

White declines to take up the gauntlet with the move 11 c4, instead preferring to complete his development and maintain his pawn centre. He reasons that Black still has to concern himself with the possibility of a subsequent c3-c4, which White will look to achieve in more favourable circumstances.

11...c4

Question: So Black plays ...c5-c4 after all. Isn't this a failure on his part? After all, he was trying to avoid this move, wasn't he?

Answer: No, not really. In fact, Black's argument is that he has gained from the transaction. What he wanted to do was play ...c5-c4, but without allowing the strong reply ♘g5, followed by the plan we saw in Planinec-Timman, in the notes to Game 3. With his pawn already on f6, Black can now close the centre without fear of this counter-plan. Having said that, however, the move 11...0-0-0 is also very playable, and would transpose into Game 3 if White then took up the challenge with 12 c4.

12 ♖e1 0-0

12...0-0-0 is also playable here, but the most common move is 12...fxe5: for example, 13 dxe5 (13 ♘xe5 ♘xe5 14 dxe5 0-0 is also comfortable for Black) 13...0-0 14 ♗f1. It is instructive to follow this line a few more moves, as we see some interesting play by Black.

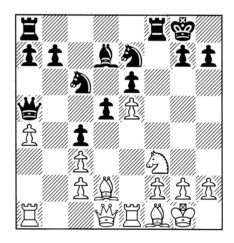

14...♖f5!

Question: Why is this good?

Answer: Black prepares to double rooks along the f-file, and also exerts pressure against the enemy e5-pawn. The latter can potentially be augmented by moves such as ...♘g6 and ...♕c7, and the e5-pawn can possibly become a serious target. This is perhaps one argument in favour of the simplifying knight capture at move 13, when White always has the possibility of f2-f4, defending the e-pawn. After 15 g3 ♖af8 16 ♗e3 ♖5f7 Black was comfortable in V.Ciocaltea-R.Vaganian, Budapest 1973.

13 exf6!?

13 ♗f1 was perhaps more consistent. The text helps Black to double rooks on the f-file.

13...♖xf6 14 ♗g5 ♖f7 15 ♕d2 ♖af8

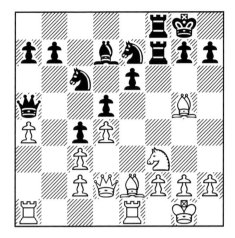

Answer: I think Black is quite comfortable here. His pieces are almost all well placed, his rooks exert pressure down the f-file, and he has pressure against the weak white queenside pawns.

Question: But what about his bad bishop on d7? And also his dark squares – the squares e5, c5, d6, etc, look like so many open wounds!

Answer: True, but one just has to get used to this in the Winawer. As we have remarked earlier, the positions are frequently unbalanced; that is to say, equal, but containing plusses and minuses on each side. Black has these weaknesses, sure, but he also has other trumps, such as the weak white queenside pawns. The bishop on d7 should not be despised, as it fulfils some useful functions – it defends the weak e6-pawn, and it also points at the a4-pawn. On a really good day, this bishop can find a new life on the kingside, after ...♗e8-g6/h5.

16 ♗h4

Question: What is this about?

Answer: It is a typical manoeuvre in such positions, the bishop aiming for g3, from where it controls e5 and attacks d6. However, Black is well placed to meet this here, since he can eliminate the bishop after ...♘f5.

16...♘f5 17 ♗g3 h6

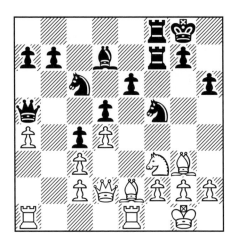

A typical move in such positions.

Question: It is just defensive, guarding against ♘g5, right?

Answer: Not entirely! As we will see, it also has the idea of a later ...g7-g5 advance.

18 ♖ad1?

This looks pretty pointless, and is a sign that White was struggling to find something constructive to do. Maybe he should have taken advantage of Black's failure to take on g3 last move, with 18 ♗e5. Black can then still eliminate the bishop, of course, but a subsequent ...♘xe5 will be met by the knight recapture on e5, which causes some problems for Black.

18...♕d8

Question: What is the point of this? Wasn't the queen well-placed on a5?

Answer: Up to a point, but with White having regrouped and brought his queen to d2, the pressure against c3 is not going anywhere. In addition, of course, the a4-pawn cannot be taken in view of 18...♕xa4?? 19 ♖a1 ♕b5 20 ♖eb1, trapping the queen. Black therefore decides that his queen has done her job on a5, at least for the time being, and so she switches to a more central position.

19 ♖b1 ♗c8

Black prefers this to 19...b6, so as to preserve the possibility of the queen returning to a5 at a later stage (see move 23).

20 ♕c1

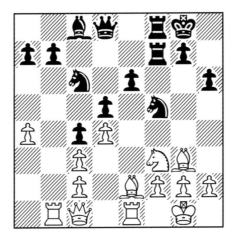

20...g5

Question: Crikey! He really did it!

Answer: Yes. This is an idea that is always in the air in these structures. Black threatens to take on g3 and push ...g5-g4, breaking through to the f2-pawn.

21 ♘e5?

This leads to exchanges which leave Black clearly better. White should probably just return the rook to f1, defending f2. Although this looks passive, it is not easy for Black to improve his position.

21...♘xg3! 22 fxg3

The tactical justification of Black's last is 22 ♘xf7? ♘xe2+, winning two minor pieces for the rook.

22...♘xe5 23 dxe5 ♛a5!

Question: What is the upshot of the last few moves?

Answer: Black has greatly improved his position. The weakness on e6 is now shielded along the e-file, the e5-pawn is isolated and weak, and the white queenside pawns are vulnerable. Black is clearly better.

24 ♛e3 b6?!

Korchnoi seeks to maintain control, but it is not clear why he did not simply take on a4, also attacking c2.

25 ♗h5 ♖f2?!

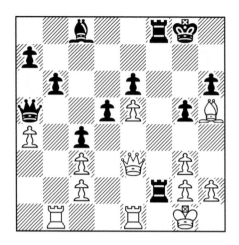

26 ⟦f1?

This allows Black a winning simplification. White should play 26 ⟦ec1, when the threat of 26 ⟗f3 forces the rook to retreat. After 26...⟦2f5 27 ⟗g6 Black cannot really avoid a repetition.

26...⟦xf1+ 27 ⟦xf1 ⟛c5!

27...⟦xf1+ 28 ⟗xf1 ⟛xa4 is certainly much better for Black, but Korchnoi realizes that the bishop ending resulting from the text is winning for Black, thanks to the weakness of the white queenside.

28 ⟛xc5

28 ⟦xf8+ ⟗xf8 29 ⟗f2 is no better after 29...⟛xe3+ 30 ⟗xe3 ⟗d7, when the a4-pawn drops.

28...⟦xf1+ 29 ⟗xf1 bxc5 30 a5

This is the point of the exchange on c5, but the a-pawn is only prolonging its life, not curing its terminal illness. The black king will march over and round it up in due course.

30...⟗d7 31 ⟗e2 ⟗f8 32 h4 ⟗e8 33 ⟗g4 ⟗e7 34 hxg5 hxg5 35 ⟗d2 ⟗d7 36 ⟗c1 ⟗f7

Now it is clear that the a-pawn is doomed, and the rest is silence.

37 ⟗b2 ⟗c6 38 ⟗a3 ⟗b5 39 ⟗b2 ⟗xa5 40 ⟗a3 ⟗b5 41 ⟗b2 a5 0-1

Although the a-pawn cannot itself be forced home, Black can create a second passed pawn on the d-file, which will be decisive.

Game 5
A.Suetin-W.Uhlmann
Berlin 1967

1 e4 e6 2 d4 d5 3 ♘c3 ♗b4 4 e5 ♘e7 5 a3 ♗xc3+ 6 bxc3 c5 7 a4 ♕a5 8 ♗d2 ♘bc6 9 ♘f3 ♗d7 10 ♗e2 c4 11 0-0 f6 12 exf6

Another different way of handling the position. In the previous game, White delayed this move until Black was able to recapture on f6 with the rook. Here, he takes at once, forcing the reply ...gxf6 which leads to another slightly different structure.

12...gxf6 13 ♖e1 0-0-0

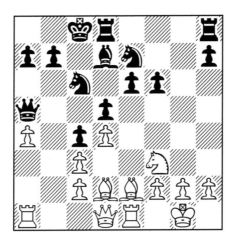

With the pawn on f6, castling short is clearly not very attractive, so this move is the most natural. The position before us could also be reached by other move orders, of course.

> **Question:** So what are the differences between this set-up
> and that which we saw in the previous game?

Answer: The pawn being on f6, rather than g7, strengthens Black's centre (especially the e5-square), and gives him the open g-file, along which he can attack the white king. White himself perhaps has slightly more chances of attacking the black king here, using the open b-file, but it is still not easy to do so, as the doubled c-pawns hamper White's communications. Very often in these structures, with the black pawn having gone to c4, White finds his position rather cut in two along the c-file, and it is rather cumbersome to shift pieces between the king's and queen's flanks. Overall, this structure with ...gxf6 strikes me as very comfortable for Black.

14 ♗f1 ♘f5

Note that one idea for Black in such positions is to bring this knight to e4, via d6. If it ev-

ever gets there, it is likely to be very powerful, so White has to fight against this plan.
15 ♕c1 h5 16 ♕a3 ♖dg8 17 ♖ab1

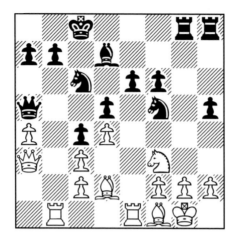

17...♘d8!

Another typical Winawer manoeuvre, worth noting.

> **Question:** What is the idea?

Answer: The knight moves away to meet the threat of 18 ♖b5. At the same time, it defends the e6-pawn, thus potentially freeing the bishop on d7 for more fruitful work, possibly taking on a4, perhaps coming to c6, to defend b7. The knight on d8 also defends b7, of course, so Black is already well prepared for the possible white attack down the b-file.

18 ♖b4 ♖h7

The rook gets ready to double on the g-file, as well as adding yet another potential defender to the b7-square.

19 h3

> **Question:** What is the point of this?

Answer: White wants to get his king off the g-file by ♔h2.

19...♖hg7 20 ♗f4 ♗c6 21 ♔h2

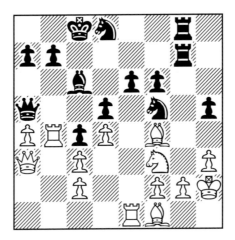

21...♔d7!

> *Question:* What's this? Surely after all the defensive moves to protect b7, the king does not need to flee the queenside?

Answer: No, that is not the idea. Black is actually using his king to defend the weakness at e6, so as to free his knight on d8 to come via f7 to d6 and ultimately, e4!

> *Question:* Hardly an everyday manoeuvre, is it?

Answer: Indeed not, but such deep manoeuvring is characteristic of these blocked Winawer positions.

22 g3?!

Uhlmann criticises this passive and weakening move, and recommends instead 22 ♖eb1, when Black must always reckon with a potential exchange sacrifice on b7.

22...♘f7 23 ♕c1

White's last intended 23 h4 and ♗h3, but now runs into 23...♘7h6! and a check on g4, so White changes his mind.

23...♘7d6 24 ♗xd6?!

This is also a huge concession. White's reluctance to let the knight into e4 is understandable, but losing his dark-squared bishop is a high price to pay. Now not only does any hope of dark-square counterplay disappear, but the g3-square loses a crucial defender.

24...♘xd6 25 ♕e3 ♘e4 26 ♘d2

This was White's idea, challenging the knight and seemingly forcing it away, but Uhlmann now exploits the hidden dynamism of his position.

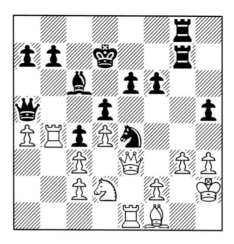

26...♕c7!

This very strong move threatens a rook sacrifice on g3, and virtually forces White to capture on e4, thus opening the diagonal of the oft-despised 'bad' bishop on c6.

27 ♘xe4 dxe4

> **Question:** But isn't Black just losing a pawn here?

Answer: He is losing the c4-pawn, yes, but this is irrelevant. He has terrible threats against the white king, such as ...h4 and ...f5-f4.

28 ♗xc4

It is hard to know what to recommend for White. The queen exchange 28 ♕f4? loses at once after 28...♕xf4 29 gxf4 e3!, and Uhlmann himself points out that 28 ♔h1 runs into 28...♖xg3 29 fxg3 ♖xg3 followed by a lethal discovered check with ...e3+. The best chance was 28 h4, but after 28...♗d5, Black prepares ...f5-f4, and White's position remains very unpleasant.

28...h4?

This natural move looks crushing, but the computer points out an unlikely tactical resource, which allows White to snatch a draw. Correct is the preliminary 28...a5, driving the white rook off the fourth rank, and only after 29 ♖bb1 h4, with a dangerous initiative.

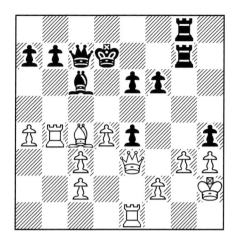

29 ♖g1?

Amazingly, White can force a perpetual check with 29 ♗xe6+! ♚xe6 30 d5+! ♗xd5 31 ♖xe4+ ♗xe4 32 ♕xe4+ ♚f7 33 ♕e6+ ♚g6 34 ♕g4+ etc.

29...f5 30 ♖bb1 hxg3+ 31 fxg3 ♖xg3!?

Uhlmann awards this an exclamation mark, but once again, the computer points out a superior defence for White. Objectively, Black should therefore have played 31...♗xa4 32 ♗b5+ ♗xb5 33 ♖xb5 b6 with a solid advantage.

32 ♖xg3 f4 33 ♖xg8?

Here, the remarkable 33 ♖f1! ♖xg3 34 ♕xf4 ♕xf4 35 ♖xf4 ♖xc3 36 ♗b3 allows White to put up tough resistance.

33...fxe3+ 34 ♚g2

No doubt missing Black's next. 34 ♚g3 is a more tenacious defence.

34...♚d6!

This nice move sets up ...♕f7, with decisive effect.

35 ♗e2?

Collapsing at once, but other moves also lose: for instance, 35 ♖f1 ♗xa4, or 35 ♖g3 ♗e8 36 ♗e2 ♕xc3.

35...♕f7 0-1

Despite the tactical opportunities missed by both players over the last few moves, this is a highly instructive game for Uhlmann's middlegame manoeuvring. Wolfgang Uhlmann was of course the world's greatest Winawer exponent for over 40 years, using it as virtually his exclusive defence to 1 e4, and winning many fine games with it. We will see several others later in this book.

Game 6
R.Byrne-V.Korchnoi
London 1979

This game was played in the BBC televised tournament, *The Master Game*, in which the players afterwards recorded an abbreviated version of their thoughts during the game. I have made use of these comments below, as they shed some interesting light on the whole Winawer variation.

1 e4 e6 2 d4 d5 3 ♘c3 ♗b4 4 e5 c5 5 a3 ♗xc3+ 6 bxc3 ♘e7 7 ♘f3 ♕a5 8 ♗d2 ♘bc6 9 ♗d3!?

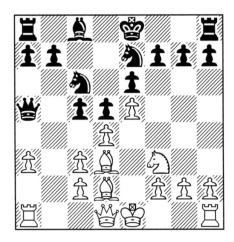

Rather an unusual move, but one with which Byrne had experimented previously. White is prepared to sacrifice a tempo, in order to provoke the advance ...c5-c4, clarifying the position.

9...c4 10 ♗f1

Question: Uh? What's this?

Answer: White's idea is to play g3 and ♗h3. We have seen in previous games how White often does this anyway, having first played ♗e2, 0-0 and ♖e1; here, he hopes to gain time on that.

10...f6!?

This is a distinctly risky move in this position, as Black's king is rather exposed after the exchange on f6. After 10...♗d7, Korchnoi was worried about the standard idea 11 ♘g5, provoking weaknesses. He therefore decided to play the provocative text, partly motivated also by the tournament situation, which required him to play for a win. It is a typical example of the kind of 'heroic defence', often practised by Lasker (Korchnoi's hero) and Nimzowitsch – Black invites difficulties, in order to achieve a fighting game, and create an imbalance, where winning chances are also available.

11 exf6 gxf6 12 ♘h4!

This is the drawback to Black's plan. Now ♕h5+ is a highly unpleasant threat. Against quiet development, Black could play ...♗d7 and ...0-0-0, reaching a position similar to the previous game.

12...0-0

Practically forced, but the king is, of course, not terribly secure on the kingside.

13 g3 ♖f7 14 ♗g2 ♗d7 15 0-0 ♘g6 16 ♘xg6 hxg6 17 h4

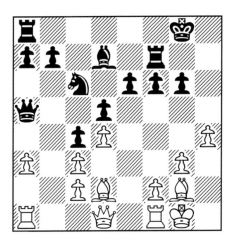

Question: I don't like the look of Black's game here!

Answer: Indeed, White's opening plan has worked out quite nicely, and he has a useful initiative. In his TV commentary, Korchnoi admitted that White's position "is clearly better – his king is better protected and he has the two bishops. They don't play right now, but sooner or later, the position will get open".

Question: So why have you included this game?
It hardly looks like model play by Black!

Answer: No, but that is in many ways *why* I have included it. It is a really instructive example of how hard these positions can be to break down, even when they go a bit wrong. The fact of the matter is that, without doing anything obviously wrong, Byrne's position seems to tread water from now on, and he is gradually outplayed. Korchnoi's handling of the position is masterly, and shows how to play such structures.

17...♖h7!

The first step. Black must prevent the advance h4-h5.

18 ♖e1!?

This can hardly be bad, but it is the start of this 'running on the spot' approach that White finds himself unwittingly following. Perhaps he should have played 18 ♗f3, enforcing h4-h5.

18...♖e8 19 ♕f3 ♔g7

White attacks things, Black defends them! At each step, White is invited to come up with something else to do.

20 ♗f4

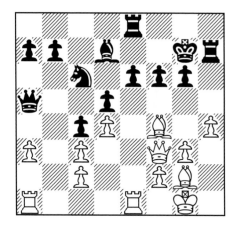

20...♘d8!

A really excellent move, and a manoeuvre which we saw to good effect in the last game also. Black needs to protect his dark squares, so the knight comes to f7. From there, it rather 'dominates' the white bishop on f4, covering the squares d6, e5, g5 and h6, which the bishop attacks.

21 ♖e2 ♘f7

> *Question:* Isn't White still better here?

Answer: Objectively, perhaps he should be, but he has real trouble finding something to do. In fact, Byrne made a memorable comment here: "It's always a problem; every time I found the same thing. It looks at times as though in this opening both sides get stuck in a sticky pudding after about 15 moves". This is rather a good description of what often happens – the heavyweight manoeuvring struggles that often arise in these blocked Winawer structures resemble a bit of a sticky pudding, with both sides finding it hard to improve their positions. But in this example, Black continues to do so, whilst White struggles.

22 ♖e3

> *Question:* That looks rather strange! The rook has only just gone to e2.

Answer: Yes, and it is a sign that Byrne was really struggling for a plan. His last move had intended 22 ♖ae1, but now he backed out, because he was afraid Korchnoi would simply take the a-pawn, when White has no follow-up. With the white queen having to guard c3, we see that two of White's most powerful pieces are tied down to defending the weak queenside pawns.

22...♖hh8

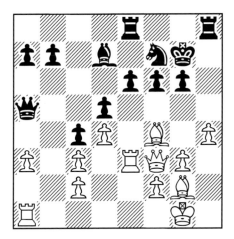

Question: Idea?

Answer: Just slightly improving his position. Korchnoi looks forward to the day when he will be able to unite his rooks behind the e-pawn. At the moment, he still has to worry about h4-h5, but the day may come, and meanwhile, he continues to invite White to think of something to do.

23 ♕e2

Question: Now what is he up to?

Answer: White intends to bring his queen to d2, defending c3 from a different square. He is still rather fumbling around for a constructive idea.

23...♗c6!

Question: Why the exclamation mark?

Answer: It is as much for psychological effect as anything else. Korchnoi reminds White that his c3-pawn is still under attack, so Black can dangle the e6-pawn under White's nose with impunity.

24 ♕d2

24 ♖xe6? ♖xe6 25 ♕xe6 ♕xc3 would leave half the white position *en prise*. The text de-

fends c3 again, but now h4-h5 is no longer supported, and Korchnoi immediately takes advantage of this.

24...♖e7! 25 ♖e2

White simply does not know what to do, whereas Black steadily improves his position.

25...♖he8

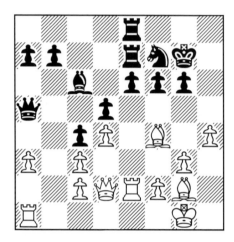

Suddenly, Black is ready to break in the centre with ...e6-e5. White has made no progress at all over the past 7-8 moves, whereas Black has regrouped most of his pieces – the knight has come to f7, the bishop to c6 and the rooks to e7 and e8.

26 g4

Rather a desperate lunge, but Byrne was by now feeling enormously frustrated by the position, and felt that he had to do something before the black pawns started to roll.

26...e5 27 ♗g3 e4 28 g5 fxg5 29 hxg5 ♗d7!

With the change in central structure, Black's bishop no longer fulfils any function on c6, and so it seeks pastures new.

30 ♗f4

The g5-pawn is now starting to be vulnerable, and so White defends it, in anticipation of his next move.

30...♗g4 31 ♖e3 ♕a6!

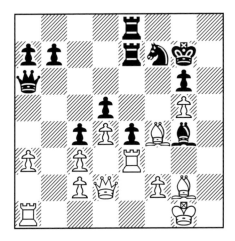

Question: What is the idea of this?

Answer: The queen has done a sterling job on a5, tying the white pieces down to the defence of the c3- and a3-pawns. Now at last she transfers to the other wing, where there are new fish to fry, namely the g5-pawn.

32 ♖g3 ♕e6 33 ♕e3 ♕f5 34 ♔f1 ♖h8

The rook is looking at h5, attacking the g5-pawn again, or at a penetration down the h-file.

35 ♔e1 ♗f3!

A very nice move. With the removal of the bishop from g2, the black rook will be able to penetrate along the h-file.

36 ♔d2

36 ♗xf3 exf3 37 ♕xe7 ♖h1+ 38 ♔d2 ♕xf4+, winning a piece, is the tactical point of Black's last move.

36...♖h4

The white army is being harried at every turn, while the poor rook on a1 has still not moved.

37 ♗b8 ♗xg2 38 ♖xg2 ♖h3

Decisive. Now the g5-pawn drops off.

39 ♖g3 ♖xg3 40 ♕xg3 ♘xg5

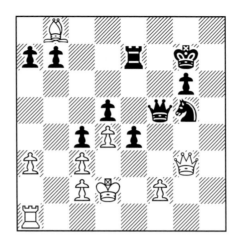

The game is basically over. White is a pawn down, and still has weaknesses on f2, c3 and a3. In addition, the black knight now penetrates very effectively on the light squares, which White's once-proud 'anti-Winawer' bishop cannot protect.

41 ♔c1 ♞f3 42 ♗xa7

White recovers his pawn, but his pieces are hopelessly scattered and inactive, whereas Black's compact army is poised to overrun the kingside.

42...♕g5+ 43 ♕xg5 ♞xg5 44 ♗b8 ♜f7 45 ♜b1?

45 ♗g3? leads to the instructive variation 45...e3 46 fxe3 ♜f1+ 47 ♔b2 ♜xa1 48 ♔xa1 ♞e4 with a textbook knight against bad bishop ending.

This is rather ironic, considering that the dark-squared bishop is supposed to be White's pride and joy in the Winawer, whereas it is Black whose bishop is traditionally bad! The pawn on e3 is useless, whilst the g5-pawn will cost White a piece.

However, 45 ♗e5+ was a little more tenacious, although 45...♔g8 (45...♔h6 46 ♔b2 ♜f3 is probably also good enough) 46 ♗g3 e3 47 fxe3 ♖f1+ 48 ♔b2 ♖xa1 49 ♔xa1 ♘e4 is still winning.

45...e3

45...♖xf2 also wins, but Korchnoi prefers to stick with the plan outlined in the previous note.

46 f4 ♘e4 47 ♔b2

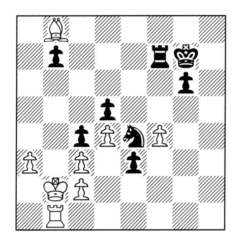

47...g5!

Forcing White to open the f-file, after which the rook supports the passed e-pawn.

48 fxg5 e2 49 ♖e1

Korchnoi points out that Black also wins after 49 ♗e5+ ♔g6 50 ♗f6 ♘xg5!: for example, 51 ♗xg5 ♔xg5 52 ♖e1 ♖e7! 53 ♔c1 ♔f4 54 ♔d2 ♔f3 55 a4 ♔f2 56 a5 ♖e4 and White is in zugzwang.

49...♖f2 0-1

There is no defence to the knight transfer to f3.

A really great Winawer game, which is enormously instructive. It shows the kind of patience Black must be prepared to show in such positions, especially when things have gone a little wrong for him. Korchnoi does not panic, but carefully covers his weaknesses, meets White's threats, and then gradually improves his position. White, on the other hand, finds it extremely hard to come up with a constructive plan, and is gradually outplayed. One should also bear in mind that Robert Byrne was no fool – a very strong and experienced grandmaster, he had appeared in the Candidates Tournament just five years before this game was played. When a player of his class finds the white side of the Winawer so hard to play, all white players should pause for thought.

Game 7
R.Byrne-R.Vaganian
Moscow 1975

1 e4 e6 2 d4 d5 3 ♘c3 ♗b4 4 e5 ♘e7 5 a3 ♗xc3+ 6 bxc3 c5 7 a4 ♘bc6 8 ♘f3 ♕a5 9 ♗d2 ♗d7 10 ♗b5

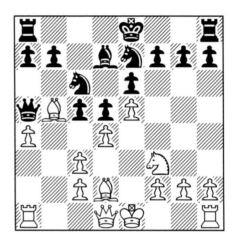

Question: Instead of 10 ♗e2. What is the idea?

Answer: The move was first played by the American Grandmaster, Robert Byrne, but most of the credit for popularising it goes to England's John Nunn. The bishop takes up a more active post, exerting greater pressure against the centre (notably supporting e5, by threatening to take on c6 at some moment).

Question: But can't Black just chase it away with ...a6?

Answer: Indeed; White hopes that this will prove a weakening, and/or a loss of tempo.
10...♕c7

Question: So what is the point of the text?

Answer: Black gets the queen out of the way of the bishop on d2, and prepares to adopt a set-up which is very similar to one we will see in the lines with an early ...♕c7 by Black – see Game 14.
The text is one of four main alternatives:
a) 10...a6 is the most principled response, simply putting the question to the bishop at

once. Byrne's original idea was 11 ♗e2, hoping that the pawn being on a6 will represent a weakness for Black, but practice has not really borne this out. After 11...f6, play proceeds much as Games 3-5. The b7-pawn may sometimes be a little weaker than usual, especially if Black castles short (a later ♖b1 by White can no longer be met by ...b6), but it is hard to believe that Black need lose a great deal of sleep over this nuance. White has also tried 11 ♗xc6, but then both 11...♘xc6 and 11...♗xc6 seem perfectly adequate for Black.

> **Question:** So 10...a6 looks like a very easy and
> straightforward response to 10 ♗b5 then?

Answer: Yes, and for that reason, it is John Watson's recommendation for Black.

b) 10...c4 is another principled response, cutting off the bishop from its home base and ensuring it must exchange itself. However, as we have already noted in this book, the pendulum of opinion has swung against the commitment ...c5-c4 in many Winawer lines, and this is no exception. An excellent practical example of the merits of White's play was the game M.Chandler-V.Ivanchuk, Manila Interzonal 1990. Chandler's opening play was frequently influenced by his friend John Nunn, and this was one successful example: 11 0-0 0-0-0

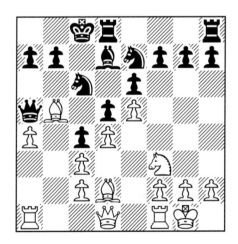

12 ♗c1! (exploiting the tactic 12...♕xc3?? 13 ♗d2 to re-route the bishop to the a3-f8 diagonal, without having to waste a tempo defending the c3-pawn) 12...f6 (another bad advert for Black's set-up was the following: 12...h6 13 ♗a3 f5 14 exf6 gxf6 15 ♖e1 ♖de8 16 ♘h4 ♕xc3 17 ♗xe7 ♘xe7 18 ♗xd7+ ♔xd7 19 ♖b1 b6 20 ♖e3 ♕a5 21 ♕g4 ♘c6 22 ♕g7+ ♔c8 23 ♘g6 ♖hg8 24 ♕xf6 and Black did not last much longer: 24...♕d2 25 ♖xe6 ♘xd4 26 ♘e7+ ♔b7 27 ♖exb6+ ♔a8 28 ♖b7 1-0 J.Nunn-S.Kindermann, Munich 1991) 13 ♕e1 ♖he8 (Psakhis gives as "a probable improvement" 13...♖de8 14 ♗a3 ♘f5 "with quite good chances of equalising") 14 ♗a3 ♔b8 15 ♗xc6! (this exchange was also seen in the previous note,

note, and is a standard feature of the variation – White times the move so as to cause Black maximum embarrassment) 15...♘xc6 (15...♗xc6? 16 exf6 gxf6 17 ♕xe6 simply loses a pawn) 16 ♕e3 ♔a8 17 ♖fb1 ♗c8 18 ♗d6 ♖d7 19 ♖b5 ♕d8 20 a5 and White had obviously achieved much of what he wants in such structures.

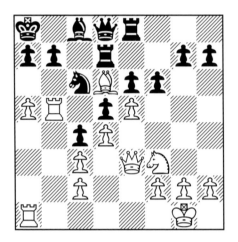

Chandler went on to win a fine game, which is worth seeing further: 20...g5 21 ♗c5 g4 22 ♗b6! ♖c7 (already desperation, but 22...axb6 23 axb6+ ♔b8 24 ♕c1 mates quickly, whilst 22...♕e7 23 exf6 ♕xf6 24 ♘e5 is also very good for White) 23 ♘e1 fxe5 24 dxe5 ♗d7 25 ♕c5 ♖e7 26 a6! bxa6 27 ♖xa6 ♗e8 28 ♗xc7 ♖xc7 29 ♕d6 ♕xd6 30 exd6 ♖b7 31 ♖xb7 ♔xb7 32 ♖a1 and Chandler won the ending.

c) 10...f6 is another critical try, apeing Black's best line against 10 ♗e2.

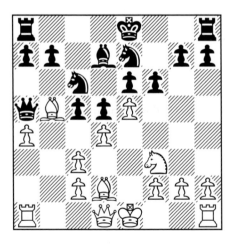

However, as already pointed out, here the bishop on b5 exerts counter-pressure against Black's pressure on e5, so it is arguably less logical to try to attack the e5 square in this line. After 11 ♕e2 ♕c7 (11...fxe5? fails tactically; after 12 ♘xe5! ♘xe5 13 ♕xe5 ♗xb5 14 c4! ♕d8

15 cxb5 White was clearly better in J.Nunn-J.Brenninkmeijer, Groningen 1988) 12 0-0 a6 13 ♗xc6 ♘xc6 14 ♗c1 cxd4 15 exf6 gxf6 16 ♘xd4 Black's position is a little rickety, J.Nunn-S.Kindermann, Vienna 1991.

Returning to Vaganian's 10...♕c7:

11 0-0 0-0

The game J.Nunn-I.Farago, Dortmund 1987, saw Black transpose into another c4-structure, with 11...♘a5 12 ♗d3 c4 13 ♗e2 0-0-0, but this one looks a little odd, since his knight is rather misplaced on a5 and the queen passive on c7. White was considerably better after 14 ♗c1 ♔b8 15 ♕d2 h6 16 ♕f4 ♗e8 17 ♕g4 ♖g8 18 ♘h4 ♔a8 19 f4 ♗d7 20 ♗a3 ♘f5 21 ♘xf5 exf5 22 ♕f3 ♗e6 23 ♖fb1, although the game was eventually drawn.

12 ♖e1

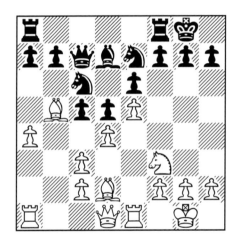

> **Question:** How is this position for Black? He looks more passive than in Byrne-Korchnoi, for example, with his queen on c7.

Answer: Black is very solid here. We will discuss this set-up in more detail in Game 14, but it is safe to say that Black has no particular problems. He intends play on the c-file, and also retains the chance of a kingside break with ...f6.

12...h6 13 ♗f4?!

13 ♗c1 is more usual here, but Black is still fine. Psakhis then gives 13...♘a5 14 ♗a3 b6 15 dxc5 bxc5 16 ♗xd7 ♕xd7 17 ♗xc5 ♖fc8 "with adequate compensation". As we will see later, such pawn sacrifices are a standard feature of this variation.

13...♘g6 14 ♗g3 ♘ce7!

The white bishop is not well placed on g3, and Vaganian starts to exploit it at once. This knight usually goes to a5 in this variation, but here, it has its eye on the enemy bishop.

15 ♗d3

White does not want to exchange light-squared bishops.

15...c4 16 ♗xg6

A concession, but as Psakhis points out, 16 ♗f1 ♕a5! leaves White really missing his dark-squared bishop on the queenside.

16...fxg6!

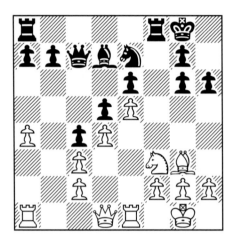

Question: That's a surprise!

Answer: It is an excellent move, after which Black takes over the advantage. He opens the f-file for his rooks, and prepares a later ...g6-g5, followed by ...♗e8-h5, when his so-called 'bad' bishop will become a very strong piece. White stands worse on both sides of the board.

17 h4

Question: Goodness me! That looks a bit much!

Answer: It is a sign of desperation. Byrne can find no other way to stop the plan of ...g5 and ...♗e8-h5, but of course, the move is seriously weakening. It is remarkable how rapidly the position has turned against White, since his ill-considered transfer of the bishop to g3.

17...♖f7 18 ♕b1 ♔h7

Question: What is the point of this move?

Answer: A good question! I am not sure it is necessary at all, but it does not spoil anything. Black improves his king, and emphasizes that he is in no great hurry. White does not really have a constructive plan.

19 ♕b4 ♘f5 20 ♗h2 ♖af8 21 ♖e2 ♗c6 22 g4?

As Psakhis puts it, "Byrne loses his nerve". On the other hand, he does not suggest what else White can do about the threat of 22...♕d8, winning the h-pawn.

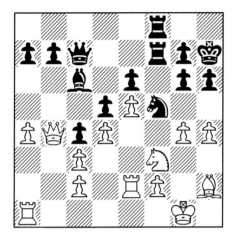

22...♘g3! 23 ♘g5+ hxg5 24 ♗xg3

White hopes to have avoided the worst, but now the black queen switches to the king-side, after which the game does not last long.

24...♕d8! 25 h5 gxh5 26 gxh5 ♖f3

Threatening ...♕e8.

27 ♔g2 ♕e8 28 ♖h1 ♕f7

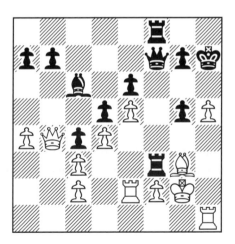

Now 29...♖xg3+ is the threat.

29 ♔h2 ♕f5 30 ♕e7 ♖f7 31 ♕d8 ♗xa4 0-1

Byrne had seen enough. One pawn has gone, and the moves ...♖xc3 and ...♕g4 will soon account for a couple more.

Game 8
V.Ragozin-M.Botvinnik
Training match, Moscow 1944

1 e4 e6 2 d4 d5 3 ♘c3 ♝b4 4 e5 c5 5 a3 ♝xc3+ 6 bxc3 ♘e7 7 ♘f3 ♛a5 8 ♛d2

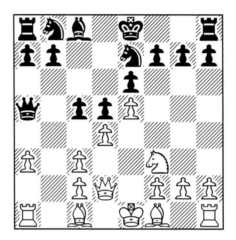

In contrast to the previous games, here White defends the c3-pawn with his queen, reserving the option of bringing the bishop to a3.

> **Question:** Isn't this more logical if White is going to play a4?

Answer: Arguably, yes, although as we have seen already, the bishop can sometimes redeploy from d2 to a3 later in the middlegame. But ♛d2 saves time, and certainly appears more logical on the surface.

> **Question:** What does "on the surface" mean?
> I sense a 'but' somewhere in the background!

Answer: Well, yes, I'm afraid so. As we will see, the bishop cannot come to a3 so easily in these lines, without allowing Black a comfortable ending. Because of this, the ♛d2 lines are not generally regarded nowadays as being so dangerous for Black.
8...♘bc6 9 ♝e2

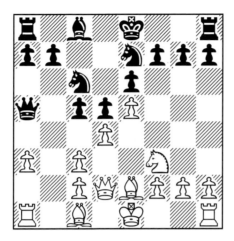

9...♗d7

> *Question:* So why doesn't Black take the ending here with 9...cxd4?

Answer: Well, he has to be careful. For a start, trading on d4 forces off the queens, but only at the cost of undoubling White's c-pawns. As we already know, the Winawer involves trading positional advantages – by taking on c3 with his bishop in the opening, Black surrenders the bishop-pair and weakens his dark squares, but in return, he mangles the white queenside pawns. Undoubling the pawns by an exchange on d4 risks throwing away his compensating advantages, and leaving White with a free bishop-pair.

> *Question:* So are you saying the endings are bad for Black?

Answer: Not necessarily! In fact, here we come to a major issue. General rules of thumb must always be treated with some caution, as chess has numerous exceptions, but we can state a useful such rule here: *the endings arising after the exchanges on d4 and d2 are usually pretty comfortable for Black, if White cannot recapture on d2 with the bishop. However, where he can play ♗xd2, Black must be rather more careful about entering the ending.*

> *Question:* Why does it make such a difference?

Answer: Basically because Black needs to be able to play a rapid ...♘a5-c4 in such endings. If he is unable to do so, the white bishop-pair can often assume considerable strength. If White recaptures with the bishop on d2, then ...♘a5 is prevented.

The classic illustration of this rule of thumb is the game V.Smyslov-R.Letelier, Venice 1950, which we will present in full. White had actually played a4 instead of ♗e2, and play then continued:

9...cxd4 10 cxd4 ♕xd2+ 11 ♗xd2!

The key point. Smyslov immediately stops the manoeuvre ...♘a5-c4.

11...♘f5

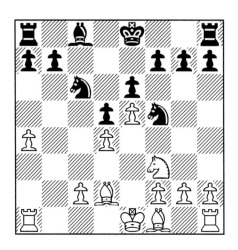

12 ♗c3!

Another excellent move. Black was hoping his opponent would defend the d4-pawn with the move 12 c3?! which would allow ...♘a5, but Smyslov is wise to that trick.

12...♗d7 13 ♗d3 ♖c8 14 ♔d2!

Again accurate. Black was threatening the cheapo 14...♘xe5, which Smyslov stops by defending his bishop. Meanwhile, Black is still prevented from playing his knight into c4.

14...0-0 15 a5!

Now ♘a5 is stopped once and for all, whilst the black b-pawn is fixed on b7, and can be attacked along the b-file.

15...♖c7 16 ♖he1!

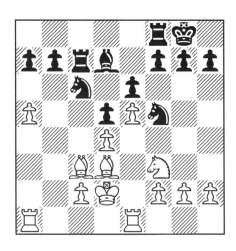

A subtle prophylactic move, directed against the ...f6-break.

Question: What is your assessment of this position?

Answer: White has some advantage. He has stopped Black's main source of counterplay, with ...♘a5-c4 and play along the c-file, and he has a potential target on b7. His also has the bishop-pair, and control of the dark squares, his traditional Winawer birthright.

16...f6?

Playing into White's hands. Smyslov suggested instead 16...a6 with the idea of ...♘a7 and ...♗b5, trying to exchange the bad bishop and increase Black's control of the light squares. White would have only a small advantage after that.

17 ♗xf5!

A nice positional idea. White surrenders the bishop-pair, in the cause of keeping the f-file closed, thus preventing Black obtaining counterplay.

Question: But now we have opposite-coloured bishops.

Answer: Yes, but with plenty of other pieces on the board, this is not such a significant drawing factor.

17...exf5 18 exf6 ♖xf6 19 ♖ab1

White now enjoys an indisputable advantage. Black has pawn weaknesses on b7 and d5, whilst the dark squares c5 and e5 are very vulnerable. Smyslov exploits these plusses in exemplary fashion.

19...h6 20 ♖b5! ♗e6 21 ♖eb1 ♖ff7 22 ♘e1!

An excellent manoeuvre. The knights heads for d3, from where it attacks the two weak dark squares on c5 and e5, and also has the option to come to f4, attacking the d5-pawn again.

22...f4

Black stops the latter idea and tries to work up some counterplay on the kingside, but his pieces are rather too passive for it to be effective.

23 f3 g5 24 ♘d3 ♔h7 25 ♖e1 ♖f6

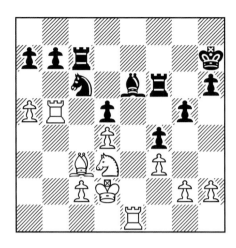

26 ♖c5!

Now specific tactical threats start to appear. The first is 27 ♘b4, winning a pawn.

26...♖c8

26...b6 is met by 27 axb6 axb6 28 ♖b5 when the b-pawn is lost, since 28...♖b7? runs into 29 ♘c5.

27 ♘b4! ♘xb4

After 27...♘e7 Smyslov points out the nice combination 28 ♘xd5 ♘xd5 29 ♖xe6! ♖xc5 (29...♖xe6 30 ♖xc8) 30 ♖xf6 ♖xc3 31 ♖d6 and White regains the piece, with an extra pawn.

28 ♖xe6! ♖xe6 29 ♖xc8 ♘c6 30 a6!

Black was hoping to hang on after 30 ♖c7+ ♖e7 but a fresh tactical blow destroys the last line of defence.

30...bxa6 31 ♖c7+ ♔g6 32 ♖d7 ♘e7 33 ♗b4

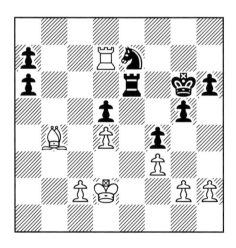

Decisive. With the loss of the d5-pawn, Black cannot stop the two connected white passed pawns.

33...♘f5 34 ♖xd5 ♘e3 35 ♖d8 ♘xg2 36 d5 ♖b6 37 ♗c5 ♖b7 38 ♖c8! ♘h4 39 ♔e2 ♘f5 40 ♖c6+ ♔h5 41 d6 ♖d7 42 ♖c7 1-0

A textbook game by Smyslov, which has taught generations of Winawer players not to exchange queens in these endings, if White can take with the bishop.

Returning to Botvinnik's 9...♗d7:

10 a4

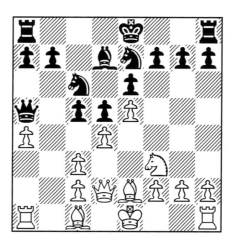

10...♖c8!?

> *Question:* So what is the point of 10...♖c8?

Answer: It is a kind of high-class waiting move. We know from above that taking the ending is not so good here, because of 10...cxd4 11 cxd4 ♕xd2+ 12 ♗xd2! à la Smyslov-Letelier.

> *Question:* But wait a minute – can't Black play 12...♖c8 in this position?
> Now he threatens 13...♘f5, when 14 ♗c3 is impossible because of
> 14...♘xe5! so White would have to play 14 c3.

Answer: A nice try, but White will answer that with 13 ♖a3! covering c3, and meeting 13...♘f5 with 14 ♗c3. Botvinnik's 10...♖c8 is in fact a more subtle version of your idea here.

> *Question:* Okay, I see. So does Black have any other moves?

Answer: Yes, he can also play 10...f6 which we will examine in Game 10.

11 0-0

This allows Black to show his idea. White has two more testing tries: 11 dxc5 (see Game 9), and 10 ♗d3!? (Game 11). Note that 11 ♗a3 would allow Black to reach the same comfortable version of the ending as occurs in the game: 11...cxd4 12 cxd4 ♕xd2+ 13 ♔xd2 ♘f5 14 c3 ♘a5, etc.

While we are talking about this position, however, I should point out one other way Black can go wrong in these endings. Even when the white bishop is on a3, rather than d2, it is important to play the move ...♘f5 early. It is often a mistake to allow White to trade both his bishops for Black's knights, and leave an ending with the white knight against Black's light-squared bishop. An instructive recent example of this was the game Y.Vovk-S.Williams, Gatwick 2012. In the position after 13 ♔xd2 in the above variation, but with the white bishop on f1 and the black rook still on a8...

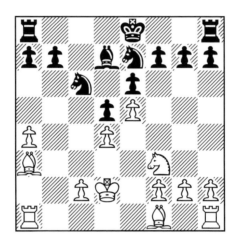

...Williams continued 12...♘a5!? (12...♘f5! 13 c3 ♘a5 is equal) 13 ♗d3 ♘c4+? (13...♘f5!), after which the Ukrainian GM seized his chance: 14 ♗xc4 dxc4 15 ♗xe7! ♔xe7 16 ♔c3.

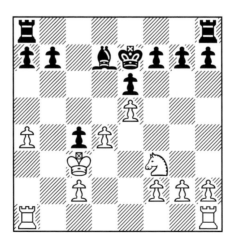

This ending is not nice for Black. Although his bishop has increased scope now the pawn has left d5, it is still inferior to the agile white knight, whilst Black has weak dark squares, a weak pawn on c4, and (most crucially) lacks effective counterplay. Vovk went on to win instructively, as follows: 16...♖ac8 17 ♘d2 ♗c6 18 f3 f5 19 a5 g5 20 ♖hb1 h5 21 ♖b4 (the c-pawn is already dropping off) 21...g4 22 ♖g1 gxf3 23 gxf3 ♖hg8 24 ♖xg8 ♖xg8 25 ♖xc4 and White proceeded to the full point.

11...cxd4!

Now Black reaches his desired endgame.

> *Question:* But isn't White ready to recapture on d2 with the bishop?

Answer: Yes, but his king is not in the centre and your tactical idea above prevents White from establishing the ♗c3/♔d2 formation which Smyslov used.

12 cxd4 ♕xd2 13 ♗xd2 ♘f5 14 c3

Now forced, since 14 ♗c3? is refuted by 14...♘xe5, which reveals the point of Botvinnik's 10th move.

14...♘a5

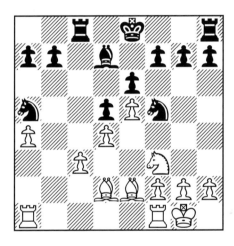

> *Question:* So Black has got his knight to a5. Why is this such a big deal?

Answer: The point is that with the pawn on c3, the white dark-squared bishop has much less scope, whilst Black has much more active play on the queenside. His knight will come to c4, he can double rooks on the c-file, etc. He has also fixed the white a-pawn on a4, at least temporarily, and he has no issues with pressure down the b-file, such as we saw in Smyslov-Letelier. A comparison between this position and Black's position in that game will clearly reveal the difference.

> *Question:* So is Black better here?

Answer: I am not sure that he is objectively better, but he is certainly comfortable. In practice, Black quite often wins such endings, although that may be because more often than not, he is the stronger player.

15 ♖fb1

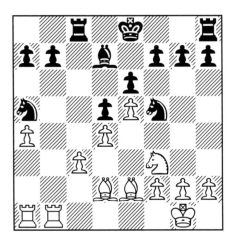

15...♖c7

> *Question:* Why didn't Black block the b-file with 15...b6 here?

Answer: He could, and that would be a perfectly valid move. Timman suggests that Botvinnik probably wanted to avoid the risk of White later breaking with a4-a5, after the black knight goes to c4.

16 ♗c1 f6

> *Question:* This looks a bit odd. Will Black really take on e5?

Answer: Probably not. The point of the move is simply to give his king a square on f7, so he can bring the king's rook over to the queenside.

17 ♗a3 h5!

Nice prophylaxis. 17...♔f7?! runs into 18 ♗b4 ♘c4 19 g4 ♘e7 20 ♗d6 winning the b7-pawn, as pointed out by Timman.

18 ♗b4 ♘c4 19 a5 ♗c6 20 ♗c5 a6

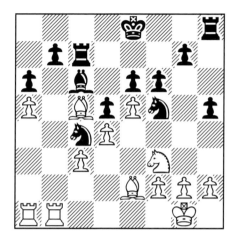

White has played well so far and held the balance comfortably.

21 ♗d3 ♔f7 22 ♖e1 ♖e8 23 ♖ab1 ♗b5 24 h3 ♘e7!

Heading for c6. White has to be careful about his a-pawn.

25 ♗xc4

As Timman points out, this is hard to avoid in the long run, if only to save the a-pawn, so White tries to stir up some queenside play while he has the chance.

25...♗xc4 26 ♗d6 ♖d7 27 ♘d2 ♖c8 28 ♖b6 ♗b5

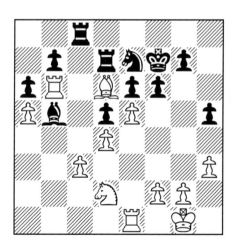

29 exf6?!

Timman is critical of this, and recommends 29 ♘b3, after which a drawish position arises following the practically forced variation 29...♖xc3 30 ♘c5 ♖xc5 31 ♗xc5 ♘c8 32 ♖xb5 axb5 33 exf6 gxf6 34 ♖b1.

29...gxf6 30 ♗b4 ♖c6 31 ♖xc6 ♘xc6 32 f4

He wants to prevent the advance ...e6-e5.

32...♘xb4 33 cxb4 ♖c7

Suddenly, Black is better and White must fight to hold the balance.

34 ♘b3 ♖c4 35 ♘c5 ♖xd4 36 ♖xe6 ♖xb4 37 f5

Timman applauds this as the best chance, although the computer disagrees, preferring 37 ♖b6 ♖xf4 38 ♖xb7+ ♔g6 39 ♖b6. Black is certainly better after 39...♖f1+ 40 ♔h2 ♖a1 41 ♘xa6 ♖xa5, but with the position that much 'smaller' (i.e. the passed pawn not so far distant from the kingside), White would have drawing chances.

37...♖f4?!

This justifies White's last. The computer's 37...♗e8 looks better.

38 ♖b6?

38 ♘xb7 should draw: for example, 38...♖xf5 39 ♖e1 ♖f4 40 ♘d6+ ♔g6 41 ♘xb5 axb5 42 ♖b1 and White can hold the rook ending.

38...♖xf5 39 ♖xb7+ ♔g6 40 ♖b6

40 ♘e6 is slightly more tenacious, but after 40...♖e5 Black should still win.

40...d4 41 ♘xa6 d3

Now the d-pawn is too strong.

42 ♘c7 d2 43 ♖d6 ♖f1+ 44 ♔h2 d1♕ 45 ♖xd1 ♖xd1 46 ♘xb5 ♖d5 47 ♘c3 ♖xa5

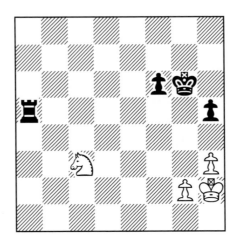

48 ♘e2 ♔f5 49 ♔g3 ♖a3+ 50 ♔h4 ♖a2 51 g4+ ♔e5 52 ♘c1 ♖c2 53 ♘d3+ ♔e4 54 ♘b4 ♖c4
0-1

The knight will be hunted to extinction on the a-file.

On the basis of this game and the notes, we now know most of the essentials of these Winawer endings arising after the queen exchange on d2. Basically, Black needs to avoid two main things – the white set-up with ♗c3/♔d2, preventing Black's ...♘a5-c4 manoeuvre (Smyslov-Letelier), and also the position where White exchanges both bishops for knights (on c4 and e7), as in Vovk-Williams. Providing he avoids both of these, Black should be comfortable in most such endings.

W.Hartston-W.Uhlmann
Hastings 1972/73

1 e4 e6 2 ♘c3 d5 3 d4 ♗b4 4 e5 ♘e7 5 a3 ♗xc3+ 6 bxc3 c5 7 ♘f3 ♗d7 8 a4 ♕a5 9 ♕d2 ♘bc6 10 ♗e2 ♖c8 11 dxc5!

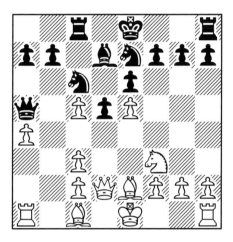

> **Question:** Why is this good?

Answer: Introduced by Vasily Smyslov, it is the most critical reply to 10...♖c8. White puts paid once and for all to any endgames after an exchange of pawns on d4.

> **Question:** Okay, but surely he mangles his pawn structure in doing so?
> And, if the idea is so good, why didn't he play it last move?

Answer: Well, to take the second question first, he is reacting to Black's last. This has deprived Black of any chance to castle queenside. In addition, as we will see, White hopes to bring his knight to d6, in which case he will gain a tempo on the rook. As for the first question, White does mangle his pawns, yes, but he gets various compensations. Firstly, he frees the square d4, as a base for his knight. From there, the knight can potentially jump via b5 to d6, or maybe to b3, from where it would defend the extra pawn on c5. A second point is that White opens the position – he rules out the move ...c5-c4, and if Black recaptures on c5, then the a3-f8 diagonal is opened for White's dark-squared bishop. He hopes that his dark-square play will more than compensate for the weak queenside pawns.

11...♘g6

> *Question:* Why doesn't Black just recapture on c5?

Answer: That would be bad after 11...♕xc5? 12 ♗a3 ♕a5 13 ♗b5 when Black will have trouble castling, as 13...0-0?? 14 ♗xc6 wins material.

12 0-0

The immediate 12 ♕e3 is also possible, hoping to transpose into Smyslov-Uhlmann below. Old analysis from the 1970s claims that Black can equalize with the pawn sacrifice 12...d4!? 13 ♘xd4 ♘xd4 14 ♕xd4 ♕xc5 15 ♗e3! (the best way to pose Black problems; he was fine after 15 ♕xc5 ♖xc5 16 f4 ♖xc3 17 ♗d3 0-0 in W.Wittmann-W.Uhlmann, telex 1990) 15...♕xc3+ 16 ♕xc3 ♖xc3 17 ♔d2 ♖c8 18 ♖hb1 ♗c6 19 ♗b5 0-0 20 ♗xc6 ♖fd8+ (allegedly a key improvement over 20...bxc6 21 ♗xa7 ♖fd8+ 22 ♔c3 with a clear advantage to White, W.Hartson-S.Webb, England 1973) 21 ♔c1 ♖xc6 22 ♖xb7 a6 (Eales).

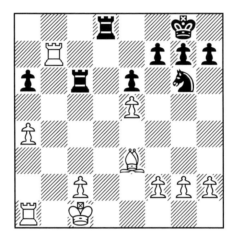

However, running this line on further reveals that after 23 f4 ♖dc8 24 ♖a2 ♘h4 25 g3 ♘f3 26 h4 ♘e1 27 ♖b6 ♖xc2+ 28 ♖xc2 ♘xc2 29 ♔d2 ♘xe3 30 ♔xe3 ♖a8 White is vastly more active in the rook ending. I would not touch this ending with a barge-pole as Black.

Instead after 12 ♕e3, Black should probably prefer 12...♘f4, when it is hard for White to avoid the repetition after 13 ♗f1 ♘g6 14 ♗e2 ♘f4.

12...♘gxe5

This is an attempt to avoid the continuation of the stem game, which went 12...0-0 13 ♕e3 ♕c7 14 ♘d4! ♕xe5 15 ♘b5 ♕xe3 16 ♗xe3 a6 17 ♘d6 ♖c7 18 a5 and White had a strong bind in V.Smyslov-W.Uhlmann, Mar del Plata 1966. Smyslov went on to win a memorable game.

13 ♘xe5 ♘xe5

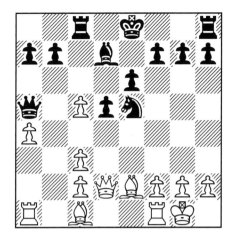

14 ♕e3

14 ♕g5 is more active, and conceals a fiendish trap: 14...♘g6 15 c4!. Now the trap is 15...dxc4?? 16 c6! winning a piece. This has caught several players, sadly the most notable being 1970s French Defence authority and Irish international John Moles, who fell for it against Gligoric in a clock simul. In his seminal volume on the Winawer, he not only quoted the game, but added the intriguing comment "in vino veritas!", presumably implying that he had consumed a drink or two when playing the Gligoric game!

Instead, 15...0-0 is best, when Moles assesses the position as equal, saying "White's extra pawn is worthless and his two bishops are not particularly dangerous." Watson analyses further: 16 cxd5 exd5 (*Fritz*'s 16...f6 17 ♕d2 ♕xd2 18 ♗xd2 exd5 19 ♗e3 ♖fe8 is also fine) 17 ♕xd5 ♗c6 18 ♕d2 and now the nice tactic 18...♕xc5! 19 ♗a3 ♕f5 20 ♗xf8 ♘f4 when both ...♕g5 and the neat ...♕h3 are threats. *Fritz* confirms that White has nothing after 21 ♖fd1 ♖xf8.

14...♘g6

Question: So what is the verdict on this position?

Answer: I think Black is fine. He has regained his pawn, and has much the sounder pawn structure. White still has the bishop-pair, and the dark squares in Black's camp look like their usual bad accident, but as Winawer players, we can live with that, can't we? In fact, Uhlmann even assesses the position as better for Black, and although, like many of his assessments in this opening, that may be a touch optimistic, it is not long before Black really does stand better.

15 ♗a3 ♗c6 16 f4

This is necessary, as otherwise Black will mobilize his central pawn majority with ...e6-e5.

16...0-0 17 ♕h3?!

This somewhat pointless queen manoeuvre looks like the start of White's difficulties. In view of what happens in a few moves' time, White should probably follow the computer's advice and secure his a-pawn, with 17 ♗b4 ♕c7 18 a5.

17...♖cd8 18 ♗b4 ♕c7 19 ♗d3 f5

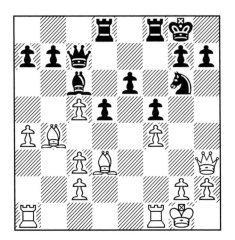

> *Question:* I am not sure I would have played that! Doesn't this make Black's bishop even worse and leave weaknesses on e6 and e5?

Answer: It is a case of attackable and non-attackable weaknesses. Black wants to stop the advance f4-f5. After the text, this is prevented forever, and the white bishop on d3 is severely curtailed in its mobility. Meanwhile, the e5- and e6-squares are easily defended, and far from easy to attack effectively.

20 ♕g3 ♖f6 21 ♕e3

Uhlmann points out that this was the last chance to play 21 a5.

21...a5

> *Question:* Doesn't this just win a pawn?

Answer: Yes, but not entirely free of charge. As Uhlmann points out, White is able to bring his dark-squared bishop to the long diagonal, and work up some initiative in compensation.

22 ♗a3 ♗xa4 23 ♗b2 ♗c6 24 c4 ♖f7 25 g3

25 ♕xe6? ♘xf4 is not good for White, but the e-pawn is now threatened.

25...♖e7

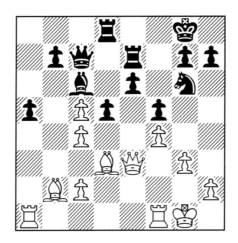

26 ♖ae1?

Uhlmann does not comment on this move (perhaps because he thought Black was just better all the way through!), but the computer suggests that it is a turning point, after which White is always struggling. It does not consider Black to have any advantage after 26 cxd5 ♗xd5 27 ♗c3 ♖a8 28 ♖a3. Indeed, such are the chains in which Black is held on the dark squares, that it is hard to see him making serious progress.

26...♕d7

Now, by contrast, White can never exchange on d5, because of the queen recapture.

27 ♕d4 a4 28 h4 dxc4! 29 ♕xd7

After 29 ♕xc4 Uhlmann intended 29...h5, but 29...♕d5 looks like a safer way to secure the advantage.

29...♖dxd7 30 ♗xc4 ♖d2 31 ♖f2

Forced, because 31 ♖xe6 loses after 31...♖g2+ 32 ♔h1 ♖xe6 33 ♗xe6+ ♔f8, and if 34 ♗d7 then 34...♖f2+.

31...♖xf2 32 ♔xf2 ♔f7

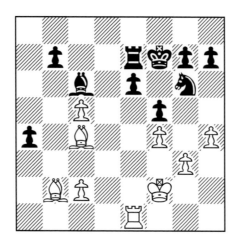

Answer: Well, my old Russian trainer Igor Belov always used to deplore the use of the word "winning" in such positions, saying: "It's only winning when you attack something big and he can't defend it!". But certainly, Black has good practical winning chances. The remainder is of peripheral interest to our main theme, which is the opening, so I will skip through the rest of the moves relatively briefly.

33 h5 ♘f8 34 ♗e5 ♖e8 35 ♗d6 ♘d7 36 g4 fxg4

Uhlmann gives 36...b5! as best: for example, 37 cxb6 ♘xb6 38 ♗a2 ♗d5 39 ♖b1 ♘c8! 40 ♗xd5 ♘xd6 "with a clear endgame advantage".

37 f5 ♘f8 38 ♔g3 ♔f6

This time, Uhlmann's recommendation is less convincing: 38...♗f3 ("!") 39 fxe6+ ♘xe6 "and Black dominates", but in fact, it is hard to see how he can untangle after 40 ♗b5 ♗c6 41 ♖f1+ ♔g8 42 ♗c4.

39 ♗e5+?

The losing move. White should hold after 39 fxe6 ♘xe6 40 ♔xg4, since Uhlmann's 40...♗f3+ ("!!") is met adequately by 41 ♔g3! ♗xh5 42 ♗b5 ♖a8 43 ♗c4: for instance, 43...♘g5 44 ♗e7+ ♔g6 45 ♔f4 h6 46 ♗d3+ ♔f7 47 ♗c4+ etc.

39...♔xf5 40 ♗xg7 ♘d7 41 ♗d3+ ♔g5 42 ♗xh7

42 h6 is slightly more tenacious.

42...♔xh5 43 ♖e2 ♔g5

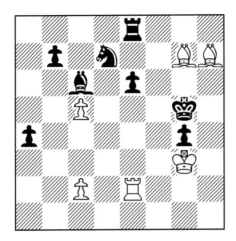

Now it is all over.

44 ♗d4 ♗f3 45 ♖d2 ♘f8 46 ♗d3 ♘g6 47 ♖h2 e5 48 ♗e3+ ♘f4 49 ♖h7 a3 50 ♗c4 ♔g6 51 ♖h2 ♖a8 52 c3 ♗d5 0-1

There is a slightly sad postscript to this game. At the start of it, Hartston needed half a point from his two remaining games, for a Grandmaster norm. After losing here, he was outplayed in the final round by Larsen, missed out on his norm, and never did become a Grandmaster.

1 e4 e6 2 d4 d5 3 ♘c3 ♗b4 4 e5 ♘e7 5 a3 ♗xc3+ 6 bxc3 c5 7 a4 ♘bc6 8 ♘f3 ♕a5 9 ♕d2 ♗d7 10 ♗e2

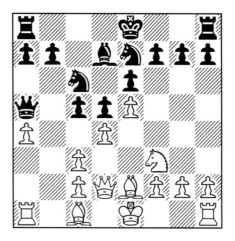

10...f6

Instead of 10...♖c8, as seen in the previous game, Black adopts a more dynamic approach, immediately attacking the white centre.

> *Question:* Is this better than 10...♖c8?

Answer: Objectively, I am not sure there is much to choose between the two moves, but 10...f6 is more dynamic, and also more risky.

> *Question:* What about the standard idea 10...c4 here?

Answer: In this position, closing the position is definitely to be frowned upon. By comparison with the examples we have already considered in this book, it is obvious that White is better off with his queen on d2 and his bishop on c1 – he is a couple of tempi up on the best he can hope for in the ♗d2 lines.

> *Question:* Yes, but how important are a couple of tempi in a blocked position?

Answer: Less important than in an open one, certainly, but still not to be despised. Examples such as Planinec-Timman showed how nice White's position can be in these structures, if he gets himself organised well; to give him some extra tempi is really asking for it.

> *Question:* So do you have an example from grandmaster practice?

Answer: Well, perhaps because 10...c4 is so illogical, there have not been many practical examples. Moles quotes a game A.Lutikov-V.Lyavdansky, USSR 1965, which went 11 0-0 0-0-0 12 ♗a3 f6 13 ♖fb1 and White was simply better. This is one case where I must just appeal to you to trust me!

11 exf6

This is the most critical. 11 0-0 fxe5 12 dxe5 (or 12 ♘xe5 ♘xe5 13 dxe5 0-0) 12...0-0 is equal.

11...gxf6

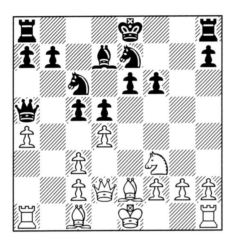

12 dxc5

> *Question:* Why is this necessary? Can't White just play 12 0-0 here?

Answer: He can, of course, but Uhlmann claims easy equality in the ending after 12...cxd4 13 cxd4 ♕xd2 14 ♗xd2 ♘f5.

> *Question:* Is that necessarily so? From the previous game,
> I thought White was doing well if he can play 15 ♗c3 in such
> a position? After all, 15...♖c8 can be met by 16 ♖a3.

Answer: Yes, but even so, without his king in the centre on d2, White does not usually have a lot in such positions. Furthermore, the exchange on f6 has changed things radically, because Black has the possibility of ...♘d6-e4. He is comfortable here.

12...0-0-0 13 0-0 e5

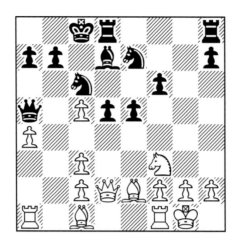

> **Question:** Well now, what is happening here? It looks rather sharp!

Answer: It is, indeed. White has an extra pawn, at least for the moment, and as always, the opening of the position potentially makes his bishop-pair stronger. On the other hand, his pawn structure on the queenside is shot away, and Black has a strong pawn centre. Chances are probably about equal, but in a very dynamic way, and any inaccurate play by either side could have serious consequences.

14 c4

14 ♗a3 is given as best by Moles. The game W.Hartston-S.Hutchings, Swansea 1972, then continued 14...♖hg8 15 ♖fb1 ♘g6 16 g3 and now 16...h5 gives counterplay, in an unclear position.

14...d4!?

> **Question:** Is this best?

Answer: Possibly not. Black seizes central space and keeps his powerful pawn centre, but remains a pawn down. In a later game, L.Stein-V.Doroshkevich, USSR Championship, Riga 1970, Black tried 14...dxc4 15 ♗xc4 ♕xc5 16 ♗b3. Now 16...♗g4?! 17 ♕h6! ♘d5?! (17...♗xf3 18 ♕h3+ with a plus) worked out badly: 18 ♘d2! ♖hg8 19 ♗a3 ♕a5 20 ♘e4 ♘d4 21 ♔h1! ♗e6 22 ♖ad1 ♕c7 23 ♘xf6! ♖g6 24 ♘xd5 ♖xh6 25 ♘xc7 ♔xc7 26 ♗xe6 ♖xe6 27 c3 with a clear advantage. Moles suggests no fewer than three improvements at move 16: 16...♘f5, 16...♘g6, and 16...e4, all of which may offer reasonable chances.

However, the computer's suggestion 14...♕xd2! 15 ♗xd2 e4 may be best of all, when Black really does have a good initiative for his pawn.

15 ♕h6

A critical try is 15 ♕xa5! ♘xa5 16 ♘d2. Uhlmann now gives 16...f5 as slightly better for

Black, but this assessment seems questionable after 17 ♘b3 which seems to favour White. *Fritz* prefers 16...♖hg8 17 g3 and only now 17...f5 18 ♘b3 ♘ac6; the point being that 19 ♗g5 is no longer possible. The position then remains unclear.

15...♘g6 16 ♘d2 f5 17 ♘b3 ♕c7

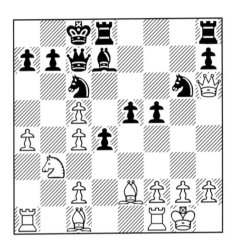

18 f4

Uhlmann hails this as the best for White, but *Fritz* likes 18 a5 a6 19 ♖d1, considering the position clearly in his favour.

18...♘b4 19 ♗d1?!

Uhlmann gives the line 19 fxe5 ♘xc2 20 ♖b1 ♗c6 21 ♖xf5 ♗e4 "with a strong attack for Black", but once again, the silicon beast is far from convinced, reckoning White is clearly better after 22 ♖f1.

19...d3 20 cxd3 ♘xd3 21 fxe5 ♕xe5 22 ♗f3!

The best. 22 ♗g5 is another important option, mentioned by Uhlmann. He analyses a long combination beginning 22...♗c6, but the computer shows his analysis to be full of holes. Instead, 22...f4! 23 ♗f3 (23 ♗xd8?? ♕e3+ mates) 23...♖de8 is equal, according to *Fritz*.

22...f4 23 ♗d2 ♗c6 24 ♗xc6?

White can win by force here with 24 ♕h3+! ♔b8 (if 24...♖d7 25 ♗g4) 25 ♗xc6 bxc6 26 ♗a5 when the rook has no retreat on the d-file.

24...bxc6 25 ♖ab1 ♖d7 26 ♕h3 ♖e8 27 ♕f3 ♕e4 28 ♘a5?!

28 ♕xe4 ♖xe4 29 ♘a5 holds the balance. Now Black starts to take over.

28...♕xf3 29 ♖xf3 ♖e2

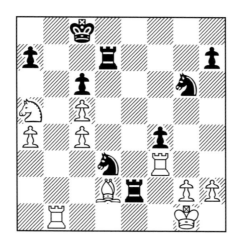

30 ♗c1?

Losing at once. 30 ♗c3 was the only move, although Black is now clearly better after 30...♘h4.

30...♘h4 31 ♖xf4

A final amusing example of the flaws in Uhlmann's pre-computer analysis of this game is his note to 31 ♖h3. He gives 31...♖xg2+ 32 ♔f1 ♖f2+ 33 ♔g1 ♖g7+ 34 ♔h1 ♖f1#, overlooking the mate in one with 31...♖e1#.

31...♖xg2+

Good enough, but there is a forced mate with 31...♖e1+ 32 ♖f1 ♘f3+ 33 gxf3 ♖g7+ etc.

32 ♔f1 ♘xf4 33 ♗xf4 ♖d3 0-1

> **Question:** Hmmm. I am not too convinced by all this! It looks as though White was just better for much of the game.

Answer: It is interesting that Moles, writing back in 1975, described this game as "difficult to analyse"; Uhlmann's efforts rather bear this out! Of course, it is easy for me to carp, sitting here, armed as I am with a 21st century computer, and I mean no disrespect to the East German GM, but it does look as though his whole assessment of Black's chances in this game was extremely optimistic. Indeed, the fact that so strong a player as Leonid Stein should have been prepared to go down the white side of the line five years later, against Doroshkevich, suggests that he also thought so. Nonetheless, I think Black is doing fine after 10...f6, if he heeds the improvements at move 14. However, there seems little doubt that 10...♖c8 is a safer way to handle the line for Black.

1 e4 e6 2 d4 d5 3 ♘c3 ♗b4 4 e5 c5 5 a3 ♗xc3+ 6 bxc3 ♘e7 7 ♘f3 ♗d7 8 a4 ♕a5 9 ♕d2 ♘bc6

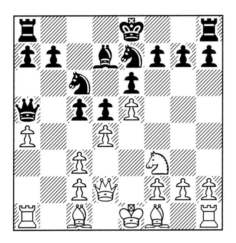

10 ♗d3

Question: Is this better than 10 ♗e2? Doesn't it invite the reply 10...c4 with tempo?

Answer: It does invite that reply, but therein lies the point. White argues that he wants to see the pawn committed to c4, and is willing to sacrifice a tempo to provoke the move. 10 ♗d3 was a favourite of Fischer's.

Question: What about 10 ♗b5 in this position?

Answer: Actually, by comparison with the similar position in the ♗d2 variation, here the move 10 ♗b5?! is dubious, for tactical reasons. Black can reply 10...♘xe5! 11 ♘xe5 ♗xb5. White can regain the pawn with 12 ♗a3 ♗a6 (*Fritz's* 12...f6 may be even better) 13 ♗xc5, but after 13...f6 14 ♘d3 ♘c6 15 0-0 ♔f7 Black was equal in E.Mnatsakanian-V.Korchnoi, Yerevan 1965, and went on to win.

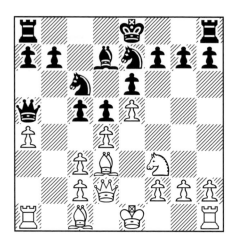

10...c4?!

Uhlmann takes the bait, but this move is no longer regarded as best, and Black usually prefers 10...f6.

> **Question:** I think I am detecting a pattern here – in most
> Winawer lines, Black seems reluctant to play ...c5-c4 these days!

Answer: I think that is definitely true. The understanding of the closed structures with ...c5-c4 has moved on over the years, and the initial impression made by Botvinnik's victories with the ...c5-c4 plan in the 1930s has now worn off. White players have a much better idea of how to handle the position and coordinate their forces, and as a result black players have increasingly shifted attention to more fluid approaches, based around ...f6 and leaving the pawn on c5. Indeed, despite his success in the present game, Uhlmann himself switched to 10...f6 in another game against Fischer, played two years after this one. Play continued 11 0-0 fxe5 12 ♘xe5 (12 dxe5 0-0 is also comfortable for Black) 12...♘xe5 13 dxe5 0-0 14 c4 ♕xd2 (14...♕c7 is more ambitious, but the text is fine for Black) 15 ♗xd2 ♗c6 16 a5 ♖ad8 17 ♗e3 d4 18 ♗d2 ♘g6 19 f4 ♘h4 and Black was fine.

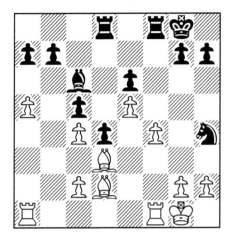

The game ended in a draw after 20 ♖f2 ♖d7 21 ♖e2 ♖df7 22 ♖b1 g5! 23 fxg5 ♗xg2! 24 ♖xg2 ♘xg2 25 ♔xg2 ♖f2+ 26 ♔g3 ♖xd2 27 ♖xb7 ♖f7 28 ♖b8+ ♔g7 29 ♖e8! ♖df2 30 ♖xe6 ♖7f3+ 31 ♔g4 ♖f4+ 32 ♔g3 ½-½, R.Fischer-W.Uhlmann, Stockholm Interzonal 1962.

11 ♗e2 f6 12 ♗a3! ♘g6?!

This early attack on e5 proves premature, because it is too dangerous to take the pawn anyway. Uhlmann recommends 12...0-0-0 13 0-0 and now Black has several options, although White remains a little better in all cases.

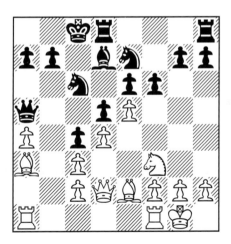

Question: Why?

Answer: Basically, he has a good set-up against the ...c5-c4 structure. His bishop is strong on a3 and his pieces are well placed. 13...♖df8, a suggestion of Botvinnik, is perhaps the most interesting of Black's tries here.

Answer: It is quite a typical manoeuvre for such blocked structures. The rook intends to come to f7. This will protect the e7-knight, threaten activity along the f-file after the exchange ...fxe5, and also frees d8 for the black knight. We saw in Game 5 that the manoeuvre ...♘c6-d8 can be useful in such positions, to defend b7 and potentially allow the light-squared bishop to take on a4.

13 0-0!

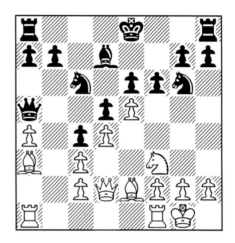

13...0-0-0

Answer: The line 13...fxe5?! 14 ♘xe5 ♘gxe5 15 dxe5 ♘xe5 16 ♕g5! ♘g6 17 ♗h5 is too dangerous for Black.

14 ♗d6

Answer: I think White is certainly somewhat better. He has defended his e5-pawn conveniently, and obtained a relatively favourable version of the blocked structure. However, once again, we see the resources of the black position being brilliantly exploited by Uhlmann, which is why I have included the game in this book.

14...♘ce7!

The knight is heading for f5, to attack the bishop.

15 ♘h4!

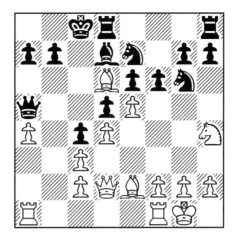

Answer: Fischer neatly exploits the tactical opportunities, to achieve his strategic objective of keeping his bishop on a strong diagonal.

15...♖de8 16 ♘xg6! hxg6 17 exf6!

Answer: Fischer is consistently pursuing the plan begun by his 15th move. He clears the h2-b8 diagonal, and intends that his bishop should remain on that diagonal when it is driven away from d6.

17...gxf6 18 h3!

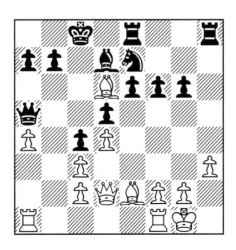

This is the point. The bishop now has a retreat on h2, and the diagonal h2-b8 is very strong.

18...♘f5 19 ♗h2 g5 20 f4?

Up to now, Fischer has played brilliantly, and has achieved a great position, but this premature attempt to shatter the black structure runs into a brilliant refutation. Instead, 20 ♖fe1! leaves White with a clear advantage. His bishops are both great, and the black king is distinctly uncomfortable.

20...♘d6! 21 ♗f3?!

This was no doubt part of Fischer's plan, but he misses the reply. He should have tried 21 fxg5!? ♘e4 22 ♕e3 (22 ♕f4 e5!) 22...♕xc3 23 ♕xc3 ♘xc3 24 ♗f3 fxg5 25 a5 (Uhlmann), when White is still slightly better, although he has lost a fair bit of his previous advantage.

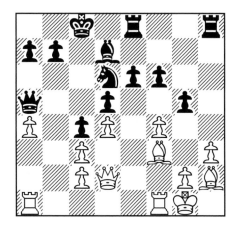

21...g4!!

> *Question:* What is this all about?

Answer: It is a brilliant positional idea from Uhlmann, which transforms the position completely. As so often in the Winawer, the strategic battle is over the activity of the white bishop pair; if White can get the bishops working, he will usually be doing well, whereas if Black can tame them, his own chances will usually be good. Here, Uhlmann sacrifices a pawn to bury the bishop on h2.

22 hxg4

22 ♗xg4? ♘e4 23 ♕e3 f5 24 ♗f3 ♕xc3 25 ♕xc3 ♘xc3 is now just better for Black.

22...f5!

The second step of the plan. Having sacrificed a pawn, Black now grants his opponent a protected passed pawn!

> *Question:* Sounds like madness!

Answer: Yes, but there be method in't! It is all about killing the white bishop-pair, especially the bishop on h2. A few moves ago, it was the pride of White's position, glaring menacingly down the open h2-b8 diagonal, towards the black king. Now it will spend the rest of the game staring at its own pawns on f4 and d4, neither of which can move and let the poor prelate back into the daylight.

23 g5

23 gxf5 exf5 just gives Black the open g- and e-files to play with.

23...♖e7

There has been a total transformation of the position. The extra pawn is hardly felt at all, whilst Black has a clear plan to strengthen his position: his bishop can come to h5, his rooks can double on the h-file, and the knight constantly threatens to jump into e4. In addition, as usual in these structures, the a4-pawn is on death row, and can only await Black's announcement of a date for its execution.

24 ♗g3 ♗e8 25 ♕e3 ♘e4 26 ♗xe4

The knight clearly cannot be tolerated on e4.

26...dxe4

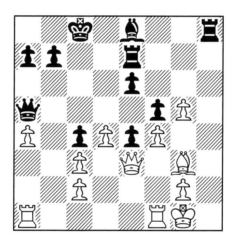

27 ♔f2

Fischer was always a great materialist, and duly clings on to his extra pawn. It was worth considering 27 d5!? to bring his bishop back to life.

27...♖eh7

27...♕d5 at once was probably more accurate.

28 ♖fb1

Passing up the last chance to liberate his bishop with 28 d5.

28...♕d5!

Slamming the door on the unfortunate prelate, which will spend the remainder of the game in cloistered inactivity. The only issue here is whether Black can actually break through and win. Given the blocked position, the game should probably end in a draw, but

Black has what chances there are.

29 ♕e1?

Fischer completely overestimates his position and misses Black's 30th. Correct was 29 ♕d2!? or 29 a5, maintaining the blockade.

29...♖h1! 30 ♕xh1??

This just loses. Uhlmann gives the line 30 ♕e3 ♖xb1 31 ♖xb1 ♗xa4 32 ♖a1 ♗xc2 33 ♖xa7 ♔b8 34 ♖a1 ♗d3 as offering better defensive chances.

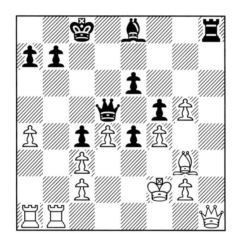

30...e3+!

This *zwischenzug* is key. Now the opening of the a8-h1 diagonal means that the oft-despised 'bad' bishop will become extremely powerful, whereas its counterpart on g3 continues to resemble a big pawn.

31 ♔g1

Instead, 31 ♔xe3? ♕e4+ 32 ♔f2 (32 ♔d2? ♖xh1 33 ♖xh1 ♕xg2+ wins) 32...♖xh1 33 ♖xh1 ♗c6! 34 ♖h2 ♕xc2+ 35 ♔g1 ♕xc3 (Uhlmann) wins a piece, and 31 ♔e2? also loses after 31...♖xh1 32 ♖xh1 ♕xg2+.

31...♖xh1+ 32 ♔xh1 e2! 33 ♖b5!?

A desperate attempt to drum up some counterplay, but it merely makes Black's task easier. Even so, after 33 ♖g1 ♕e4 34 ♖ac1 ♔d8 Uhlmann considers White's position to be hopeless. The bishop will come to c6 and the c3-pawn will drop, after which the c2- and d4-pawns will follow.

33...♗xb5 34 axb5

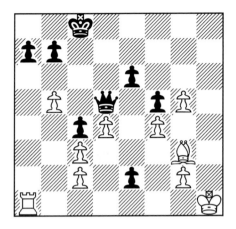

34...♛xb5!

Trading the e-pawn for a passed a-pawn.

35 ♖e1 a5 36 ♖xe2 a4 37 ♖xe6 a3 38 g6

Both 38 ♖e5 ♛xe5, and 38 ♖e1 a2 39 g6 ♛a6 40 g7 ♛h6+ (Uhlmann) also lose.

38...♛d7!

But not 38...a2?? 39 g7 a1♛+ 40 ♔h2

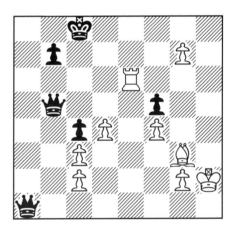

when it is White who wins!

39 ♖e5 b6!

Depriving White of the move ♖a5, and with it, his last chance.

40 ♗h4 a2 41 ♖e1 ♛g7 42 ♖a1 ♛xg6 0-1

43 ♖xa2 ♛h5 44 g3 ♛f3+ 45 ♔h2 ♛xc3 46 ♗f6 b5 (Uhlmann) leaves White helpless.

This is one of the great Winawer games, thanks to Uhlmann's brilliant strategic idea at move 21. The battle to tame the white bishop-pair is central to the Winawer, and this is a memorable example, which every black player should bear in mind.

Game 12
R.Felgaer-V.Korchnoi
Bled Olympiad 2002

1 e4 e6 2 d4 d5 3 ♘c3 ♗b4 4 e5 ♘e7 5 a3 ♗xc3+ 6 bxc3 c5 7 a4

White's other main alternative here is 7 h4.

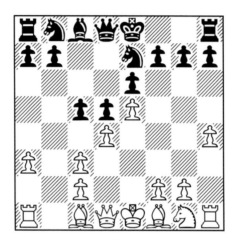

Question: Another non-developing move! What is the idea?

Answer: White logically aims to weaken further the kingside dark squares, which are always likely to be the Achilles' heel of Black's position in the Winawer. If permitted, the pawn will come all the way to h6. Positionally, the idea is well founded, but as you will note, the problem is that White neglects his development. Black has a number of approaches: 7...♕a5 (7...♕c7!? 8 h5 h6 9 ♘f3 b6 is also playable) 8 ♗d2 ♘bc6 9 h5.

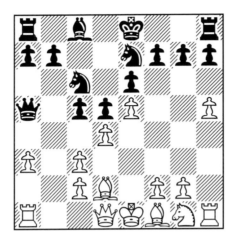

This is the parting of the ways. Essentially, Black has three options here.

a) 9...cxd4 10 cxd4 ♕a4 is one line. Black attacks the d4-pawn and intends to follow up with ...b6 and ...♗a6, exchanging White's key attacking bishop. The critical line now is Kasparov's dynamic pawn sacrifice 11 ♘f3 (11 c3 ♕xd1+ 12 ♖xd1 h6 is no problem for Black, nor is 11 ♗c3 b6) 11...♘xd4 12 ♗d3.

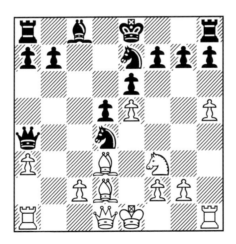

Question: So what does White have for his pawn?

Answer: He has caught up in development and hopes that his dark-squared bishop will develop active play. Typical ideas include ♖h4 (usually prefaced by ♔f1, to avoid the tactic ...♘xf3 with check), h6, etc. G.Kasparov-V.Anand, Linares 1992, continued 12...♘ec6 (12...h6 13 ♔f1 ♘xf3 14 ♕xf3 is another approach, when the analysis runs deep in the sharp lines after 14...b6 15 ♕g3 ♗a6! 16 ♕xg7 ♗xd3+ 17 cxd3 ♖g8 18 ♕xh6 ♕d4, etc) 13 ♔f1 ♘xf3 14

♕xf3 b6 15 h6. White has good compensation, although the position is extremely sharp. This is not a line Black can afford to enter without deep preparation.

b) The quiet approach is 9...h6!?. White retains a kingside space advantage, with the so-called Quartz Grip on the kingside potentially offering long-term chances in the endgame, but on the other hand, Black secures his dark squares against further significant weakening and can develop calmly with ...♗d7 and ...0-0-0. Psakhis then gives 10 ♘f3 ♗d7 11 a4 0-0-0 12 ♕c1 f6, assessing the position as equal.

c) 9...♗d7 is the course preferred for many years by Uhlmann, as well as other strong players, such as Psakhis, Lputian and Grischuk.

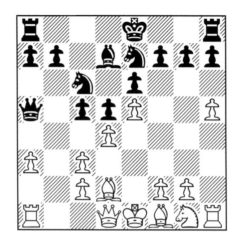

Black simply continues developing, placing his faith in that aspect of his position. After 10 h6 gxh6 White has:

c1) 11 ♘f3 0-0-0!? (despite being so comprehensively outplayed in the present game, Short retained his faith in the h4-plan, and later used it to beat Lputian, who preferred the immediate 11...♘g8!? 12 c4 – playing to open the game to the maximum – 12...♕c7 13 cxd5 exd5 14 dxc5!? 0-0-0 15 ♗e2 ♗g4 16 ♔f1 h5 and Black was doing perfectly well N.Short-S.Lputian, China 2004) 12 ♗d3 (12 a4 ♖dg8!? 13 ♖xh6 ♘f5 14 ♖f6 ♕d8 15 ♗e3 ♖g6 16 ♖xf7 ♗e8 17 ♖xf5 exf5 18 g3 ♗d7 19 ♕d2 ♖hg8 was reasonable for Black in V.Bologan-W.Uhlmann, Dresden 1997, although White eventually won; 12 ♖xh6 ♘g8 13 ♖h4 f6 also gives Black reasonable counterplay) 12...c4 13 ♗e2 ♘g8!.

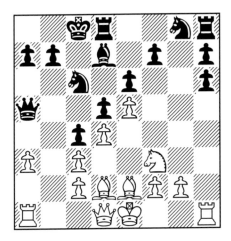

Question: That looks funny!

Answer: It is a typical idea in this line. Black is not so much concerned with trying to hang on to the h6-pawn, as preparing the break ...f6. After 14 ♔f1 f6 15 ♕e1 fxe5 16 ♘xe5 ♘xe5 17 dxe5 ♘e7 18 ♗xh6 ♖hg8 Black stood well in N.Short-L.Psakhis, Port Erin 1999. He went on to outplay his powerful opponent totally, before collapsing in time-trouble and losing.

c2) 11 ♖b1 is a newish and fairly critical idea here. White activates the rook on the b-file, attacking b7, and setting up ideas of ♖b5. He has scored quite well with this, and the best line for Black is not entirely clear at present. A reasonably solid approach is 11...♕c7 (11...0-0-0 12 ♖b5 ♕xa3 13 ♖xc5 a6 14 ♕b1 ♔c7 15 c4 b6 16 cxd5! bxc5 17 d6+ ♔c8 18 ♖h3 ♕a4 19 ♖b3, D.Vocaturo-T.Hillarp Persson, Reykjavik 2009, with an unclear position, is an example of the sort of sharp play than can ensue) 12 ♘f3 ♘g8 13 ♖b5 c4 14 ♕b1 0-0-0, K.Nemcova-D.Petrosian, Dubai 2011, with a position that is not entirely clear, but where Black's dark squares look weaker than usual in such structures. As I say, 11 ♖b1 is a critical test for this whole 9...♗d7 rapid development approach.

In summary, the early h4 plan remains an interesting and unclear way for White to proceed. The line with 9...h6 is probably the way for Black to play, if he wants a quiet position, without needing to prepare sharp, forcing lines.

Returning to Felgaer's 7 a4:

7...♕a5 8 ♕d2 ♘bc6 9 ♘f3 f6

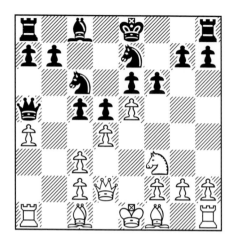

Question: This is another new move order, isn't it?

Answer: Yes. Instead of 9...♗d7, Black immediately attacks the centre.

Question: So what is the difference?

Answer: I am not sure that it will always make a huge difference from the line with 9...♗d7 10 ♗d3 f6. Assuming that Black ends up playing his bishop to d7 fairly soon, then a transposition is likely, but, as the present game shows, there can be important differences.
10 ♗d3

Korchnoi had used the 9...f6 move order before. In particular, he demonstrated one of its advantages after 10 ♗a3. Rather than enter the standard Winawer ending with 10...cxd4 (comfortable though that should be for Black), he can do even better: 10...fxe5! 11 dxe5 ♕xa4! (once again, Korchnoi exploits the pin on the a-file to annex a pawn; here, the fact that White is one move further from castling than would be the case if the moves ...♗d7 and ♗e2 were already played, means that Black has time to extract his queen, before the threat of ♗xe7 becomes real) 12 ♗e2 b6 (simply defending the extra pawn) 13 c4 (13 0-0 ♕e4 was presumably the idea; White can gain a tempo or two on the queen, but he has no way to achieve anything concrete, and a pawn is a pawn – all in all, a typical Korchnoi pawn-grab) 13...♘d8 14 0-0 ♕d7.

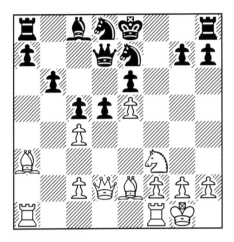

Black has had to resort to one or two contortions to escape with his booty intact, but White was unable to take advantage of his small development lead. After 15 ♘g5 h6 16 ♘h3 0-0 17 ♖fd1 ♘dc6 18 ♗b2 ♗b7 19 ♘f4 d4 in F.Kuijpers-V.Korchnoi, Wijk aan Zee 1971, Black just had a solid extra pawn and a clear advantage.

However, in view of what happens in the main game, perhaps White should prefer the safer 10 ♗e2.

10...fxe5 11 dxe5 0-0 12 0-0

It is hard to suggest any other move for White, but now there follows a typical and strong Winawer exchange sacrifice.

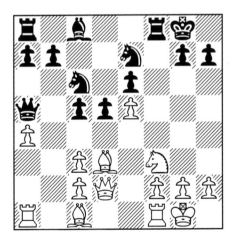

12...♖xf3!

This cries out to be played.

13 gxf3 c4 14 ♗e2 ♘xe5

Question: So what is going on?

Answer: I think Black has a very attractive position. He has one pawn for the exchange, and has exposed the opponent's king. Even more importantly, as we pointed out in Game 2, in such Winawer structures the lack of open files means that rooks often struggle to become fully effective. That is the case here, with Black's knights proving very adept in the blocked structure. The computer may assess the position as slightly in White's favour, but I think that, in practice at least, Black has the easier position to play. The further course of the game bears this out.

15 ♗a3 ♘f5 16 f4 ♘g6 17 ♗g4 ♘gh4 18 ♗b4 ♕c7 19 a5 ♕f7

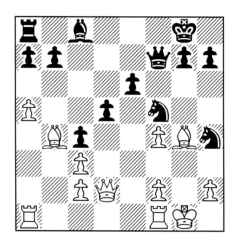

White has secured his queenside from the typical pressure exerted by the enemy queen from a5, but instead, Black switches his attention to the other wing.

20 f3 ♗d7 21 ♖ae1 ♕g6 22 ♔h1 ♗c6 23 ♕f2 d4!

Once again, this positional pawn sacrifice just begs to be played. The bishop on c6 now becomes a powerful piece, bearing down the long diagonal. There is also the incidental threat of ...♕xg4, hence White's next.

24 ♗xf5 ♘xf5 25 cxd4 ♗d5

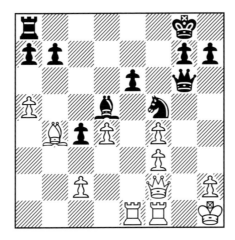

Question: White has a whole extra exchange, so shouldn't he be better?

Answer: In most positions, he would be of course, but here the rooks just lack effective scope. It is hard to argue that the rook on e1 is really a better piece than the knight on f5. That is the secret of such positional exchange sacrifices in the Winawer.

26 c3 ♕h5 27 ♖e5 ♕h6 28 ♖e4

Question: White offers the exchange back?

Answer: Indeed! This is the acknowledgement that the rook is no stronger than the black minor piece.

28...♕h3

Black blithely ignores the rook.

29 ♖g1 b6 30 ♕g2 ♕h5 31 a6 ♖c8

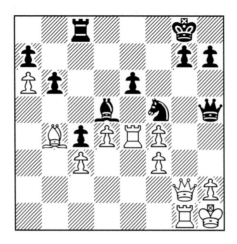

32 ♗d6??

White tries to exploit the tactics to transfer his bishop to e5, but in fact, this move is just a losing blunder. After a move such as 32 ♖f1, the balance would be maintained. White cannot really do anything, but it is also hard for Black to strengthen his position.

32...g6

Now that the mate threat on g7 is disposed of, Black threatens both ...♘xd6 and ...♘h4. White cannot defend against both.

33 ♗e5 ♘h4 0-1

White's position caves in on the long diagonal.

This game is another nice illustration of the positional exchange sacrifice in these Winawer structures. The relatively blocked structure, with its lack of open files, means that knights are frequently as effective as rooks. White was holding the balance until his blunder near the end, but Black always had full compensation for his material investment.

Game 13
J.Vidarsson-C.Ward
Reykjavik 1998

1 e4 e6 2 d4 d5 3 ♘c3 ♗b4 4 e5 c5 5 a3 ♗xc3+ 6 bxc3 ♕a5

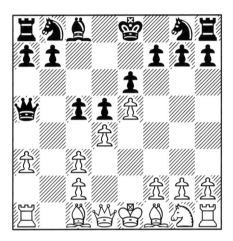

Question: Yet another move order!

Answer: Yes! This is a line which has become very popular in recent years, as a way of avoiding the problems of 6...♘e7 7 ♕g4. This move order actually goes back to the 1950s, when it was used regularly by Lajos Portisch. In the 1960s, it attracted notice in the games of the colourful US Virgin Islands player, Bill Hook, who played it in a famous game against Bobby Fischer. For these reasons, John Watson calls it the Portisch-Hook Variation, a nomenclature which I have no difficulty following.

Question: So what is the point?

Answer: With his early queen manoeuvre, Black aims to bring quick pressure against the white pawns, hoping thereby to restrict White's options. Firstly, Black attacks c3, which needs to be defended. Black then intends to follow up with ...♕a4, which attacks d4 and c2, and also blockades the white a-pawn, thus preventing the standard plan of a4 and ♗a3.

Question: So do you think this line is an improvement on the usual 6...♘e7 line?

Answer: I am not sure I would be that categorical, but the early ...♕a5 is certainly a very logical way to play as Black, and I am surprised that it has taken so long to become popular.

7 ♗d2

Question: Is 7 ♕d2 also possible here?

Answer: Of course. Now 7...♕a4?! makes less sense, since d4 and c2 are both defended, and 8 dxc5 looks an effective reply. 7...♘e7 is likely to transpose into lines we have already examined, but Black can also pursue other plans, one of the main ones being 7...♘c6 8 ♘f3 b6.

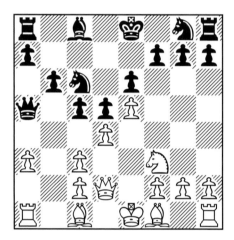

Black hopes to trade off his bad bishop by ♗a6. One oft-quoted example then is J.Poulton-N.Pert, British League 2002, which went 9 dxc5 bxc5 10 a4 ♗a6 11 ♗xa6 ♕xa6 12 ♗a3 ♖c8 13 ♕d3 and now Watson gives 13...♕a5 with a good game for Black. Overall, 7 ♕d2 looks no threat at all to Black.

7...♕a4 8 ♕g4

This is the most aggressive reply. White insists on forcing his opponent to reveal how he plans to defend the g7-square.

The other major option for White here is 8 ♕b1.

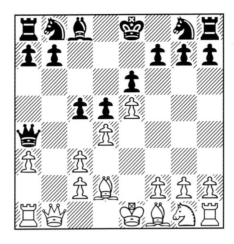

Answer: Basically, White wants to use the threat of 9 ♗b5+ to force Black to close the position with 8...c4 (8...a6?! is not very attractive after 9 ♕b3).

Question: But this is just a standard structure, isn't it?

Answer: Yes, but White has clarified things. In addition, he has relieved the pressure against d4, which is often a feature of the Portisch-Hook variation, and he has stopped the standard plan of ...b6 and ♗a6, exchanging off the bad bishop. On the other hand, Black has his queen blockading the white queenside on a4, and he is relieved of any worries about ♕g4, probing the kingside.

Question: So how should we assess the position?

Answer: I think chances are about equal. A typical recent example, featuring a top player as White, was the game P.Svidler-D.Lima, Khanty-Mansiysk 2011: 9 h4 (White has many possible set-ups, of course, but Svidler's choice here is the most popular) 9...♘c6 10 h5 h6 11 ♘f3 ♗d7 12 g3 0-0-0 13 ♗h3 (the most active formation; White has gained space on the kingside with the h-pawn march, and now he takes aim at the e6-pawn, hoping to discourage Black from breaking with ...f6) 13...♘ge7 14 0-0 ♖df8 15 ♖e1

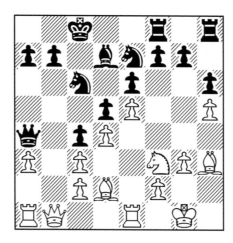

15...g5 (Watson suggests 15...g6 as "more active") 16 ♘h2 f5 17 exf6 and now Watson's suggestion is 17...♖xf6 18 f4 gxf4 19 ♗xf4 ♖g8 with counterplay. White has made progress in activating his dark-squared bishop, but at the cost of weakening his king position. 8 ♕b1 is a critical try against the Portisch-Hook, and forces a closed, heavyweight struggle, but the average Winawer player should be used to such battles. Objectively, the game is close to equal.

Now back to 8 ♕g4, after which Black has a major choice to make.

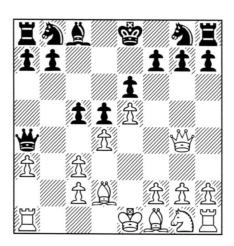

8...g6

Question: That looks incredibly ugly!

Answer: I agree! Weakening the dark squares even further in this way is grossly unaesthetic and creates permanent, long-term weaknesses. However, it does defend g7, without giving up castling rights. Black intends to castle long, securing his king, and hopes that his positional gains on the other wing will give him an adequate game.

Question: But surely White will infiltrate on f6 or h6, won't he?

Answer: Black intends to leave his knight on g8 for the time being, to cover those squares. Meanwhile, he will pressurize the white centre and queenside pawns, in order not to give White a free hand on the kingside.

The other option is 8...♔f8.

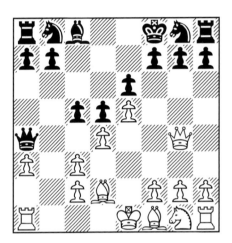

Question: But now Black cannot castle!

Answer: True, but he has avoided a permanent weakening of his kingside dark squares. He hopes that his king will prove safe on f8. Meanwhile, White must decide what to do about his hanging c2-pawn, hence 9 ♕d1.

Question: This is all pretty confusing! Why retreat the queen again?

Answer: White's argument is that his queen has done her job on g4, by provoking the enemy king into moving. Now the queen returns to guard the centre. This is the most popular move here, and was Fischer's choice in the game against Hook.

Alternatively, White can defend everything with the clumsy-looking 9 ♖a2, after which a famous Hook scalp continued 9...♘c6 10 ♘f3 b6 11 ♗d3 ♗a6 12 0-0 ♗xd3 13 cxd3 c4 14 dxc4 ♕xc4 15 ♖aa1 ♘a5, V.Liberzon-W.Hook, Nice Olympiad 1974, with a comfortable position for Black, who eventually scored a famous victory.

Fischer-Hook continued 9 ♕d1 b6. This is the standard plan in such positions. Black proceeds to exchange light-squared bishops. Another logical treatment is 9...♘c6, increasing the pressure against d4. A high-class example from a few years ago then continued 10 ♘f3 ♘ge7 11 ♕b1 c4 12 h4 ♗e8 13 h5 h6 14 g4 ♔d8 15 g5 hxg5 16 ♘xg5 ♔e8 (to and fro; the blocked position makes such manoeuvring viable) 17 ♗e2 b6 18 ♗g4 ♗d7 19 ♕d1 ♘g8 20 ♗e3 ♘h6 and Black had good chances in S.Karjakin-P.Nikolic, Wijk aan Zee 2005.

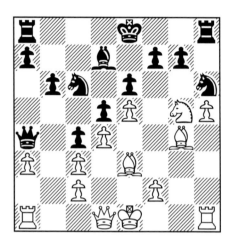

He went on to stand clearly better, before falling for a tactic and losing.

Note that White's last move, 9 ♕d1, defended not only c2, but indirectly d4 as well: 9...cxd4 10 cxd4 ♕xd4?? 11 ♗b4+.

After 9...b6, Fischer went 10 h4.

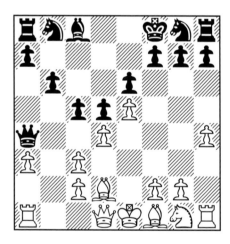

Question: Still not developing any pieces!

Answer: Once again, the relatively closed nature of the position makes such extravagances possible. As we have already seen, h4-advances are another common theme in these

Winawer structures. White hopes to push the pawn all the way to h6, weakening the enemy dark squares further, whilst the rook can often develop via h4.

10 c4 is a critical alternative.

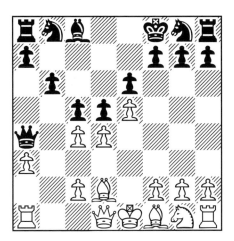

Question: What is the point?

Answer: White seeks to open the position, to activate his bishops and get at the uncastled black king. However, one adequate solution is 10...♘e7 11 cxd5 ♕xd4 12 dxe6 ♕xe5+ 13 ♗e2 ♗b7 14 ♗f4 ♕c3+ 15 ♗d2 ♕e5 16 ♗f4 ♕c3+ 17 ♗d2, as in A.Grischuk-Y.Shulman, Khanty-Mansiysk 2005.

After 10 h4, 10...♘e7 was Hook's choice against Fischer. 10...♗a6 is also fine for Black: 11 ♗xa6 ♘xa6 (equally good is 11...♕xa6: for example, 12 h5 h6 13 ♖h4 ♘e7 14 ♖f4 ♘bc6 as given by Moskalenko, when Black is doing well) 12 h5 h6 13 ♖h4 ♖c8 14 ♖f4 cxd4 15 cxd4 ♖xc2 (or 15...♘e7 16 ♕f3 ♔e8 17 c3 ♖f8 18 ♘h3 ♘b8 19 ♕g4 ♖g8 20 ♕f3 ♖f8 21 ♕g3 ♖g8 22 ♕f3 and ½-½ in I.Cheparinov-P.Nikolic, Wijk aan Zee 2005) 16 ♗c3 ♕b3 17 ♖f3 ♘e7 18 ♖b1 ♕a2 19 ♖a1 ♕b3 20 ♖b1 was agreed drawn in P.Konguvel-V.Moskalenko, Badalona 2006.

R.Fischer-W.Hook, Siegen Olympiad 1970, proceeded 11 h5 h6 (almost always necessary; the pawn cannot be allowed to come to h6) 12 ♖h4 ♗a6 13 ♗xa6.

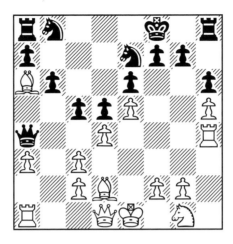

The game went 13...♘xa6 with unclear play, but Watson suggests that 13...♕xa6 followed by ...♕c4 would be even better.

After that long digression, we now return to Ward's 8...g6:

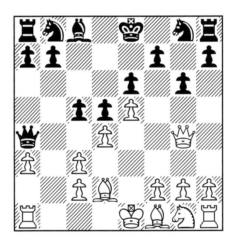

9 ♖a2

White has many options here, just as after 8...♔f8. However, Black's plan is largely the same – if he can take on c2, he usually does so; if not, he generally plays ...b6, ...♗a6 and prepares queenside castling. Let us look at some of the options:

a) 9 ♖c1 defends c2 more naturally than the game move, but of course, it involves sacrificing the a3-pawn. Now 9...♘c6 10 ♘f3 h6!?.

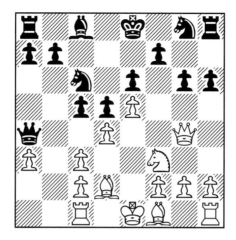

Question: What is this for?

Answer: Black just covers the dark squares a little more, taking g5 from White. 10...b6 is also perfectly reasonable.

11 ♗d3 c4 12 ♗e2 ♗d7 13 ♕f4 ♖h7

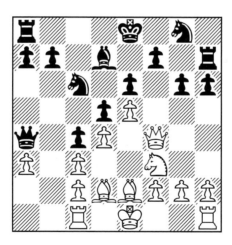

Now we see the other point of Black's 10th. The rook defends f7, so Black can castle long.

Question: It all looks very clumsy!

Answer: It does, but such manoeuvres are often possible in blocked positions. Don't forget that Black is effectively a pawn up already, since he will be able to take on a3 whenever he feels like it. "A pawn ahead is worth a little trouble", as they say.

B.Parma-L.Portisch, Bled 1961, proceeded 14 h4 0-0-0 15 0-0 ♕xa3 16 ♖a1 ♕f8 17 ♘h2 f5 18 exf6 ♘xf6 with an unclear position.

b) 9 h4 is a natural way to attack the kingside, but now Black sets up a light-square blockade: 9...h5 10 ♕g3 ♘e7 11 ♘f3 b6 12 ♗d3 ♗a6 13 ♕g5 ♘d7.

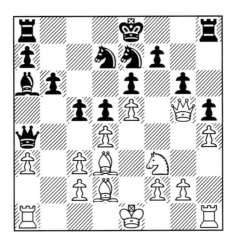

The other knight covers f6 instead! M.Jimale Abdulle-W.Hook, Bled Olympiad 2002, continued 14 g4 ♗xd3 15 cxd3 c4 (a typical idea in such structures; once the exchange of bishops has taken place on d3, this move secures an outpost for Black on c4) 16 gxh5 ♖xh5 17 ♕e3 ♕a6 18 dxc4 ♕xc4 19 ♕e2 ♖c8 20 ♕xc4 ♖xc4, and Black was better in the ending (weak pawns on a3, c3 and h4, plus a bad white bishop) and went on to win a long game.

c) 9 ♕f4.

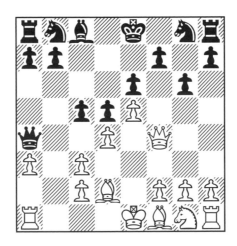

Question: What is this – a pawn sacrifice?

Answer: Indeed. The strong Cuban GM Dominguez has played this twice, so it deserves respect: 9...♕xc2 (the critical move, else White has just improved his queen position free of charge) 10 ♘f3 b6 (10...c4 11 ♗e2 h6 12 0-0 ♘c6 was unclear in L.Dominguez Perez-W.Arencibia Rodriguez, Havana 2008) 11 dxc5 bxc5 12 ♖c1 ♕e4+ 13 ♕xe4 dxe4 14 ♘g5 f5 15 exf6 ♘xf6 16 ♗c4 ♗a6 17 ♗a2 ♘bd7 18 ♘xe6 ♖c8 was unclear and eventually drawn, L.Dominguez Perez-R.Vaganian, Barcelona 2007.

d) 9 ♕d1 is probably soundest, but less threatening than the ♕f4 plan. After 9...b6 (9...♘c6 10 ♘f3 b6 11 h4 h5 – 11...cxd4!? is more critical – 12 dxc5 bxc5 13 ♗e3 c4 14 ♗e2 ♘ge7 15 0-0 was V.Bologan-L.Psakhis, Internet (blitz) 2004, and now 15...♘f5 is unclear) White has:

d1) 10 h4 was once Magnus Carlsen's choice, but after 10...♗a6 11 ♗xa6 ♘xa6 12 h5 cxd4 13 hxg6 fxg6 14 ♖h4 ♘e7 15 cxd4 ♖c8 16 c3 ♘c5! 17 ♖h3 ♕xd1+ 18 ♖xd1 Black had no problems in A.David-L.Psakhis, Bad Wiessee 1999.

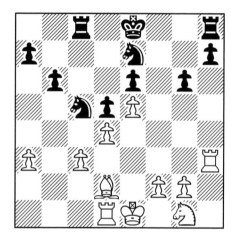

Black's treatment here, allowing h5xg6 and recapturing ...fxg6, is quite notable. Psakhis is one of the world's premier French Winawer experts, and his handling of the positions is always worth a close look.

d2) After 10 ♘f3 ♗a6 11 ♗e2 ♗xe2 12 ♕xe2 c4!? (12...♘c6 also looks fine for Black) 13 0-0 ♕xc2 14 a4 ♘c6 15 ♖fc1 ♕f5 16 ♗e3 h6 17 ♘h4?! ♕e4 18 g4? g5 19 ♘g2 ♘ge7 Black was clearly better and went on to win in A.Hunt-N.Pert, Witley 1999.

> **Question:** So which do you prefer, 8...g6 or 8...♔f8?

Answer: I am honestly not sure. 8...g6 certainly offends my eye, but, interestingly, it was the choice of Portisch himself, and I have great respect for his positional judgement. Black certainly has a safer king after 8...g6, and, as Nigel Short likes to point out, checkmate ends the game – it is no good accumulating positional advantages, if your king gets mated! That is one argument for 8...g6, rather than 8...♔f8. In truth, I think both lines are equally possible, and the choice is largely one of taste.

Finally, we return to 9 ♖a2:

9...c4

9...b6 à la Hook, is more natural. Ward's treatment is always an option in such positions, but strikes me as rather passive.

10 ♕d1 ♘c6 11 ♗e2 ♗d7

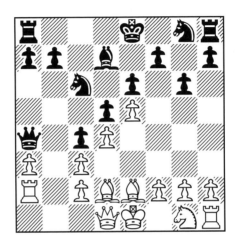

12 g4?

Question: What is this?

Answer: I think this is just rather a rash lunge. White should just develop normally with 12 ♘f3 0-0-0 13 0-0 when he must be somewhat better, although the usual problem of breaking down the solid black structure is still there, of course. The queen's blockading post on a4 is useful here, but the fact that the only kingside break with ...f6 involves such weakening of the dark squares and the e6-pawn means that it is hard to create any active counterplay.

12...f6

Now that White has so weakened himself with 12 g4, this is justified.

13 ♘f3 0-0-0 14 h4 h5!

White's play has been extremely optimistic. Where is he going to put his king? The answer is "Nowhere" – it just has to remain in the centre, and Black will open lines there and attack it.

15 gxh5 ♖xh5 16 exf6 ♖f5 17 ♖g1

Missing his chance. There was the tricky tactic 17 ♘e5! ♘xf6 (if 17...♖xf6 18 ♗g5) 18 ♘f7, after which Black must shed an exchange with 18...♘e4 19 ♘xd8 ♘xf2 20 ♕b1 ♘xd8, with an unclear position.

17...♘xf6

Now Black simply stands better. The white king is a sitting duck in the centre of the board.

18 ♘g5 ♖f8 19 ♗e3 ♕a5!

Nicely luring the white queen on to the fatal square d2.

20 ♕d2

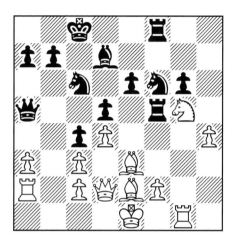

20...♖xg5!

The decisive blow. The knight jump to e4 is devastating.

21 hxg5 ♘e4

The rest is rather gory, so I would suggest you remove any children from the room, before playing through the remaining moves!

22 ♕c1 ♕xc3+ 23 ♗d2 ♕xd4 24 ♗e3 ♕c3+ 25 ♗d2 ♕h3 26 c3 ♕h2 27 ♖f1 ♖xf2 28 ♖xf2 ♕xf2+ 29 ♔d1 ♘a5 30 ♕c2 ♕g1+ 0-1

31 ♗e1 ♘f2+ 32 ♔d2 ♕xg5 is mate.

This main game was rather one-sided, after some over-optimistic play by White in the early middlegame, but nonetheless I think the Portisch-Hook system is a very viable way to play for Black. If the latter is looking to avoid lots of forcing lines, such as arise after 6...♘e7 7 ♕g4, it is ideal, as it relies much more on general plans.

1 e4 e6 2 d4 d5 3 ♘c3 ♝b4 4 e5 ♘e7

Answer: It can be, but usually, as here, it just amounts to a transposition.
5 a3 ♝xc3+ 6 bxc3 c5 7 ♘f3 ♛c7

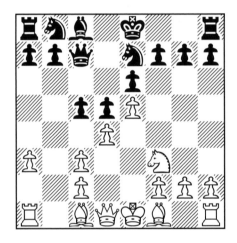

Answer: This is the start of another system entirely. Rather than place the queen on a5, Black puts it on c7. From there, it still exerts pressure down the c-file (...cxd4 is sometimes a threat), but also attacks e5. It is less threatening than 7...♛a5, but is a very solid and re-spectable system. It enjoyed great popularity in the late 1960s and early 1970s, and was later revived with success in the 1980s/90s, by the then leading GMs Yusupov and Predrag Nikolic. It remains a reliable and, in my view, underrated line for Black.

The real significance of this system with ...♛c7 is in terms of the move order 4...c5 5 a3 ♝xc3+ 6 bxc3 ♛c7. This is a weapon against an early ♛g4. Black intends to meet 7 ♛g4 by moving his f-pawn, when the queen defends g7 along the rank. This line is examined in Game 19. However, if White meets this line with 7 ♘f3, then after 7...♘e7, we reach the game position.

8 a4

8 ♝d3 is a tame move, which allows Black to implement his main idea: 8...b6!, revealing

a key point of these ...♛c7 systems. Black prepares to exchange his traditionally bad light-squared bishop, by means of ...♝a6. In general, if he can achieve this without suffering any immediate consequences, then he stands comfortably. Not only has he offloaded his own potentially bad bishop, he has also deprived White of one of his key attacking pieces, after which castling short becomes much safer for Black.

8...b6 9 ♝b5+

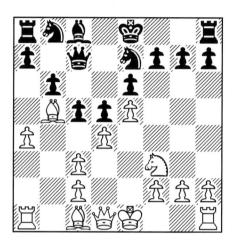

Question: What's this – "patzer sees a check, patzer gives a check"?

Answer: Not at all. This move actually embodies quite a subtle idea. White is trying to prevent Black from implementing his ...♝a6 plan, to exchange bishops.

Question: But how can he do that? Surely ...♝a6 will be possible, after the check has been blocked?

Answer: Well, as John Nunn always used to say to me, when I tried to spout general principles, "What move are you going to play?"

Question: Well, how about just 9...♞bc6 then?

Answer: Okay, but now you can't play ...♝a6, because it will be en prise!

Question: Oh, I see. Okay, I will play 9...♞ec6 instead, and then I can follow up with ...♝a6.

Answer: Yes, but now you have removed the only minor piece that defends your kingside. You will get to make the bishop exchange, sure, but your kingside is rather bereft. The old game A.Lein-A.Bastrikov, USSR 1959, continued 10 0-0 ♗a6 11 ♘g5! h6 12 ♘h3 and moves such as ♕g4 and/or ♘f4-h5 are in the air. This is not terribly comfortable for Black.

> *Question:* You have an answer to everything, don't you! All right, let's play simply 9...♗d7 and now we will exchange bishops on b5 instead!

Answer: "Cherez moi troop!", as they say in Russian ! ("Over my dead body!"). The point of White's idea is now revealed:

9...♗d7

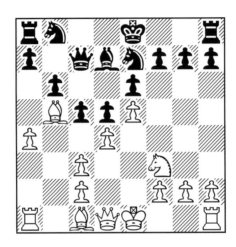

10 ♗d3!

This is the key – now the black bishop has been lured away from the a6-square, White can retreat his bishop to d3, and the exchange of bishops has been avoided, albeit at the cost of a tempo.

10 0-0 is less logical, and does not offer any advantage, although it is not entirely without venom and is worth a more extended look: 10...♗xb5 11 axb5.

> *Question:* Doesn't Black now have a backward a-pawn?

Answer: He does at this moment, but after 11...a5! he does not any more! Play might continue 12 ♘g5 (White again adopts this standard way of generating kingside play; it is his only hope, as Black has solved his positional issues on the queenside, and will stand very comfortably if he is allowed simply to castle short and play ...♘d7, ...♖c8, etc) 12...h6 13 ♘h3 ♘d7 14 ♘f4.

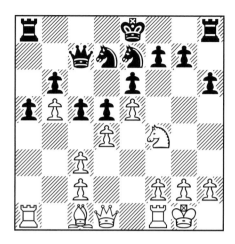

Now 14...0-0 is good enough for equality: for example, 15 ♘h5 ♔h8! 16 ♕g4 ♖g8 17 ♕h3 ♘f8 and Black was extremely solid in B.Ivkov-R.Byrne, Sousse Interzonal 1967, but 14...cxd4 is more critical, and possibly objectively stronger: 15 cxd4 ♕c4 16 ♗a3. Here is the rub. White will generate play on the dark squares. A famous game L.Stein-R.Byrne, Sousse Interzonal 1967 (played a few rounds before Ivkov-Byrne above – 14...0-0 was Byrne's attempted improvement) ended in drastic defeat for Black, but improvements are possible: 16...♘f5 17 c3 g6 (17...h5!? 18 ♘xh5 ♕xc3 19 g4 ♕h3! – Moles) 18 ♕f3 ♕xb5 (and here Moles suggests 18...h5!?) 19 g4 ♘e7 (19...♘h4!? is Moles's final suggestion) 20 ♖fc1 ♖c8 21 ♖ab1 ♕c4? (21...♕a6) 22 ♘g2! ♖c6 23 ♘e3 ♕a4 24 ♖a1 ♕b5

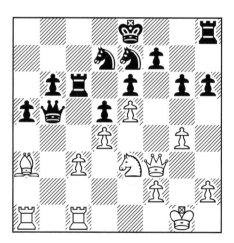

25 c4! 1-0. Black actually resigned, chiefly in view of the line 25...dxc4 26 ♘xc4 ♖xc4 27 ♕a8+ ♘c8 28 ♕xc8+ ♖xc8 29 ♖xc8#. However, although this game gave Black's line, starting at move 14, a bad reputation, it remains far from clear, as the various suggested improvements show.

Now back to the main line.

10...♘bc6 11 0-0

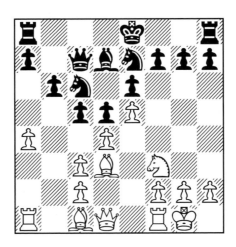

Question: So what is happening in this position?

Answer: I think chances are about equal. Black has developed his pieces, and has the standard queenside structural advantage. He will castle short, play ...♘a5 and possibly ...♖c8, with counterplay on the queenside. The kingside thrust ...f7-f5 is another key idea. For his part, White has his bishop-pair, chances of kingside play, and hopes to activate his queen's bishop on the dark squares. It is a typical Winawer fight.

12...h6

Question: Is this necessary?

Answer: Indeed it is, at least if Black wants to castle short. The immediate 11...0-0? allows the old Greek Gift sacrifice: 12 ♗xh7+ ♔xh7 13 ♘g5+ ♔g6 14 ♕d3+ ♘f5 (or 14...f5 15 ♗f4 ♕b7 16 ♕g3) 15 g4 with a dangerous initiative.

12 ♖e1

The older line, which has similar ideas, starts 12 ♗a3 ♘a5 13 ♘d2 0-0 14 dxc5 bxc5 15 ♘b3! (this forces the exchange on b3, straightening out White's pawns) 15...♘xb3 (15...♘b7? leaves the knight misplaced on b7) 16 cxb3

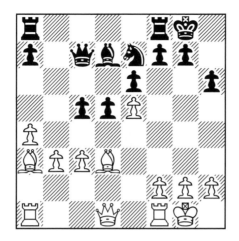

16...f6! (this active move was an improvement on 16...♖fc8?! which landed Black in trouble after 17 ♖e1 ♘g6 18 ♗c1 ♘xe5 19 ♗f4 f6 20 ♖e3 ♗e8 21 ♕e2 ♖ab8 22 ♗c2 c4 23 b4 ♖d8 24 ♖xe5 fxe5 25 ♗xe5 ♕d7 26 ♗xb8 ♖xb8 27 ♕e5 and Black never escaped his chains on the dark squares in A.Williams-R.Keene, British Championship, Eastbourne 1973) 17 exf6 ♖xf6 18 c4?! (18 b4 c4 19 ♗c2 ♗e8 is unclear) 18...d4 19 b4 cxb4 20 ♗xb4 ♘c6 21 ♗a3 e5 22 ♖b1 ♘a5 23 ♗e4 ♗c6 24 ♗d5+ ♔h8 25 f4 ♖d8, C.Pritchett-G.Botterill, British Championship, Brighton 1977. Chances are about equal, although White soon went wrong and lost.

The reader will note the many references in this section to the English Oxbridge generation of the late 1960s and early 1970s – Keene, Whiteley, Hartston, Botterill, Williams, Moles etc. These players contributed greatly to the theory of this ...♕c7 set-up.

12...0-0

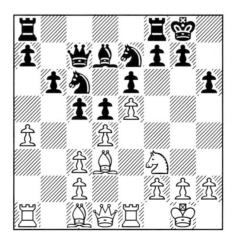

13 ♗a3

As in the previous note, White looks to activate his bishop on its traditional a3-f8 di-agonal. The alternative is 13 ♗f4, which is similar to Game 7. White wants to use his bishop on the kingside with ♕d2 and a possible sacrifice on h6. White's kingside chances should not be underestimated, but it seems that Black defends adequately after 13...♘g6 14 ♗g3 cxd4.

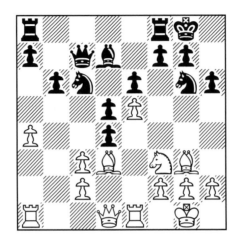

15 ♘xd4 ♘a5 (a standard idea in this line; the knight heads to c4, whilst the queen's pressure down the c-file is unmasked) 16 ♕g4 (16 ♖e3 ♘c4 17 ♗xc4 ♕xc4 18 h4 ♗xa4 19 h5 ♘e7 20 ♗f4 was unclear, and eventually drawn in J.Nunn-P.Nikolic, Amsterdam 1988) 16...♕xc3 17 ♖ad1 (17 ♘e2 ♕c7 18 ♗xg6 fxg6 19 ♕xg6 ♗c8! is equal, as given by Atalik) 17...♘c6 18 ♘b5 ♕b4 gives White compensation for the pawn, but no more than that.

Question: Why not straighten out the pawns with the other recapture at move 15?

Answer: The problem is that 15 cxd4 ♘b4! eliminates White's key light-squared bishop.

Question: Isn't the immediate bishop sacrifice on h6 possible at move 13?

Answer: A good question. It took some years for the English theorists to work out that it was unsound, but it appears that White has insufficient compensation for the piece after 13 ♗xh6 gxh6! 14 ♕d2 ♔g7 15 ♕f4 ♘g8!.

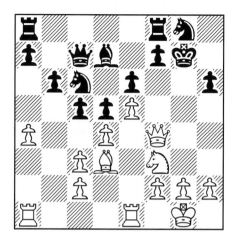

Following 16 ♖e3 ♘ce7 17 ♘h4 ♘g6 18 ♖g3 ♗e8 19 ♖e1 c4 20 ♗xg6 fxg6 21 ♕g4 ♘e7 22 ♕xe6 ♕d7 Black soon won in R.Sutton-J.Moles, Skopje Olympiad 1972.

Yet another impressive demonstration of the English players' mastery of this variation was the game C.Zuidema-A.Whiteley, Cala Galdana 1974, which saw the white player massacred: 13 ♕d2 f5 14 exf6 ♖xf6 15 dxc5 bxc5 16 ♕e3 c4 17 ♗f1 ♖af8 18 ♗a3 ♖8f7 19 ♖ad1?! ♕a5 and White was already dropping a pawn, with no counterplay on the kingside.

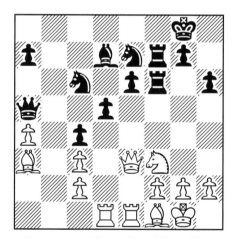

He tried to save himself tactically, but without success: 20 ♕c5 ♕xc3 21 ♗xc4 dxc4 22 ♖e3 (22 ♖xd7? ♖xf3) 22...♕xc2 23 ♖xd7 and now the exchange sacrifice finished him off: 23...♖xf3! 24 gxf3 ♕b1+ 25 ♔g2 ♖f5 0-1.

13...♘a5

This is basically forced, to defend the c-pawn.

14 dxc5 bxc5 15 ♘d2

Again, a standard manoeuvre. White frees the way for his queen to come to g4 and his rook via e3 to g3.

15...♗xa4

Critical, although French expert Igor Naumkin has played 15...♘g6 here, which also seems adequate.

16 ♕g4!

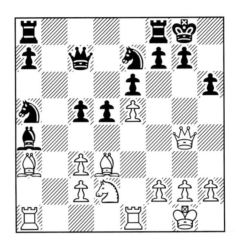

This move is the most critical. J.Nunn-A.Yusupov, Linares 1988, was equal/unclear after 16 ♗xc5 ♕xc5 17 ♖xa4 ♕xc3 18 ♖e3 ♔h8!. Black eventually won, and although this was not directly the result of the opening, it is notable that Nunn later switched to 16 ♕g4 here.

> *Question:* This is all a bit obscure. What is going on?

Answer: Basically, White has sacrificed a pawn, for a kingside attack. He will follow up with ♘f3 and ♗c1, and try to blast Black off the board on the kingside.

> *Question:* So is he better?

Answer: I don't believe so, but such a position is very concrete, and careful analysis is needed. On the basis of the game under consideration, Black seems to be holding at least, but he needs to play accurately. White has actually scored very well in practice from this position, but Black's 16th move may change that.

16...♗e8!

Atalik attributes this to the Russian GM, Sergey Ivanov (another Winawer expert, whose games are always worth looking at). Previously, the usual move had been 16...♗d7, when 17 ♘f3 ♖ab8 (17...♘c4 18 ♗c1 f5 19 exf6 ♖xf6 20 ♗xc4 dxc4 21 ♕xc4 was better for White in J.Nunn-P.Nikolic, Wijk aan Zee 1992, whilst the point of Black's 16th move in the game is shown if Black here tries: 17...♘ac6? aping Atalik's play in the main game; this now fails, because after 18 ♗xc5 ♘xe5 19 ♘xe5 ♕xc5, the bishop on d7 hangs) 18 ♗c1 ♔h8 19 ♕h3! ♘g8 20 g4! ♗b5 21 g5 ♗xd3 22 cxd3 was A.Colovic-D.Komarov, Barletta 1999, where White's attack was too strong.

17 ♘f3 ♘ac6

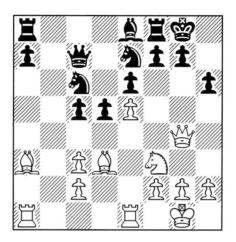

18 ♗c1?!

The natural follow-up, but Atalik, annotating the game in *ChessBase Magazine*, suggests it may be the cause of White's troubles. Instead, he analyses 18 c4 ♘b4 19 cxd5 ♘exd5 20 ♗e4 ♗c6 21 ♗c1 and now both 21...♖ae8 and 21...♔h8 are enough for equality, but no more. Indeed, after the latter, 22 ♕h5 ♔g8 23 ♕g4 ♔h8 could produce an immediate draw.

18...f5 19 exf6

19 ♕g3 ♔h8 is adequate for Black.

19...♖xf6

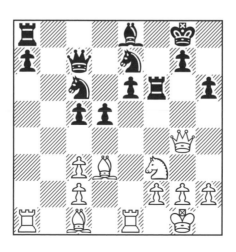

20 c4

20 ♖xe6? ♗d7 21 ♗xh6? ♖xh6 (Atalik) is the tactical point of Black's play.

20...♗g6

Atalik mentions 20...♗d7 as an alternative, whilst the computer likes 20...♖b8. In all cases, White has enough kingside play to compensate for his pawn minus, but no more than that.

21 ♗b2!?

Atalik records that his opponent was unable fully to calculate the consequences of 21 ♖xe6. The point is that after 21...♕d7 22 cxd5 the reply 22...♗xd3 is forced, because 22...♘xd5? allows the winning queen sacrifice 23 ♖xf6!! ♕xg4 24 ♖xg6 ♕c8 (if 24...♕h5 25 ♖xc6) 25 ♗xh6 with a decisive advantage. After 22...♗xd3, 23 cxd3 ♘xd5 24 ♖e4 ♕xg4 25 ♖xg4 is equal.

21...♗f5

Atalik says he assumes White had missed this, but in fact, Black has no advantage anyway.

22 ♕h5?

Now Black assumes the advantage. As Atalik points out, White had to exchange queens with 22 ♕g3 ♕xg3 23 hxg3 when the position is equal.

22...d4

Now the white dark-squared bishop is shut out of the game.

23 ♗a3

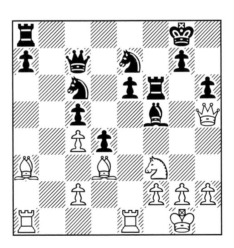

23...♘g6

Atalik awards this two exclamation marks, and claims that after 23...♕d6 24 ♘d2, "I will not get much", but the computer disagrees: 24...♘e5 25 ♗xf5 exf5 26 f4 ♘d7 just seems to leave Black a pawn up, with a clear advantage.

24 ♗xf5 exf5 25 ♗xc5 ♘f4 26 ♖e8+

After 26 ♕h4 ♖g6, the white queen is done for after ...♖g4.

26...♖xe8 27 ♕xe8+ ♔h7 28 ♖e1?

Here, the computer agrees with Atalik, that White is still holding after 28 ♕e1!. The text loses.

28...♕a5!

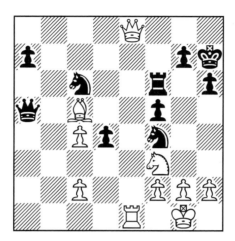

This extremely strong move leaves the white bishop without a safe square anywhere on the board!

29 ♗xd4

29 ♗f8 ♘g6! traps the bishop, whilst 29 ♗e7 ♖g6 30 g3 ♕c3 is "Goodnight Vienna".

29...♘xd4 30 ♘xd4 ♖e6! 0-1

This nice interference/back rank motif decides the game.

Rather a cataclysmic finish, but the analysis shows that White has enough for his pawn in this line, if no more than that. Overall, the ...♕c7 lines are a very solid and respectable way for Black to play.

1 e4 e6 2 d4 d5 3 ♘c3 ♗b4 4 e5 c5 5 a3 ♗xc3+ 6 bxc3 ♘e7 7 ♘f3 b6

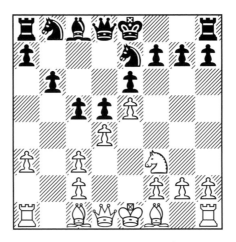

Question: Yet another different set-up!

Answer: Yes! One of the great advantages of the Winawer is that Black's position is extremely flexible and allows numerous plausible ways of handling the line.

Question: This time, I think I understand the idea! Black
intends ...♗a6, exchanging off his bad bishop?

Answer: Correct. We saw this plan in the previous game, but with Black's queen already on c7.

Question: Isn't this more logical? After all, if Black intends to play ...b6 and
...♗a6, why not do so at once, and keep flexibility with the queen?

Answer: That is a very fair point. However, as we pointed out in the notes to the previous game, the real significance of the ...♕c7 line is the move order 6...♕c7, intending 7 ♕g4 f5. With the move order in the present game, Black saves a tempo on ...♕c7, but he has to have another way to meet 7 ♕g4.

8 ♗b5+

We also saw this idea in the previous game. White intends to avoid the exchange of bishops. Other moves offer White nothing.

8...♗d7 9 ♗d3 ♗a4

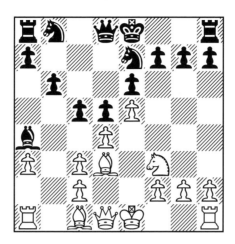

Answer: Well, this is the advantage of the tempo saved on not playing ...♕c7. The white pawn has not had time to advance to a4, so this blockading move becomes possible.

Black can also flick in the preliminary 9...c4, blockading the queenside once and for all, and then after 10 ♗f1 play 10...♗a4. Indeed, this was originally the main line, but in recent times, Black has started to delay ...c4.

Answer: Mainly to preserve flexibility. Black reasons that,,,c5-c4 is a move he will always be able to play anyway, so it makes some sense to hold it back, so as to complicate White's task. The latter has to select a development plan, taking into account the possibility of both ...c5-c4, and also some other line, such as ...cxd4 or just development by Black. At some point, if White has committed himself, Black can then play ...c5-c4, hopefully in more favourable circumstances.

But while we are talking about the blocked positions after ...c5-c4, we may as well introduce an idea, which we will see repeatedly in such positions. It is a manoeuvre first played, I believe, by Yusupov. After 9...c4 10 ♗f1 ♗a4: 11 h4 (11 g3 is met in similar fashion: 11...h6 12 ♗h3 ♔d7 13 0-0 ♕g8 14 ♘e1 ♔c7 15 ♘g2 ♘d7 16 f4 g6 17 ♘e3 h5 18 ♗g2 b5 19 h3 f5 20 exf6 ♘xf6 21 ♕e2 ♔d7 22 ♖e1 ♘f5 23 ♘f1 ♖e8 was agreed drawn in F.Jenni-A.Yusupov, German League 2002) 11...h6 12 h5 ♔d7!.

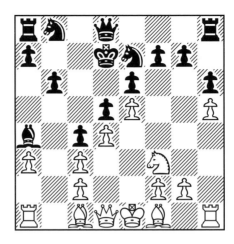

Question: Good grief! What an extraordinary move. What on earth is Black up to?

Answer: This plan has become almost a reflex action for Black in such positions. Of course, it looks strange to move the king so early, and forego castling, but with the position so blocked, the king is as safe as houses on d7.

Question: Okay, that may be so, but I still don't see why Black does not just prepare ...0-0-0

Answer: You will see why in a moment. Black has plans for his queen, namely 13 ♗f4 ♕g8!. Here it is! The queen is heading for the square h7, from where it will join in with its bishop on a4, in attacking the c2-pawn!

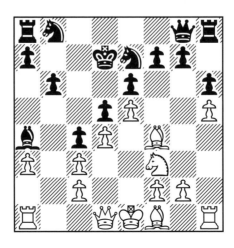

Answer: Maybe, but in such a blocked position, it is not clear what else the queen can do. The pawn on b6 prevents her reaching a5. The double attack on c2 is quite a nuisance for White, who has to devote a rook and maybe his queen to defending the pawn. In addition, from h7, the black queen always has the possibility of jumping into the game, via f5 or e4. This plan with ...♗a4, ...♔d7 and ...♕g8-h7 has now been played numerous times in this lines, and is known as a sound idea.

Answer: Ah, well that is another matter. The truth is that these blocked positions are quite drawish. That is another reason why Black tends to delay ...c5-c4 these days, in the hope of preserving more dynamism in the game. I cannot pretend that this 7...b6 system is a great winning weapon for Black, but it is excellent if he wants a solid position.

A.Shirov-A.Yusupov, Moscow Olympiad 1994, continued 14 g3 ♕h7 15 ♖c1 ♘bc6 16 ♗g2 a5 17 ♘h2 b5 18 ♕d2 ♘f5 19 0-0 ♘fe7 20 ♘g4 ♖ag8 21 ♗f3 ♔c8 22 ♔g2 ♔b7 23 ♖fe1 ♖d8 24 ♖e2 ♔a6 25 ♖h1 ♘c8 26 ♘e3 ♘b6 27 ♖ee1 ♕g8 28 ♘g4 ½-½. This was a typical game for the line – if White does not do anything silly, it is hard for either side to make progress.

Returning to Vitiugov's 9...♗a4:

10 h4 h6

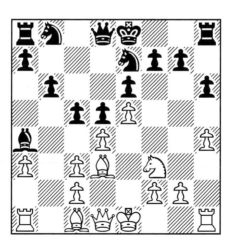

11 ♗f4

After the logical follow-up 11 h5, Black has a choice. He can close the position with 11...c4 (as he can do at almost any move, of course), and then play reverts to very similar patterns to those in the last note: for example, 12 ♗e2 ♔d7 13 ♗f4 (13 ♘h4 ♕g8 14 ♗g4 ♕h7 15 ♖a2 ♘a6 16 ♖h3 ♘c7 17 ♔f1 ♖af8 was yet another Yusupov example, also won by Black after a long battle, K.Georgiev-A.Yusupov, Las Palmas 1993) 13...♕g8 14 ♘d2 ♕h7 15 ♖a2 ♘a6 16 g4 ♘c7 led to a long manoeuvring battle and an eventual draw in the game V.Bologan-N.Vitiugov, Russian Team Championship 2010. 11...♘bc6 12 ♖h4 c4 13 ♗e2 ♔d7 14 ♗e3 ♕g8 15 ♕d2 ♕h7 16 ♖c1 ♔c7 17 ♖f4 ♖af8 was similar in A.Sokolov-A.Yusupov, 1st matchgame, Riga 1986, one of the first games with the ...♔d7 and ...♕g8 plan. Black eventually won.

Alternatively, he can keep things fluid with 11...♕c7 12 0-0 ♘d7 13 ♖e1 a6.

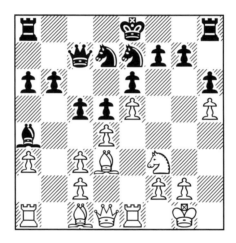

Question: What is the idea of this move?

Answer: It is another idea worth noting. Black intends ...♗b5, forcing the exchange of bishops after all. It is frequently seen in these lines where Black does not close the game with ...c5-c4. After 14 ♘h4 ♗b5 15 a4 ♗xd3 16 cxd3 0-0 Black was doing fine, and the game was eventually drawn, Z.Lanka-N.Sedlak, Lienz 2011.

11...♘bc6

Once again, the standard idea 11...c4!? 12 ♗e2 ♔d7 is perfectly possible, whilst the game Z.Lanka-I.Farago, Austrian League 2011, proceeded in similar fashion to Lanka-Sedlak in the previous note: 11...♕c7 12 ♕d2 ♘d7 13 h5 a6 14 g4 (this time White adopts a much more aggressive plan, ruling out short castling for both sides; however, Black is still okay) 14...♗b5 15 ♔f1 ♗xd3+ 16 cxd3 ♖c8 17 ♔g2

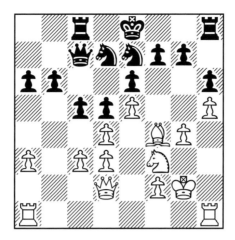

17...c4 (an idea we have seen before after cxd3 – Black secures an outpost on c4 and pressure down the c-file) 18 ♖hc1 cxd3 19 ♕xd3 ♕c4 20 ♕e3 b5 and another long battle was eventually drawn.

> **Question:** The words "long battle" seem synonymous with this variation!

Answer: That is true. The positions reached are real heavyweight stuff.
12 h5 a6!?
Now we know what the point is – Black wants to exchange bishops on b5.
13 ♕b1
Stopping the bishop exchange. The other way of trying to do so, 13 ♕e2?? c4, happens in a lot of online blitz games!
13...♕c7 14 0-0 ♘a5 15 ♖a2!

> **Question:** What is the point?

Answer: White has several ideas – he overprotects c2, and prepares ♖b2, attacking b6.
15...♖b8?!
This proves a waste of time. In *ChessBase Magazine*, Vitiugov recommended 15...0-0, when chances are balanced.
16 ♖e1

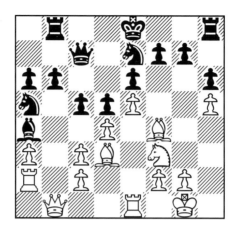

16...♔d7?!

> *Question:* Cripes! This looks a bit optimistic here, with the centre still not closed.

Answer: I totally agree. It really looks a bit much to me. 16...0-0 is still perfectly satisfactory.
17 ♖b2

Now 18 ♗xa6 is a threat, since Black cannot cut the bishop off with 18...b5.
17...c4

Because 17...♘c4?! fails to 18 ♗xc4 dxc4 19 dxc5 bxc5 20 ♖d1+ ♔c8 (20...♘d5?? 21 ♖xd5+ wins) 21 ♘d2 with a strong attack, the text is forced.
18 ♗e2

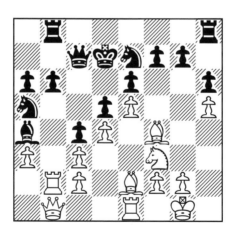

> *Question:* OK, we have finally reached the standard
> blocked structure. Isn't Black fine here?

Answer: Well, the problem is that he has made a lot of moves which do not really fit. His queen is much less active on c7 than h7, for example, and his knight on a5 is doing nothing. White certainly has a better version of the structure than he normally gets. Indeed, Vitiugov went so far as to assess the position as clearly better for White. Having said that, the further course of the game goes to show how hard it can be for White to make progress in such positions, even when he starts with a favourable version.

18...♘ac6 19 ♕c1 b5!?

This is a typical part of the plan of pushing the queenside pawns, but it also shuts the bishop on a4 out of the game.

20 ♘h2!

The knight is on its way to e3, which is frequently a good post for it in these lines.

Question: Why is that?

Answer: From e3, the knight frees up the kingside pawns to advance, with g4, f4 and f5. The knight also attacks d5, f5, etc, and defends c2.

20...a5

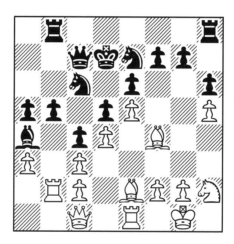

21 ♖a2!

I like this move.

Question: Why?

Answer: It is a neat piece of prophylaxis against the advance ...b5-b4. Black cannot play this, until he has ensured his bishop will not hang after axb4.

21...♕d8 22 ♗g4 ♕g8!

The black queen heads for her traditional post on h7, albeit rather late.

23 ♘f1 ♔c7 24 ♘e3 ♔b7 25 ♗h3 ♘c8 26 ♗g3 ♘b6

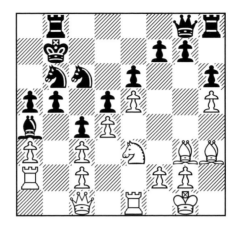

27 f4?

f4-f5 is White's main plan, but he mistimes it. Vitiugov recommended 27 ♗h4!?.

27...f5! 28 ♕d1?!

The second mistake. White loses the thread. 28 ♗h4 was Vitiugov's recommendation.

> ***Question:*** But surely White should be opening
> the position with 28 exf6, shouldn't he?

Answer: That is the move he would like to play, but here, after 28...gxf6 29 ♗h4 f5, Black is fine. The e6-pawn is easily defended, White's f4-f5 advance has been killed forever, and his dark-squared bishop is now obstructed by his own pawn on f4.

28...♘e7 29 ♖f1

Perhaps White should try 29 ♔h2!? g5 30 hxg6 ♘xg6 31 ♕h5 (Vitiugov).

29...g5 30 hxg6 ♘xg6

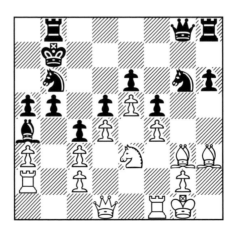

31 ♗xf5!?

Inarkiev realises that he has lost much of his advantage, and tries to force matters. Instead, 31 ♔h2 h5 is equal.

31...exf5 32 ♘xf5 ♔a6 33 ♕f3?!

The game now starts to be affected by time-trouble. This allows Black to advance the h-pawn and start counterplay. 33 ♕h5 maintains the balance.

33...h5! 34 ♘e3 h4 35 ♗h2 h3 36 g4 ♘h4 37 ♕g3 ♖b7 38 f5 ♘g2

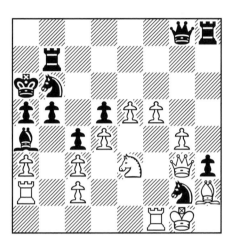

39 g5?

Losing at once. Correct was 39 ♘xg2 hxg2 40 ♖f2! ♖bh7 41 ♖xg2 ♖h3 42 ♕f4 ♖xc3 and Black retains some advantage, but the position is still very unclear.

39...♖h5 40 g6 ♘xe3 41 ♕xe3 ♖f7!

Now the white kingside pawn chain collapses.

42 f6 ♕xg6+ 43 ♗g3 h2+ 44 ♔h1 ♖h3 45 ♖f3 ♗xc2 0-1

This heavyweight battle is absolutely typical of the 7...b6 line. It is a very respectable and solid way for Black to play, and White has a very tough time breaking his opponent down, even if the latter commits a few inaccuracies. The main drawback of 7...b6, from Black's standpoint, is that it is quite hard to play for a win, unless White goes crazy. To win such blocked positions, the black player needs the patience of Job and the positional understanding of Petrosian – rather like Artur Yusupov, in fact!

1 e4 e6 2 d4 d5 3 ♘c3 ♗b4 4 e5 c5 5 a3 ♗xc3+ 6 bxc3 ♘e7 7 ♕g4

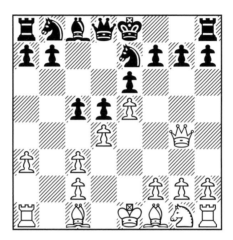

This move initiates White's sharpest response to the main line Winawer. His queen comes out to attack the key square g7, which has been weakened by the early development of Black's dark-squared bishop.

7...cxd4

And this, in turn, starts Black's sharpest and most uncompromising reply. He sacrifices his kingside pawns, to destroy the white central pawn structure, and set up an extremely double-edged position. Quieter alternatives, principally 7...0-0, are examined in Game 18.

8 ♕xg7 ♖g8 9 ♕xh7 ♕c7 10 ♘e2 ♘bc6 11 f4 ♗d7

11...dxc3 12 ♕d3 d4 is a trendy line at present, and is examined in the next game.

12 ♕d3 dxc3

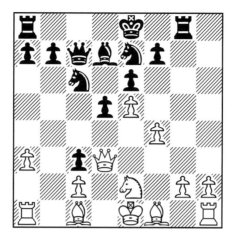

This is the principal *tabiya* of the whole variation.

> **Question:** What on earth is going on? Black seems to be on
> the verge of losing a pawn, with his kingside destroyed!

Answer: Both of those things are true, but Black has various forms of compensation.

> **Question:** Such as?

Answer: Firstly, he is ahead in development, which is certainly not to be sniffed at, in such a sharp and open position. Secondly, his king will be pretty safe after ...0-0-0, whereas White's king may struggle to find a safe haven. He cannot easily castle kingside, because moving his king's bishop is likely to leave the g2-pawn hanging, and even if he does manage it, the open h- and g-files mean that Black is likely to have serious counterplay on that wing.

> **Question:** But what about the white kingside pawns?
> Isn't the passed h-pawn just going to overwhelm Black?

Answer: It may look that way at first, but in practice, it is often very hard to make effective use of these pawns, at least in the middlegame. White is likely to be too busy trying to hold back the black counterplay, and shield his own king.

> **Question:** Okay, but isn't Black going to lose his
> c-pawn and thus be a pawn down as well?

Answer: Yes, but he will then have counterplay down the c-file as well.

> **Question:** Hmm. I am still a bit sceptical!

Answer: That is understandable. The position is hard to judge at first sight, and it is only after seeing some of the concrete problems both sides face, that one can start to appreciate the strength of the black position, in particular. Indeed, many GMs still do not believe in the black position, and the strong American Grandmaster, Yasser Seirawan, has even gone so far as to claim that Black is objectively lost! That is an extreme claim (Seirawan is notorious for his materialism), but it is fair to say that most GMs would prefer the white side of the position. Computers have made people more sceptical of such long-term material sacrifices, and 7 ♕g4 is undoubtedly the critical response to the Winawer. It is because of many black players' reluctance to play this sharp variation that move orders such as the Portisch-Hook line have become popular in recent years.

13 ♘xc3

This is a major parting of the ways, with White having many alternatives here. Of course, it is impossible to give a detailed theoretical coverage of the whole line in a book such as this, but we will look at a few sample lines, with a view to illustrating some of the typical ideas for both sides.

a) With 13 ♖g1 White declines to take on c3, instead leaving the pawn alone and concentrating on trying to advance his kingside pawns.

> **Question:** But why not take the pawn?

Answer: Well, as we will see, taking on c3 often allows Black counterplay on the c-file, after a later ...♖c8. It also takes time, which further delays White's development. By leaving the c3-pawn alone, White instead attends to his own plans.

Black responds 13...d4.

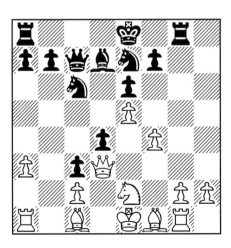

Question: Huh? Isn't that en prise?

Answer: Yes, but it is a typical pawn sacrifice in such positions. 14 g4 (after 14 ♘xd4 ♘xd4 15 ♕xd4 ♗c6 Black has excellent compensation, in the shape of splendidly active pieces, and the white king stuck in the centre; moves such as ...♘f5, ...♖d8, etc. are in the air) 14...0-0-0 15 h4 ♘d5 (15...♕b6 is also a good move here, defending d4 and preparing ...♘d5) 16 ♘xd4 ♘xd4 17 ♕xd4 ♗c6 18 ♗e2 (18 ♕xa7 f6 starts central counterplay) 18...f6! (now we see the drawbacks of White's plan with g4 and h4, his king is denuded and very exposed, if the centre opens up; Black is willing to invest several pawns for that purpose) 19 h5 (19 exf6 e5! is Black's idea; after 20 ♕xe5 ♕b6 followed by ...♖ge8, he has fierce counterplay) 19...♕h7 20 ♖a2 (20 exf6!) 20...♕e7 21 exf6 ♘xf6 22 ♕xc3 ♘e4 23 ♕h3.

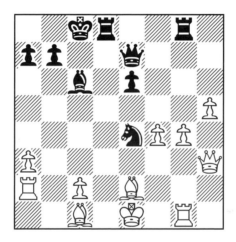

Thus far we are following A.Rasmussen-N.Zhukova, Athens 2008. Now 23...e5 would have resulted in a typically chaotic and unclear position for this variation. White has two extra pawns, but his king is a permanent problem and Black has a strong initiative.

b) 13 h4 is another variation on the plan seen in the last game. White again ignores the c3-bait and starts pushing his passed h-pawn, hoping to tie down the black forces to stopping the pawn, and thus hamper Black's counterplay in that way. Play goes 13...♘f5 (another typical theme in this variation; advancing the h-pawn weakens g3, to which Black immediately directs his knight) 14 ♖b1 d4 15 h5 0-0-0 16 ♖g1.

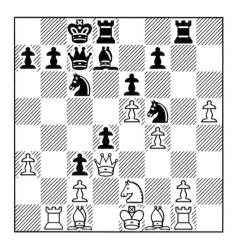

Question: What a mess!

Answer: After a while spent studying this variation, such positions start to look perfectly normal! Both sides have played logically enough – Black has finished his development, whilst White has advanced his h-pawn. Now he wants to join up with g2-g4, also attacking the active black knight.

Black can now go 16...♚b8.

Question: That looks incredibly slow, if not to say,
complacent in such a sharp position.

Answer: In fact, it is quite a standard idea. Black gets his king into a more secure spot, and also envisages a possible ...♝c8, ...b6, and ...♝b7 manoeuvre. However, he has alternatives:

b1) 16...♞ce7?!.

Question: What is the point?

Answer: It is another thematic idea in such lines. The knight frees c6 for the bishop, whilst itself preparing to come to d5, when the black knights would be ready to jump into e3. White cannot really allow this, so his next is virtually forced. However, Black's 16th has the drawback of depriving his knight of the e7-square, and is probably less good in this position.

So 17 g4 ♞h6.

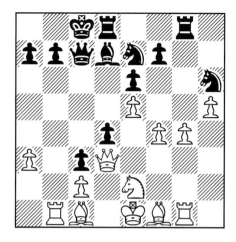

Question: Isn't the knight badly placed here?

Answer: It is quite precarious, yes. It attacks g4, and if the g-pawn advances, then the knight returns to f5. The problem comes if White manages to secure the g4-pawn and then play f4-f5. O.Korneev-A.Kveinys, Nova Gorica 2004, continued 18 ♗h3 ♗c6 19 ♖g3.

Question: What's wrong with 19 f5 here?

Answer: Black has prepared the sacrifice 19...exf5! 20 ♗xh6 ♗e4 21 ♕g3 (21 ♕d1 d3 is crushing) 21...♗xc2 22 ♖c1 d3 with excellent compensation for the piece.

After 19...♗d5 20 ♘xd4 ♗c4 21 ♕xc3...

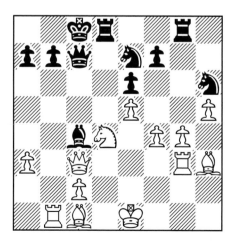

...Kveinys found 21...♖xd4, a typical tactic: 22 ♕xd4 ♘ef5 23 ♕c3 ♘xg3 24 ♕xg3 ♗e2

(ingenious, but it should not be sufficient) 25 g5 ♗xh5 26 ♖b3 ♔b8 27 ♗g2?? (27 ♕c3 would be better for White) 27...♕xc2 (suddenly, the game is over) 28 ♖xb7+ ♔c8 29 ♔f1 ♗e2+ 30 ♔g1 ♕d1+ 31 ♔h2 ♘g4+ 32 ♕xg4 ♗xg4 33 ♗e3 ♕e1 0-1. In my experience, this is a typical scenario for this variation – examining the game afterwards, with the aid of a computer, suggests that White is objectively better, but one slip proves fatal. Over the board, White's position is extremely hard to handle.

b2) 16...f6 would be thematic, when the position is unclear after 17 g4 ♘h6 18 exf6 ♖xg4 19 ♖xg4 ♘xg4 20 ♘xd4 ♘xd4 21 ♕xd4 ♗e8, but let's go back to 16...♔b8:

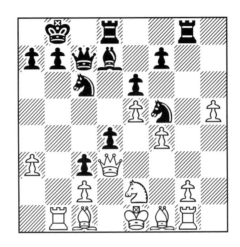

V.Vehi Bach-F.Vallejo Pons, Palma de Mallorca 2009, proceeded 17 g4 ♘h6 18 g5?! (see the previous note; 18 ♗h3 looks stronger, when Black must constantly worry about the position of the knight on h6) 18...♘f5 19 ♗g2 ♘a5 (another thematic idea – the knight looks at c4-e3; however, 19...b6 followed by ...♗c8, is safer here, reaching the position seen after move 21) 20 ♖b4 (20 ♗e4 is stronger) 20...♘c6 21 ♖b1 b6 22 ♗e4 ♘ce7 23 ♔f2 ♕c5 24 ♘g3 ♗a4! (yet another standard idea in this line; now there is a strong threat of 25...♗xc2, and White finds himself struggling) 25 ♔g2? (25 ♗xf5 was best, but after 25...exf5 White is in trouble anyway, as his light squares are a disaster) 25...♘e3+ (decisive) 26 ♗xe3 dxe3 27 ♕a6 ♗c6 28 ♔h3 ♖d2 29 ♖be1 ♘d5 30 ♔g4 ♗b5 0-1. Another excellent example of how easily things can go wrong for White.

c) 13 ♘g3.

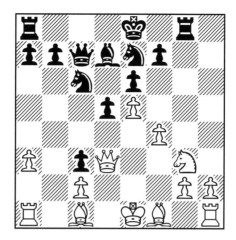

Question: This looks like a sensible move. By blocking the g-file, White wants to follow up with ♗e2 and 0-0. How does Black meet this?

Answer: The key idea is to remove the knight from g3: 13...0-0-0 14 ♕xc3 ♘f5! and this is how. The exchange on f5 damages the black pawn structure, but removes the key knight from g3. A sample game, involving French aficionado John Watson on the black side, continued 15 ♘xf5 exf5 16 ♗d2 ♗e6 17 ♗d3? (17 ♔f2 is objectively better, although human players are naturally averse to such king moves) 17...♖xg2 18 0-0-0 d4 19 ♕b2 ♘a5 when Black was clearly better, and went on to win.

d) 13 ♗e3 d4!? (once again, this thematic pawn sacrifice is interesting, although there is nothing wrong with the natural 13...♘f5) 14 ♗xd4 (the top-level stem game with 13...d4 continued 14 ♗f2 0-0-0 15 ♘xd4 ♘xd4 16 ♕xd4 b6 17 ♗h4 ♗b5 18 ♕e4 ♗xf1 19 ♖xf1 ♖d5 20 ♗xe7 ♕xe7 and Black had compensation for the pawn, and even went on to win the heavy piece ending B.Spassky-V.Korchnoi, 2nd matchgame, Belgrade 1977) 14...♘xd4 15 ♘xd4 0-0-0.

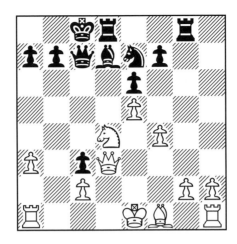

Once again, Black has excellent compensation for the pawn – the open lines and exposed white king, together with Black's significant lead in development, give him an excellent game. After 16 ♕c4? (returning the pawn to bail out into an ending, but now White is just worse) 16...♕xc4 17 ♗xc4 ♖xg2 18 0-0-0 ♗a4 Black won in D.Papakonstantinou-E.Rozentalis, Vrachati 2011.

e) 13 ♖b1 is probably the most respected of the non-captures on c3. The rook takes up a useful post, aiming down the b-file, preventing ...♕b6, and also setting a nice trap. 13...0-0-0 (13...♘f5?! is well met by 14 h3! followed by g4; by contrast, simple development with 14 g3 gave Black good, and thematic, counterplay in the old game L.Shamkovich-W.Uhlmann, Sarajevo 1963, which continued 14...d4 15 ♗g2 0-0-0 16 ♔f2 ♘a5 17 ♖d1 ♗c6 18 ♗xc6 ♕xc6 19 ♕f3 ♕c5 20 ♖d3 ♖d7 21 g4 ♘h4 22 ♕g3 ♖h8 23 h3 ♘c6 24 ♖b3 ♕c4 25 ♘g1 a5! with a nice advantage to Black) 14 ♘xc3 ♘a5 (the trap set by White's 13th move is 14...a6?? 15 ♕xa6!).

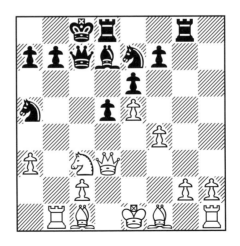

Now White has several options:

e1) 15 ♘b5 leads to little after 15...♗xb5 16 ♖xb5 (16 ♕xb5?! ♕xc2 is a dubious pawn sacrifice) when 16...♚b8 transposes to variation 'e2' below.

e2) 15 g3 ♚b8 16 ♘b5 ♗xb5 17 ♖xb5 ♖c8 (or 17...♘c4 18 ♗e2 ♖c8 19 0-0 ♘f5 which was equal, and quickly turned into advantage for Black after 20 ♖f3 ♖g6 21 ♗b2?! ♕c6 22 ♖b4 ♕c5+ 23 ♚h1 ♖h8 24 ♗f1 ♘xg3+ 25 ♖xg3 ♕f2 26 ♖g2 ♖xg2 27 ♗xg2 ♘e3 28 ♖xb7+ ♚c8 29 ♖b8+ ♚c7 30 ♖b7+ ♚d8 and 0-1 in M.Sergeeva-S.Ganguly, Abu Dhabi 2007) 18 ♗e3 b6 with equality, L.Dominguez Perez-Y.Shulman, Buenos Aires 2005.

e3) 15 ♖g1 ♚b8 16 g4 d4 17 ♘e4 ♗a4 18 ♖b2 a6 19 ♘d6 ♘f5! 20 ♘xf5 exf5 21 ♗d2 ♗b5 22 ♕xf5 ♘c4 was unclear in L.Dominguez Perez-Zhang Pengxiang, Linares 2002, eventually won by Black.

e4) 15 h3! is the critical move: 15...♚b8 16 g4 ♖c8 17 ♘b5 ♗xb5 18 ♖xb5, as in L.Dominguez Perez-D.Stellwagen, Wijk aan Zee 2009.

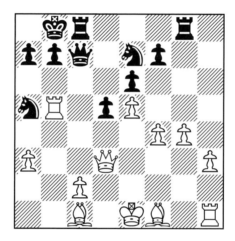

Now Postny has suggested 18...♘c4!? 19 ♗e2 ♕c6 20 ♖b1 ♕c5 followed by ...♘c6-d4 with compensation.

f) 13 ♕xc3!? is the other way to take the pawn. On c3, the queen pins the enemy knight on c6, thus restricting possible ...♘a5 ideas. White also retains control of the crucial square d4, unlike in the line beginning 13 ♘xc3. Black has:

f1) 13...♘f5 14 ♖b1.

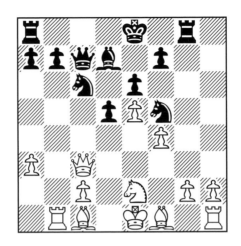

Question: Why this?

Answer: We have seen the idea many times already. The rook takes up an active post and restricts the activity of the black queen. The text has been regarded as best here, ever since the old game R.Bogdanovic-W.Uhlmann, Sarajevo 1963, which continued 14 ♗d2 ♛b6! 15 a4 ♖c8 16 a5 ♛d8 (the queen has been driven back, but now threatens to emerge on the other flank, via h4; Black had good play, and went on to win in powerful style) 17 ♛d3 a6 18 ♖a3 ♘a7 19 ♖c3 ♗b5 20 ♖xc8 ♛xc8 21 ♛c3 ♗c4 22 g3 ♘b5 23 ♛b2 ♛c6 24 ♖g1 ♖h8 25 ♖g2 d4! 26 ♖f2 ♛h1 27 g4? (27 ♛b4) 27...♖xh2 28 gxf5 ♖xf2 29 ♔xf2 ♛h2+ 30 ♔e1 ♛h4+ 31 ♔d1 ♛f2 32 ♗e1 ♛xf1 33 ♘g3 ♛f3+ 34 ♔c1 ♛e3+ 35 ♔d1 ♘c3+ 36 ♗xc3 dxc3 37 ♛b6 ♛d2# (0-1).

After 14 ♖b1 Black can go 14...♖c8.

Question: Why not castle long?

Answer: As we have just seen, that is a viable option too, but Black reasons that, with the c-file open, he does better to bring his rook there straightaway, with the idea of counterplay against c2.

S.Karjakin-P.Harikrishna, Bilbao 2007, continued 15 ♖g1 d4 16 ♛d3 ♘ce7 17 g4.

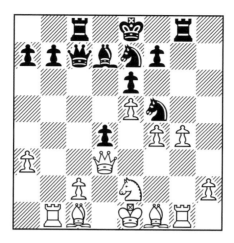

Now Black should have tried 17...♗a4 18 ♖b2 ♗xc2 19 ♕b5+ ♔f8 with an unclear position.

f2) 13...0-0-0 is another option: for example, 14 ♖b1 ♘f5 15 ♖g1 d4 16 ♕d3 ♘a5 (the sharp counterattack 16...f6 17 g4 ♘h4 18 exf6 e5 must always be considered in such positions, but it came up short in I.Kurnosov-N.Vitiugov, Ramenskoe 2006, after 19 ♔f2 ♗e6 20 ♗h3 ♖h8 21 c3 ♕f7 22 cxd4 exd4 23 g5; however, 16...♗e8!? is also worth considering, followed by ...f6) 17 g4 ♗a4 18 c3

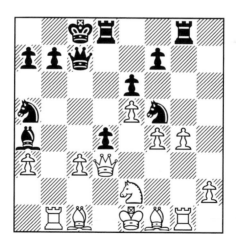

18...♗c2! (a nice tactical idea, and yet another which crops up in various lines) 19 ♕xc2 d3 20 ♕a2 ♕c5! 21 ♖g2 ♘e3 22 ♘g3 ♖xg4 23 ♖f2 ♘ac4 with an unclear position, where chances are about equal, A.Volokitin-S.Ganguly, Moscow 2007.

After this extremely long digression, we return to the main game and 13 ♘xc3:

13...a6

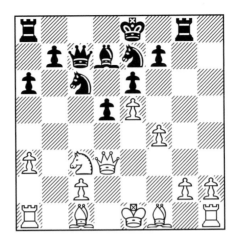

14 ♖b1

A major alternative here is Spassky's 14 ♘e2.

> **Question:** What is the point? It looks an odd move.

Answer: White reasons that the knight will be threatened along the c-file after ...♖c8, so he moves it away in advance. In addition, he takes control of the d4-square. This move caused a few problems for Black when first introduced in the 1980s, but it does look rather odd to spend a tempo, returning the knight to a clumsy square, where it shuts in the king's bishop. Black should be able to find adequate counterplay against such extravagance:

a) 14...0-0-0 15 g3 d4 16 ♕c4 ♘f5 17 ♗g2 ♘a5 18 ♕xc7+ ♔xc7 19 ♖b1 ♗c6 20 ♗xc6 ♔xc6 was equal in V.Anand-V.Ivanchuk, Nice (rapid) 2009.

b) A good alternative is 14...♘f5 15 h3 which was tried in A.Volokitin-Hou Yifan, Wijk aan Zee 2009, and now 15...♘a5! 16 g4 ♗b5 17 ♕c3 ♕xc3+ 18 ♘xc3 ♗xf1 19 ♖xf1 ♘d4 gave Black equal chances in the old game J.Timman-N.Short, Rotterdam 1988.

14...♘a5

14...♖c8 is also a very logical continuation. After 15 h4 ♘f5 (immediately targeting g3, which White's next defends) 16 ♖h3 ♘ce7 (16...♘cd4?! 17 h5 and now Black lost at once after the blunder 17...♕c5? 18 ♖xb7 ♘b5?? 19 ♘e4 1-0 in F.Nijboer-J.Timman, Hilversum 2006; Black clearly needs an improvement at move 17, if this set-up with 16...♘cd4 is to remain playable, but I have to admit, it is not immediately obvious what this improvement is) 17 ♗d2 (one point of Black's last is revealed after 17 h5 ♘h6! followed by ...♘ef5, when the knights blockade the kingside pawns effectively, D.Velimirovic-J.Levitt, Pinerolo 1987) 17...♘h6 the position is typically unclear.

15 h4 ♘f5

15...♖c8 was tried in J.Zawadzka-E.Berg, Warsaw 2008. After 16 ♖h3 ♘f5 17 h5 Black played the interesting idea 17...♔f8!?.

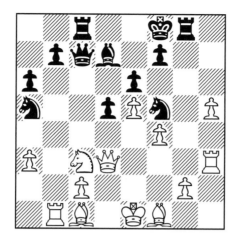

Following 18 h6?! (maybe this should be held back, so as to prevent the following manoeuvre) 18...♖g6 19 a4 ♔g8 (a most interesting set-up, as the black king manages to play a role in holding up the white kingside pawns, whilst the pawn on h6 itself prevents the white pieces attacking the enemy monarch; objectively, it is rather hard to believe, but in the game. Black soon got on top) 20 h7+ ♔h8 21 ♔d1 ♘c4 22 ♕e2? ♘g3 23 ♕f2 ♘xf1 24 ♕xf1 d4 and Black was winning.

16 ♖h3

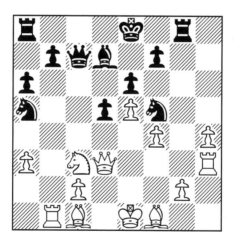

16...0-0-0

A similar example was 16...♕c5 17 h5 0-0-0 18 ♗d2 ♘c4 19 h6 ♖g6 20 h7 ♖h8 and now the blunder 21 ♕f3? (21 ♘e4 dxe4 22 ♕xc4 ♕xc4 23 ♗xc4 ♖xg2 is equal) walked into the sucker punch 21...♘xd2 22 ♔xd2 ♖xh7!. White then decided to go down in a blaze of glory, but resigned after 23 ♗xa6 (23 ♖xh7 ♖g3 wins) 23...bxa6 24 ♘xd5 ♖xh3 25 ♘b6+ ♔d8 26 gxh3 ♕d4+ 27 ♔e2 ♖g3 in D.Petrosian-S.Lputian, Yerevan 2006.

17 h5 ♘c4 18 ♖b4

18 h6 ♖g6 19 h7 ♖h8 was played in a blitz game also involving Grischuk.

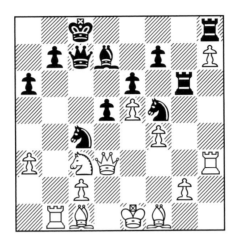

Answer: He has marched almost all the way, but the final step will be the hardest. White
hopes that his advanced h-pawn will tie Black down and disrupt his coordination, thereby
depriving him of counterplay, but objectively this is not the case. Black can cope with the
pawn and still keep adequate activity. Objectively, chances are about equal. 20 ♘e2 (20
♕f3 is a critical move, trying to get in the advance g2-g4, but Black is fine after 20...♖g7 21
g4 ♘e7) 20...♗b5 21 ♘d4

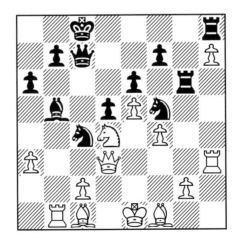

21...♘xe5! 22 ♕d1?? (22 ♕c3 ♘xd4 23 ♕xd4 ♗xf1 24 ♔xf1 ♕c4+ 25 ♕xc4+ ♘xc4 is only slightly better for Black) 22...♗xf1 23 ♔xf1 ♕c4+ 24 ♘e2 ♕e4 and Black was winning in S.Karjakin-A.Grischuk, Moscow 2008.

Meanwhile, 18 ♕f3 again hopes to achieve g2-g4, but 18...♗c6 objectively leaves White with nothing better than repeating moves. Instead, White tried to do so with 19 ♕e2? against a youthful Caruana, but after 19...♘g3 20 ♕d3 ♘xf1 21 ♔xf1 (21 ♕xf1 ♘xe5 22 fxe5 d4 is even worse) 21...d4 22 ♘e4 ♖g4 Black was already better, and after 23 ♘g3 in B.Bruned-F.Caruana, Collado Villalba 2005, he could have won at once with 23...♘e3+ 24 ♗xe3 dxe3 25 ♕xe3 ♗xg2+!.

18...♗c6 19 ♘e2 ♗b5 20 a4

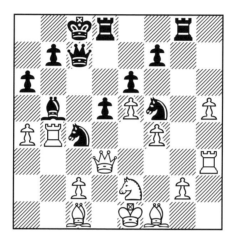

20...♕c5

> *Question:* Just a moment – isn't 20...♘xe5 on here?

Answer: It is possible, and was played in the stem game from this position, V.Hort-W.Uhlmann, Hastings 1970/71. However, after 21 ♕c3 ♗xe2 22 fxe5 ♗xf1 23 ♕xc7+ ♔xc7 24 ♔xf1, Moles' assessment is that "White has anything that's going", and Hort did in fact go on to win.

Moles himself suggests 20...♗c6, with the threat of 21...a5, followed by 22...♗xa4, but *Fritz* is unimpressed: 21 h6 a5 22 ♖b1 ♗xa4 23 h7 ♖h8 24 g4 with advantage to White. Grischuk's choice looks best, as he takes control of the key square d4, with tempo.

21 ♕c3?

After this mistake, Black seizes the advantage. 21 ♗a3 had been tried in J.Becerra Rivero-Y.Shulman, Tulsa 2008, which continued 21...♗c6 22 ♕c3 ♖g4 (it is a recurring pattern in these lines that Black makes good use of the squares g3 and g4, weakened by the early advance of the white h-pawn) 23 h6 ♖h8 24 h7? (this just exposes the h-pawn) 24...♖g7 25 ♖b3 ♕a7 26 ♗c1 ♗xa4? (26...♖gxh7 is just better for Black) 27 ♕b4?? (27 ♘g3 is unclear) 27...b5 28 ♖h5 a5 29 ♕c3 ♖gxh7 and Black won.

Finally, 21 ♗d2 is the computer's preference, with equal chances after 21...♗c6.

21...d4 22 ♕b3 ♘a5 23 ♖xb5

Desperation, but White has nothing better. His position collapses after both 23 ♕b1 ♗xe2 24 ♔xe2 (if 24 ♗xe2 ♖xg2) 24...♖g3, and 23 ♕a3 ♗xe2 24 ♔xe2 ♘c4 25 ♕b3 d3+.

23...♘xb3 24 ♖xc5+ ♘xc5

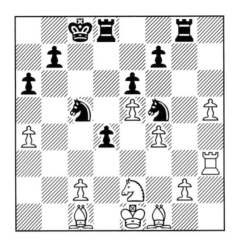

Black has won the exchange for a pawn. White has two bishops and his kingside pawns, but the latter are well controlled and Black's pieces are very active. He has a clear advantage, which Grischuk has no particular trouble converting.

25 ♘g1 ♖g3 26 ♗a3 d3

26...♘xa4 is also good.

27 ♖xg3

27 cxd3 ♘xd3+ 28 ♗xd3 ♖dxd3 is slightly more tenacious, but should also lose.

27...♘xg3

The computer points out the typically incisive 27...d2+ 28 ♔d1 ♘e4! 29 ♖f3 ♘f2+! 30 ♖xf2 ♘e3+ which is objectively even better, but I don't think we can really criticise Grischuk for missing this!

28 cxd3 ♘xa4 29 ♘e2 ♘xh5 30 g4 ♖xd3 31 gxh5 ♖xa3 32 h6 ♖a1+ 33 ♔f2 ♖d1 34 h7 ♖d8

Just in time! The remainder requires no comment.

35 ♘d4 ♘c5 36 ♘f3 ♔d7 37 f5 exf5 38 ♗h3 ♔e7 39 ♗xf5 a5 40 ♗b1 a4 41 ♘d4 ♖h8 42 ♘f5+ ♔f8 0-1

Game 17
S.Kuipers-D.Stellwagen
Dutch League 2011

1 e4 e6 2 d4 d5 3 ♘c3 ♗b4 4 e5 c5 5 a3 ♗xc3+ 6 bxc3 ♘e7 7 ♕g4 ♕c7 8 ♕xg7

8 ♗d3 is a major alternative here.

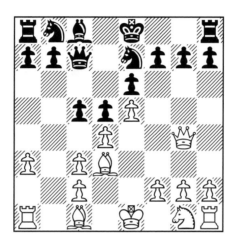

Question: Is that entirely logical? I thought the whole point of 7 ♕g4 was to take on g7?

Answer: It is, but the point is that White does not necessarily have to do so at once. The g7-pawn is not easy to defend, so White reasons that he can afford to bring the bishop out first. The idea is to avoid having to shut this bishop in with ♘e2, as happens in the main line.

8 ♗d3 is a very sharp and dangerous line, for which Black needs to be well prepared. He has two main approaches:

a) 8...cxd4 9 ♘e2 dxc3 10 ♕xg7 ♖g8 11 ♕xh7 (11 ♕h6 intending to take on h7 with the bishop, is another sharp line; theory considers that Black is okay after 11...♘bc6 12 ♗f4 ♗d7 13 ♗xh7 ♖xg2 14 ♗g3 0-0-0 when he will sacrifice the exchange on g3 to win the e5-pawn, with typical Winawer compensation) 11...♕xe5 12 ♗f4 ♕f6.

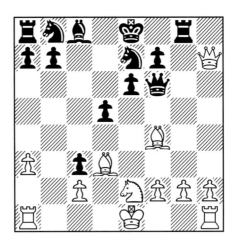

Question: What is going on here?

Answer: The position is very sharp. White has temporarily sacrificed a pawn, but he has activated his dark-squared bishop much more than he usually manages in these lines, and he has the typical kingside pawn phalanx. Objectively, Black is probably fine, but the position is extremely sharp and preparation can run very deep in such lines. Watson gives extensive coverage in *Play the French 4*, and any black player intending to go down this line should study his analysis carefully.

b) 8...c4 is the quieter solution, avoiding forcing lines, in favour of a typical closed Winawer struggle. Strangely, Watson makes no mention of this in his latest French volume, although he covered it in the first edition. Objectively, Black may be slightly worse in these lines, but it is a typical structure, where the black player should feel at home, and he does avoid a lot of sharp preparation. 9 ♗e2 ♘f5 10 ♘f3 ♘c6 and now 11 ♘h4 ♘ce7 12 ♗g5 is a suggestion of Psakhis, but I don't see that Black has any real problems after 12...0-0 or 12...♘xh4 13 ♕xh4 h6 14 ♗d2 ♘f5 15 ♕h3 ♗d7.

In this line, Black pays his money and takes his choice. In purely objective terms, 8...cxd4 is probably the best move, but the positions are very sharp and require detailed preparation. Given that 8 ♗d3 is only a fairly obscure sideline, many Black players may be reluctant to spend much time on such preparation, in which case 8...c4 is the pragmatic choice.

8...♖g8 9 ♕xh7 cxd4 10 ♘e2

Believe it or not, White does have an alternative here, in 10 ♔d1.

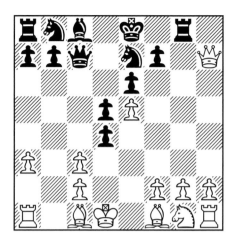

Question: That looks insane!

Answer: Maybe, but there is some logic to it. White sidesteps the threat of a lethal check on c3, without committing his knight to e2. He wants to play the knight to the more active square f3, from where it will have the idea of jumping to g5. The main line goes 10...♘bc6 11 ♘f3 dxc3 12 ♘g5 ♘xe5 13 f4 (13 ♗f4 ♕b6! is a neat tactical solution to Black's problems) and now 13...f6! is fully adequate: for example, 14 fxe5 fxg5 15 ♕h5+ ♔d8 16 ♗xg5 ♕c5! and Black will untangle with ...♗d7 and ...♔c7. He has material equality, and the white king is likely to end up the more exposed of the two monarchs.

10...♘bc6 11 f4 dxc3 12 ♕d3

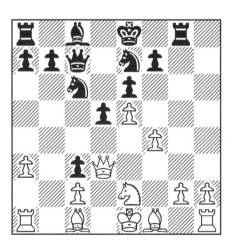

12...d4!?
This is the move that gives Black's move order its independent significance.

Question: So what is the point? Doesn't 12...d4 just give away a pawn?

Answer: Yes! We saw in the previous game that this type of pawn sacrifice is a thematic idea in the variation. Black opens lines, especially the d-file and the long diagonal h1-a8, for his pieces. With the move order in the game, Black does this at once, delaying the developing move ...♗d7. The bishop will usually come to d7 later anyway, although occasionally, it develops by means of ...b6 and ...♗b7. This system with 12...d4 has become quite popular in recent years, and is covered in detail by John Watson in the latest edition of his seminal work *Play the French*. Watson uses 12...d4 as his main line recommendation. Instead, 12...♗d7 would transpose to the previous game.

13 ♘xd4

Taking the pawn is the most natural response, but others are also possible:

a) 13 ♖b1 is a thematic move in such positions, as we know from Game 16, but in this line, it allows Black to exploit one of the advantages of not having played ...♗d7. 13...b6! logically neutralizes the pressure along the b-file, as well as preparing ...♗b7 and ...0-0-0. With the long diagonal already opened by ...d5-d4, the bishop clearly belongs on that line. 14 ♖g1 ♗b7 15 g4 0-0-0 16 ♕c4 ♖d5 (Watson gives 16...♘a5 17 ♕xc7+ ♔xc7 as better for Black, which it is, but there is nothing wrong with Grover's move either) 17 ♖g3 ♖gd8 18 h4?! ♖a5!.

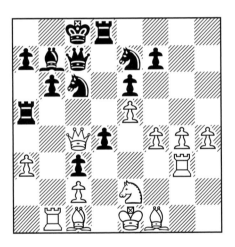

Question: That looks a bit funny. Why is it so strong?

Answer: It is rather counter-intuitive to put the rook on a5, but the point is that the threat of ...♗a6 is extremely hard to meet. 19 ♕d3 ♗a6 20 ♕h7 was E.Barbosa-S.Grover, Chennai 2011, and now simply 20...♘d5 gives Black a clear advantage.

b) 13 h4 is another typical white plan in such positions, as we know. In response 13...b6 is again good. As Watson emphasises, this is usually the move Black wants to play, unless

White does something specific to prevent it. Now:

b1) 14 ♘xd4 ♘xd4 15 ♕xd4.

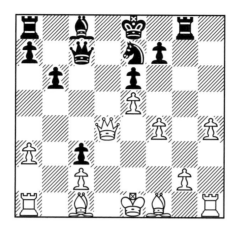

Question: So White is a pawn up?

Answer: Yes, but just as in the main game, Black has excellent compensation in the form of the open lines and exposed white king: 15...♘f5 16 ♗b5+ ♗d7 17 ♕xd7+ ♕xd7 18 ♗xd7+ ♔xd7. Despite the pawn minus, Black has positional compensation (weakness on g2, active knight, etc) and chances are balanced. The high-level game V.Bologan-G.Kamsky, Reggio Emilia 2009/10 confirmed this: 19 ♔f2 ♖g4 20 ♗e3 ♖ag8 21 ♖ag1 ♘xh4 22 g3 ♘f5 23 ♖h3 ♔e7 24 ♔f3 ♘xe3 25 ♔xe3 ♖d8 26 ♖h2 ♖gg8 27 g4 ♖d2 28 ♖xd2 cxd2 29 ♔xd2 ♖h8 30 f5 exf5 31 gxf5 ♖h5 32 ♖f1 ♖h4 33 ♔e3 ♖a4 34 ♖d1 ♖xa3+ 35 ♔e4 ♖a4+ 36 ♖d4 ♖xd4+ 37 ♔xd4 f6 38 e6 ♔d6 39 ♔c4 a6 40 ♔b4 ♔c6 ½-½.

b2) 14 h5 ♗b7 15 h6 0-0-0 16 h7 ♖h8 is perhaps a more logical follow-up to White's 13th.

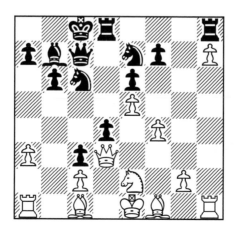

Watson regards it as critical and devotes a lot of analysis to it, assessing the position as "dynamically equal". After 17 ♖h3 he suggests *Fritz's* choice 17...♘d5, when 18 ♘xd4 ♘de7! is an amusing follow-up. White has problems on the d-file, and 19 ♘b5 ♖xd3 20 ♗xd3 (20 ♘xc7?? ♖xh3 wins) 20...♕b8 is roughly equal.

c) 13 ♘g3 is a critical attempt to exploit Black's move order.

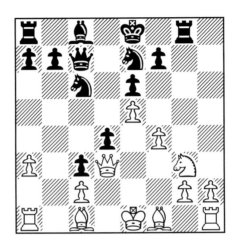

Question: What is the point?

Answer: White takes advantage of the fact that Black's last move gave up control of e4. The knight threatens ♘e4-d6+. After 13...♗d7 (13...b6 is now too slow, since after 14 ♘e4 checks on d6 and f6 are already threatened) White has:

c1) 14 ♘e4 0-0-0 15 ♘d6+.

15 ♖b1 has also been tried.

Question: With the idea that the threat of ♘d6+ is stronger than its execution?

Answer: Indeed, but Black can strike with the thematic piece sacrifice 15...♘xe5 (15...♘f5 is also playable) 16 fxe5 ♕xe5.

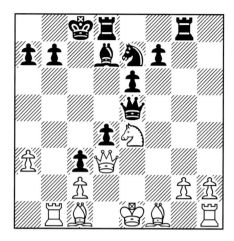

Question: What is going on here?

Answer: Black has two pawns for the piece, the white king is very exposed, and the black central pawns threaten in the near future to sweep down the board. Black is just better here, I believe, and especially in an OTB game. White's position is hard to defend. After 17 ♕e2 ♗c6 18 ♘g3 (18 ♘f2 is mentioned by Watson, but simply 18...♕d5 keeps a strong initiative) 18...♕d5 (18...♕xe2+ is also fine for Black, but the text is more fun!) 19 ♕f2 (19 ♖b4!? ♘f5 20 ♔f2 is the computer's unlikely suggestion; then 20...♘d6 21 ♗f4 f6 22 ♗xd6 ♕xd6 still looks better for Black) 19...f5 20 ♖b4 a5 21 ♖c4 e5 (21...b5 was also good) it was "wagons roll!" in the game T.Calistri-D.Bunzmann, French League 2007.

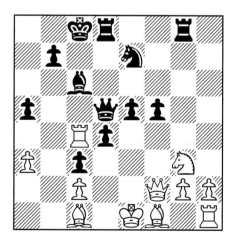

Black went on to win.

Returning to the immediate check, and then 15...♔b8 16 ♖b1.

Question: Why not simply 16 ♘xf7 with an extra pawn?

Answer: This is similar to the main line, after 16...♖df8 17 ♘d6 ♘f5.

After 16 ♖b1 Black has:

c11) 16...♗c8 was played in D.Neelotpal-S.Sengupta, Mumbai 2003, but *Fritz* is unconvinced about the black position after 17 ♘xf7 (17 g3 ♖xd6!? 18 exd6 ♕xd6 19 ♗g2 b6 20 0-0 ♘f5 21 a4 ♗b7 gave Black compensation for the exchange in V.Artemiev-D.Petrosian, Izhevsk 2011) 17...♖df8 18 ♘d6 ♘g6 (18...♘f5 19 ♘xf5 ♖xf5 is like the main line, but worse; after 20 g3 b6 21 ♗g2 ♗b7 22 0-0 it is questionable whether Black has enough for the pawn) 19 ♕e4 ♘h4 20 g3 ♘f5 21 ♗g2 ♔a8 22 ♘xf5 exf5 23 ♕d3 ♗e6 and although Black eventually drew, the silicon monster wants nothing to do with his position after 24 0-0.

c12) 16...b6 17 ♘xf7 ♖df8 18 ♘d6 ♘f5 19 ♘xf5 ♖xf5.

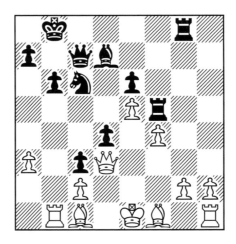

Question: So why is this any better than the analogous line with 16...♗c8?

Answer: The difference is tactical; after 20 g3 Black has the strong reply 20...♘xe5! 21 fxe5 ♗c6!. This is the point – with the bishop on c8 and pawn on b7, the bishop could not come to the long diagonal at once. After 22 ♖g1 ♗e4! 23 ♕c4 (23 ♕xd4 ♗xc2 24 ♖b4 ♖d8 is decisive) 23...♕xc4 24 ♗xc4 ♗xc2 and Black's extra pawn (soon to be two) plus initiative adds up to the advantage.

c2) Another logical move is simply 14 ♗e2, taking advantage of the fact that 13 ♘g3 defended the g2-pawn. White simply wants to castle short, solving the traditional problem of his king's exposure in the centre. This has been played by Karjakin, and so must be taken seriously: 14...♕b6 (a useful move order point; Black stops the move ♖b1) 15 0-0 0-0-0 16 ♘e4 ♘d5!? (16...♔b8 17 ♘d6 ♗e8 is Watson's recommendation, but I prefer *Fritz's* 16...♘f5, with an unclear position) 17 ♘d6+ (17 ♕b5 ♕xb5 18 ♗xb5 ♔c7 was equal in M.Khachiyan-

Y.Shulman, Saint Louis 2009) 17...♔b8 18 ♘xf7 was Karjakin's choice against Kamsky. After 18...♖df8 19 ♘d6 ♘ce7 20 ♗f3 ♗c6...

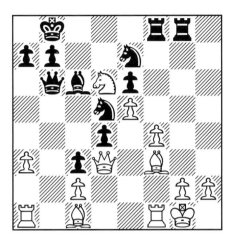

...and now, instead of Karjakin's 21 a4?! ♘b4 22 a5 ♕c5 23 ♕h7 (S.Karjakin-G.Kamsky, Nalchik 2009), when 23...♘f5 is slightly better for Black, 21 g3! is critical. Watson then analyses 21...♘f5 (both captures on f4 favour White: 21...♘xf4 22 ♗xf4 ♖xf4 23 ♗xc6 ♖xf1+ 24 ♖xf1 ♘xc6 25 ♕h7, and 21...♖xf4 22 ♗xf4 ♘xf4 23 ♕d1 d3+ 24 ♔h1 dxc2 25 ♕xc2) 22 ♘xf5 ♖xf5 as equal; Black threatens ...♗b5, and after 23 ♗xd5 ♗xd5 his monster bishop guarantees at least equality.

After that important digression, we can return to the annexing of the d-pawn:

13...♘xd4 14 ♕xd4 ♗d7

The immediate 14...♘f5?! allows the annoying 15 ♗b5+.

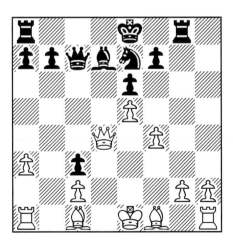

This is the main *tabiya* for the 12...d4 variation.

Question: So what is going on?

Answer: As we have already seen, Black has sacrificed a pawn, in order to open central lines for his pieces. He has the long diagonal a8-h1, along which lies the g2-pawn, already attacked once by the rook on g8. The open d-file is also available for a black rook, although the fact that a7 would hang prevents an early ...0-0-0. The knight will jump to f5, gaining a tempo on the white queen. White's issue is how to develop his pieces and get his king into shelter. The pressure against g2 makes it hard to develop the bishop from f1, and the move g3 always runs into an attack along the long diagonal, displacing the rook on h1.

15 ♖g1

15 ♖b1 is the other main move here. We are familiar with the general idea in such positions – the rook takes up an active post, pressurizing b7 in some lines, and also tames some of the black queen's activity, by taking away the b6-square. A high-class practical example then continued 15...♘f5 16 ♕f2 ♕c6.

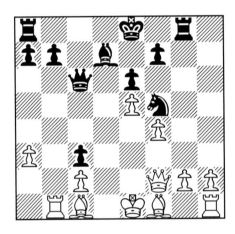

Question: That is a bit of a surprise. I was expecting the bishop to go to this square.

Answer: That is also a perfectly reasonable alternative, but quite often in this variation, it is the queen which uses the c6-square. From there, as well as pressurizing g2, the queen can jump effectively into d5, e4, and sometimes a4.

Play may go 17 ♖b4 (stopping the check on e4, but exposing the rook; 17 ♖g1 could well end in an immediate draw after 17...♕e4+ 18 ♕e2 ♕d4 19 ♕f2 ♕e4+ – indeed, from a winning viewpoint, this whole variation has the drawback that, in many lines, Black has little alternative but to take a draw by repetition, if White offers it) 17...♕d5.

Question: What is the idea of this?

Answer: It is another thematic idea in these lines. Black prepares ...♗c6, establishing a battery along the long diagonal, and securely defending b7. Another point is to add protection to the d4-square, which allows the black knight to jump there in many lines.

18 ♖g1 ♗c6 19 ♖c4 (19 ♗d3 amounts to a transposition after 19...0-0-0,since then 20 ♕xa7? ♖xg2 21 ♖xg2 ♕xg2 favours Black; it is noteworthy how well the bishop on c6 defends the black king in such positions) 19...0-0-0 20 ♗d3 ♔b8 21 ♖xc3.

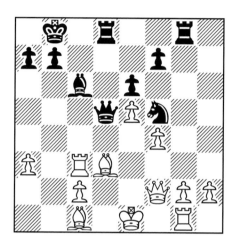

Question: Two pawns up!

Answer: Yes, but the pawns are hard to make effective use of at present, and the white king is condemned forever to remain in the centre. After 21...♕a2, practice shows that Black has enough counterplay. As Watson points out, this position has been known from at least 1965, since it can arise by transposition from the 12...♗d7 lines. After 22 ♗e3 (otherwise, the threat of 22...♕a1 is awkward to meet) 22...♘xe3 23 ♕xe3 ♖xg2 24 ♖xg2 ♗xg2 the position is balanced. The game we are following ended in a draw after 25 ♔f2 ♗c6 26 ♗e4 ♗xe4 27 ♕xe4 ♕b1 28 ♖e3 ♖c8 29 ♖e2 ♖h8 30 ♕g2 ♕c1 31 ♕g3 ♕h1 32 ♔e3 a6 33 ♖d2 ♕c1 34 ♔e2 ♕h1 35 ♔e3 ♕c1 36 ♔e2 ♕h1 ½-½ S.Mamedyarov-E.Alekseev, Ohrid 2009. Wild though the position looks, this was a pretty correct game by both sides, and a draw is highly likely in this variation.

15 ♗e3 is also a natural move, intending 15...♘f5 (15...b6 is a Watson suggestion, which perhaps keeps more tension) 16 ♕c5. Watson then suggests 16...♕c6!.

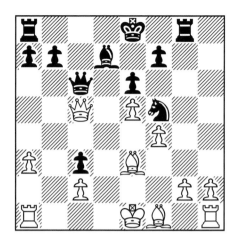

Question: That is a surprise! I would not have thought Black wanted to exchange queens, given that he is a pawn down and much of his counterplay is directed against the exposed white king.

Answer: That is a fair assumption, but White's development difficulties are the other major aspect of Black's compensation, and those persist into many of the endgames. 17 ♕xc6 (17 0-0-0 has also been tried, when *Fritz* likes the clever 17...♕b6!, which practically forces the follow-up 18 ♕xb6 axb6 19 ♗xb6 ♖xa3 20 ♔b1 ♖a4 when the double threats of ...♖b4+ and ...♖xf4 regain the pawn, again with easy equality) 17...♗xc6 18 ♔f2 ♘xe3 19 ♔xe3 0-0-0 20 ♖g1 ♖d2 21 ♖c1 ♗a4, gives enough play to hold the balance easily.

Returning to 15 ♖g1:

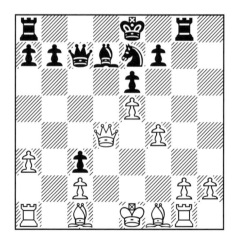

15...♘f5

Obviously the most natural, but Black has also tried 15...♖h8 here.

Answer: It looks a bit strange, but Black wants to provoke the advance of the white h-pawn, which weakens g3. I am not sure how good it is objectively, but it has had a couple of successful GM outings, beginning 16 h3 ♘f5 17 ♕f2 and now:

a) 17...♕c6 18 ♗d3 ♕d5 19 ♖b1 ♗c6 with a typical set-up for the variation. Once again, it is worth following the game to the end: 20 ♗xf5?! (this exchange removes the active black knight, but at the cost of a total surrender of the light squares; it is well-known that in middlegame positions with opposite-coloured bishops, the holder of the initiative has effectively an extra piece, and this is soon seen here) 20...exf5 21 ♖b3 0-0-0 22 ♕e2 ♖hg8 23 g4 fxg4 24 hxg4 ♖h8 25 ♖xc3 ♕d4

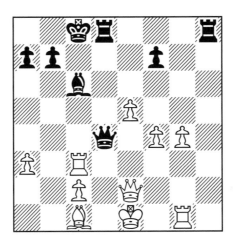

26 ♕e3? (26 ♖xc6+ is a better try) 26...♕d1+ 27 ♔f2 ♖h2+ and once again, White suddenly finds himself busted. It is a familiar scenario in this line. 28 ♔g3 ♖dh8 29 f5 ♕d5 30 ♔f4 f6 31 ♖c5 fxe5+ 32 ♕xe5 ♖f2+ 33 ♔e3 ♕f3+ 34 ♔d4 ♖d8+ 35 ♔c4 ♖xc2+ 36 ♔b4 ♖xc5 37 ♕xc5 a5+ 38 ♕xa5 ♖d4+ 0-1 T.Michalczak-T.Hillarp Persson, Reykjavik 2011.

b) As usual, Black's alternative plan is 17...♗c6, which has been played by the veteran Cuban GM and French Winawer expert, Nogueiras. After 18 g4 ♘h4 19 ♖g3 ♕a5 20 ♖d3 (*Fritz* likes White after 20 ♗e2 0-0-0 21 ♖b1, but it is not clear how much better he is after, say, 21...♔b8 or 21...♕d5) 20...♖d8 21 ♕g3 ♖xd3 22 ♕xd3 ♔f8 23 ♔f2 ♔g7 White should be somewhat better, but as usual, things can easily go wrong in such positions, which is what happened: 24 ♕g3?! (24 ♗e3) 24...♘f3 25 ♗d3 ♖d8 26 ♗e3?.

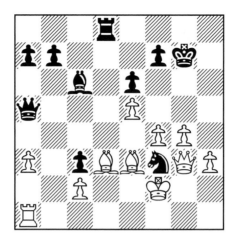

Now Black struck with 26...♖xd3! 27 cxd3 ♕b5! and White is lost, thanks to the comically helpless position of his queen. 28 ♖a2 ♕b2+! 29 ♖xb2 cxb2 30 f5 b1♕ 31 ♕f4 ♕g1+ 0-1 I.Ortiz Suarez-J.Nogueiras Santiago, Havana 2010. Rather a typical game for such lines – White looks as though he should be better, but one slip and it is all over for him.

16 ♕f2 ♕c6 17 ♗d3

17 g4 ♕e4+ 18 ♕e2 (18 ♗e2? ♘d4) 18...♕d5 is equal.

17...♕d5

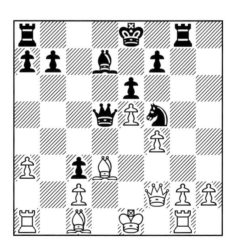

18 ♖b1

18 a4 has also been tried.

Question: With what points?

Answer: White has two ideas: ♖a3xc3, similar to the game, and also ♗a3.

18...♗c6 (Watson advocates 18...0-0-0 with the idea of 19 ♖a3 ♔b8 20 ♖xc3 ♗xa4) 19 ♖a3 ♖h8 (19...♕a5!? is suggested by *Fritz*) 20 h3 ♕a5 21 ♗xf5 exf5 22 ♕d4 ♖d8 23 ♕xc3 ♕d5 is another opposite-coloured bishop structure.

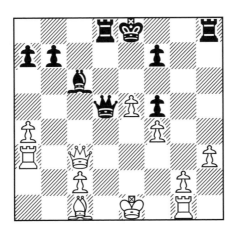

White has two extra pawns, but Black is not without play: 24 ♗d2 (24 ♔f2 is *Fritz's* preference) 24...♖g8 25 g3 ♕e4+ (25...♖xg3! forces an immediate draw, with 26 ♖xg3 ♕h1+ 27 ♔f2 ♕h2+ 28 ♔e1 ♕h1+, since 26 ♕xg3? ♕xd2+ 27 ♔f1 ♕c1+ wins) 26 ♔d1 ♖d4 27 ♖e1 ♕d5 28 ♔c1 and White was objectively better, although once again, that did not stop him losing in D.Svetushkin-S.Grover, Kavala 2010.

Instead, 18 ♗e3 allows Black to regain the pawn at once with 18...♘xe3 19 ♕xe3 ♖xg2 20 ♖xg2 ♕xg2 21 ♗e4 ♕xh2 22 0-0-0, as in R.Robson-S.Shankland, Milwaukee 2009. Now the computer's 22...♗c6 holds the balance: for example, 23 ♗xc6+ bxc6 24 ♕d4 a5! (a real computer move; the point is to stop ♕b4 in various lines) 25 ♖g1 ♕d2+ 26 ♕xd2 cxd2+ 27 ♔xd2 ♔d7 and the rook ending is equal.

18...♗c6 19 ♖b3 0-0-0 20 ♖xc3 ♔b8

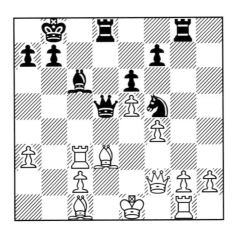

Question: Once again, Black is two pawns down! Is he really okay in this position?

Answer: Practice confirms that he is. His active pieces, and the insecure enemy king, give Black enough compensation to hold the balance.

21 ♖c4

Lots of moves are possible here, but the scenario is basically the same – Black has enough to hold the balance. Let's look at a few examples from practice.

a) 21 g3 ♘d4 22 ♗e3 ♘f3+ 23 ♔d1 ♘xg1 (the computer's 23...♕a2! looks like a more convincing way to hold the balance) 24 ♗xa7+ ♔a8 25 ♕xg1.

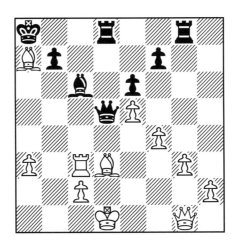

With three pawns for the exchange, plus the strong dark-squared bishop, White has more than enough compensation, and Black is struggling to maintain the balance here. 25...♗b5 26 ♗b6 ♗xd3 27 cxd3 (27 ♖xd3 ♕b5 28 ♖d6 ♖c8 29 ♔c1 ♕b3 was equal in M.Pacher-T.Petrik, Banska Stiavnica 2011) 27...♖c8 28 ♕d4 ♕b5 29 ♕b4 ♕xb4 30 ♖xc8+ ♖xc8 31 axb4 and White is better, although he ended up only drawing in T.Michalczak-L.Johannessen, Rogaska Slatina 2011.

b) 21 ♖c5!? ♕a2 22 ♖xc6!? bxc6 23 ♕c5 ♖xd3! 24 cxd3 ♖xg2 25 ♖xg2 ♕xg2 is basically just a draw, S.Ganguly-Y.Shulman, Ningbo 2011.

c) 21 ♕c5 ♖xg2 22 ♕xd5 ♖xg1+ 23 ♔f2 ♖dg8!!

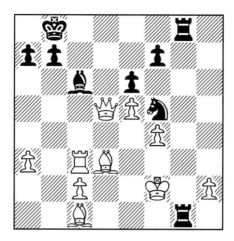

Question: Wow! That is quite a move!

Answer: Yes, although it is only equal!

24 ♕d8+! ♖xd8 25 ♔xg1 is equal, although Black later managed to mate her opponent in A.Muzychuk-K.Lahno, Moscow 2010.

21...b6 22 g4 ♗b5 23 ♖c3 ♘d4 24 ♗xb5 ♕xb5

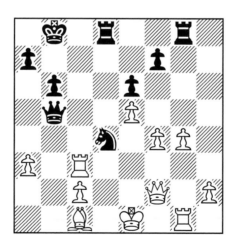

Black is holding the balance, but it should be no more than that.

25 ♕f1 ♕a5 26 ♗d2 ♕a4

Watson claims that 26...♕d5 27 ♕g2 ♕a2 28 ♕e4 ♖d5 "gives Black excellent chances", but in fact, 29 ♖gg3 is just equal, according to *Fritz*.

27 ♗e3??

27 ♕d3 ♘b5 28 ♖c4! ♕a6 29 ♕e2 ♘xa3 30 ♖c3 maintains equality, as shown by the

computer. But this line is enough to show how carefully White has to play, even with two extra pawns. The text is a losing blunder.

27...♘xc2+ 28 ♔f2 ♘xe3 29 ♖xe3

White must lose the f4-pawn, since 29 ♔xe3 ♕d4+ drops a whole rook.

29...♕xf4+ 30 ♔e2 ♕xh2+ 31 ♖g2

If 31 ♕f2 ♖d2+.

31...♕h7

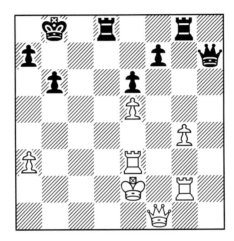

In heavy-piece endings, king safety is paramount, and here, White has a hopelessly exposed king, as well as being material down.

32 ♔f3 ♖d4 33 a4 ♖gxg4 0-1

Question: So what are we to make of these crazy 7 ♕g4 ♕c7 lines?
It looks as though everything hangs by a thread?

Answer: I think that is absolutely right. I myself played these lines for some 20 years. In all honesty, I never entirely believed my position, yet I scored an incredible 86% as Black! I lost quite a few post-mortems, where opponents eventually managed to show they had stood better at some point (often quite a lot better), but in the games themselves, I nearly always managed to come out on top. We have seen quite a few examples in the foregoing as well, even with GMs on the white side. I think the big lesson of this is that Black's position is much easier to play than White's, in a practical OTB game.

Question: Why?

Answer: I think it is because almost all players find it much easier to spot their own tactical opportunities than to anticipate their opponent's. To play the white side of this variation successfully, White needs to be able to spot all of his opponent's resources, and very few players are able to do this, even at GM level. One slip is all it takes to bring the white position crashing down, because his king is always so draughty in these positions. The black player just needs to be alert to his own chances, which most players (myself included!) find much easier.

> **Question:** What about the theoretical issue of whether
> to play the old 12...♗d7 lines, or the modern 12...d4?

Answer: I myself always played 12...♗d7, but that was just because 12...d4 had not become popular when I was active as a player. At the time of writing, 12...d4 looks to be in pretty decent shape, and I think this would be my choice now.

Game 18
V.Atlas-S.Kindermann
Austrian League 2006

1 e4 e6 2 d4 d5 3 ♘c3 ♗b4 4 e5 c5 5 a3 ♗xc3+ 6 bxc3 ♘e7 7 ♕g4 0-0

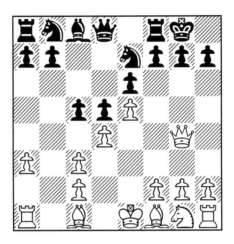

Question: This looks like a much safer way to play
than 7...♕c7. But isn't Black 'castling into it'?

Answer: Right on both counts! If Black can get away with it, then 7...0-0 is really the move
he would like to play. He does not sacrifice any material, and he avoids having his kingside
pawns wiped out. The problem is, he is castling into quite a strong attack.

Question: Is 7...♘f5 possible here?

Answer: It is another move Black would like to play, if he could, because it defends g7 without
committing the king to the kingside. However, the move has been out of favour for
some 50 years now! After 8 ♗d3, the threat is to take on f5 and g7, so the reply is forced:
8...h5 (the immediate 8...♕h4?? drops a piece after 9 ♗xf5) 9 ♕f4! cxd4 (9...♕h4 10 ♘e2!
♕xf4 11 ♘xf4 ♘e7 12 ♗e2! h4 13 ♘h5 ♔f8 14 ♗g5 is clearly better for White, M.Tal-
T.Petrosian, USSR Championship, Moscow 1983, as here is 12...g6 13 dxc5!) 10 cxd4 ♕h4
(this way, Black avoids the dxc5 capture mentioned in the previous note, but on the other
hand, White's doubled pawns have been straightened out) 11 ♕xh4! (now this is strongest)
11...♘xh4 12 ♗g5! ♘f5 (12...♘xg2+ 13 ♔f1) 13 ♘e2 ♘c6 14 c3 and Black never escaped
from the dark-square chains, D.Yanofsky-W.Uhlmann, Stockholm Interzonal 1962.

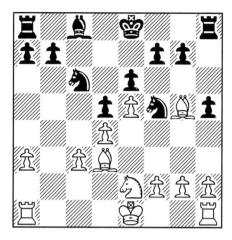

This game was immensely influential, and the move 7...♘f5 has never really recovered.

Question: What about 7...g6, similar to the Portisch-Hook lines?

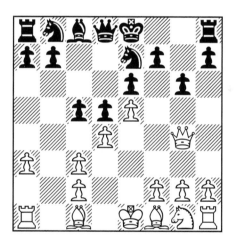

Answer: In this position, 7...g6? is just plain bad, I believe. As noted in the context of the Fischer-Hook line, when he plays ...g6 in such positions, Black usually needs to leave his knight on g8 for some time, to cover the f6- and h6-squares. Combining ...g6 with ...♘e7, as here, looks terrible, and indeed, there are no worthwhile practical examples, so bad does it look!

On the other hand, the alternative Fischer-Hook treatment, 7...♔f8, is also playable here, and had a brief spell of popularity in the 1980s. However, I don't think it is as good as in the Portisch-Hook Variation.

Answer: Since here the black queen is not blockading the white queenside on a4, White can reply 8 a4! and bring his bishop to the strong square a3. It is not the end of the world for Black, but I see no reason for him to play this way – if he wants to play a ...♔f8 variation, then the Portisch-Hook system seems a much more logical form in which to do so.

8 ♗d3

This has emerged in recent years as definitely the most dangerous move, and the only one to pose Black real problems. The older line was 8 ♘f3 ♘bc6 9 ♗d3 f5 10 exf6 ♖xf6 11 ♗g5.

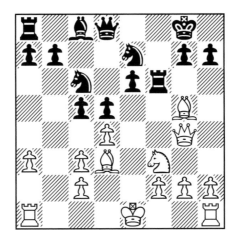

However, this lost ground rapidly in the 1980s, once it was realized that Black can reply 11...e5!

***Question:** Is that really playable? It looks as though it should lose to something!*

Answer: That is why it took literally decades before black players realized it was feasible! But once one examines the tactics with an open mind, it soon becomes apparent that Black is fine in all variations:

a) 12 ♕h4 e4 is the first point. Black will win two pieces for the rook.

***Question:** But isn't his king exposed?*

Answer: Not seriously, because most of White's developed minor pieces end up disappearing from the board! 13 ♗xf6 gxf6 14 ♕xf6 exd3 (14...♕f8 is also adequate, but the text is simpler) 15 cxd3 cxd4 16 ♘xd4 ♘xd4 17 ♕xd4 ♘c6 and Black is fine.

b) 12 ♗xh7+ ♔xh7 13 ♕h5+ ♔g8 14 ♗xf6 gxf6 15 dxe5 ♕f8! is no problem for Black.

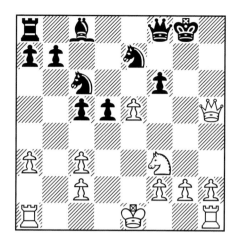

For example, 16 exf6 ♕xf6 17 0-0 ♗f5 and although Black's king is bare of pawn cover, his pieces do an excellent job of guarding His Majesty. White has a couple of extra pawns, but his queenside pawns are weak. Chances are balanced.

c) 12 ♕g3 looks strong, because 13 ♗xf6 seems to be a powerful threat, but Black has the excellent (if forced) reply 12...♖xf3! 13 gxf3 c4 14 ♗e2 ♕a5 15 ♗d2 ♘f5 and Black is actually better.

8...f5

A major parting of the ways. As we will see, the absence of the knights from f3 and c6 favours White in this line, by comparison with the variation just examined in the last note.

> ***Question:*** Doesn't 8...♘bc6 9 ♘f3 f5 transpose to the last note?

Answer: Yes, but after 8...♘bc6, White has the much more dangerous try 9 ♕h5!. Now the only move is 9...♘g6 (9...h6 was played quite a few times at GM level, until White finally proved that it loses by force: 10 ♗xh6! gxh6 11 ♕xh6 ♘f5 12 ♗xf5 exf5 13 0-0-0 f4 14 ♘h3 ♘e7 15 ♘g5 ♗f5 16 g4! ♗e4 17 ♖he1 ♕b6 18 e6 ♗g6 19 ♖d3 1-0 S.Maus-R.Hübner, Lugano 1989).

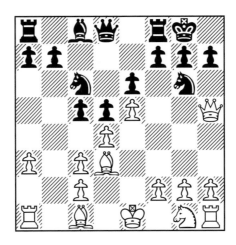

Answer: 9...♘g6 was popularised by the German Grandmaster Gerald Hertneck, and quickly became the main line. Black defends the mate threat, without creating any structural weaknesses, and he always has the option of ...c4, driving the white bishop off the b1-h7 diagonal.

Question: It looks as though he should be fine.

Answer: The trouble is, after a huge amount of practical testing, White has perfected a plan, which offers him attacking chances, and the analysis of which runs literally to move 35 and beyond. Theoreticians still argue about whether White is better or not, but it is clear that Black is playing for a draw in this line, and from most players' viewpoint, it is not terribly attractive to have to memorise 40-odd moves of theory, in order to reach a possibly tenable position. The basic line runs as follows: 10 ♘f3 ♕c7 11 ♗e3! (the most subtle; White delays castling, since the moment he castles short, Black closes the position with ...c5-c4: for instance, 11 0-0 c4 12 ♗xg6 fxg6! and he has no real problems) 11...c4.

Question: Is this forced?

Answer: Not exactly, but Black is running out of waiting moves. 11...♘ce7 was tried, but 12 h4 still keeps some advantage.

The main line goes on 12 ♗xg6 fxg6.

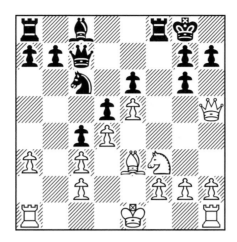

Question: Why this recapture? What happened to capturing towards the centre?

Answer: In this line, Black almost always has to take with the f-pawn, because 12...hxg6? 13 ♕h4 leaves him struggling with the threat of ♘g5.

After 13 ♕g4 we reach the basic position of this variation. By leaving his king in the centre, White has preserved the possibility of h4-h5, levering open the h-file. As I said above, the analysis of this position runs extremely deep, and there is still no final verdict, but it is easy to see that Black's position lacks dynamism (he has no pawn breaks, now that he has had to take back with the f-pawn), and he lacks counterplay. It is just a question of whether White can create serious attacking chances or whether Black will hold him off and draw.

A recent example, featuring one of the staunchest defenders of the position on the black side, was the game D.Svetushkin-A.Dgebuadze, Livigno 2011, which continued 13...♕f7 14 ♘g5 ♕e8 15 h4 h6 16 ♘h3 ♗d7 17 ♕e2 b5 (this queenside pawn advance is the only chance of counterplay) 18 g4 ♘e7 19 h5 gxh5 20 g5 hxg5 21 ♘xg5 g6 22 ♔d2 a5 23 ♖ag1

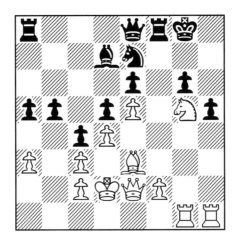

23...♖f5?! 24 ♘f3 ♕f8?! 25 ♘h4 ♕g7 26 ♗g5 ♖xg5 27 ♖xg5 and White eventually won.

Question: So are you saying the Hertneck System is bad?

Answer: No, but I just don't think it very attractive in a practical sense. Black ends up defending a blocked position, in which White has most of the winning chances that exist, and which has also been analysed almost to death. By all means play the line if you like it, but it is not really my cup of tea.

We now return to 8...f5:

9 exf6 ♖xf6 10 ♗g5

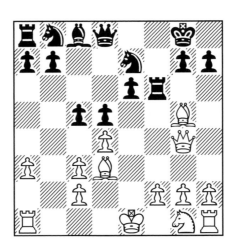

The best move. 10 ♕h5 allows Black to meet the mate threat with 10...h6! when he stands perfectly satisfactorily.

10...♖f7

Now we see the difference from the knights not being on f3 and c6: 10...e5? is simply bad after 11 ♕g3 when there is no exchange sacrifice on f3.

11 ♕h5!

Again the most precise. 11 ♕h4 h6! is less of a problem for Black.

11...g6

Forced (or is it? – see below!), but severely weakening the dark squares.

> *Question:* But why is this necessary? What is wrong with 11...h6 as in previous variations?

Answer: The problem is tactical. White has 12 ♗h7+! ♚xh7 (the computer regards 12...♚f8 as perfectly playable, so maybe this line is worth another look for Black) 13 ♕xf7 hxg5 14 ♘f3 ♘bc6 15 ♘xg5+ ♚h6 16 ♘xe6 ♗xe6 17 ♕xe6+ ♘g6 which is regarded as good for White, although admittedly, looking at it again, it also may not be so bad for Black. Perhaps 11...h6 is not as bad as has hitherto been assumed?

12 ♕d1

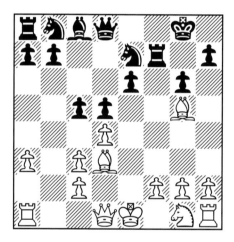

This is more or less a *tabiya* for the line starting with 8...f5.

> *Question:* And what is going on?

Answer: In many ways, it is a typical Winawer. White has the bishop pair-and Black's dark squares are weak (especially so here, with the move ...g6 played). On the other hand, White has the traditional weak queenside pawn structure. Most GMs would probably take the view that White is somewhat better, but even if that is so, it is not clear that he has a huge amount. Winawer players should be reasonably happy with this type of position.

12...♕a5

The alternative, which has been widely played here, is 12...♘bc6 13 ♘f3 ♕f8.

Question: That looks a slightly funny square for the queen.

Answer: It is rather unusual to see the queen on f8, certainly, but in this position, it makes some sense. Black covers the sensitive dark squares around his king. He can follow up with ...h6, ...♕g7, and then ...♗d7 and ...♖af8, for example. One recent practical example, by a regular practitioner of the line, went 14 0-0 c4 15 ♗e2 h6 16 ♗c1 ♔h7 17 a4 ♗d7 18 ♖b1 b6

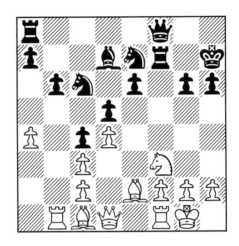

19 a5 bxa5 20 ♗a3 ♖d8 21 ♖e1 ♗c8 22 ♗c5 ♕g7 23 ♗f1 ♘f5, with an unclear position in M.Zoldan-M.Drasko, Cento 2011. Black went on to win, but he was far the stronger player. Overall, the ...♕f8 lines are a respectable way to play, but White should be a little better, at least.

13 ♗d2

13 ♕d2 is also possible. Then Watson quotes a Kindermann recommendation 13...c4 14 ♗e2 ♘f5, intending ...♘d6. Once again, we have a typical Winawer struggle, where Black's dark squares are horrible, but he has the usual structural compensation.

13...♘bc6 14 ♘f3

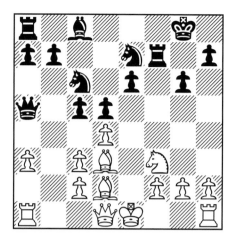

14...♛c7

Question: What is the point of this? It looks rather
odd to retreat to c7, rather than, say, a4.

Answer: 14...♛a4 is a possible move and has also been played, but the text has been the most popular in recent years. Black plans to keep his pawn on c5 and to advance ...e6-e5, not something he is usually able to do in the Winawer.

Question: Doesn't that risk opening the position for White's bishops?

Answer: Yes, it does, but on the other hand, Black frees his own pieces too, and also rids himself of the structural weakness on e6. In the resulting positions, practice suggests that chances are fairly balanced.

14...c4 is once again a major alternative, with the standard blocked Winawer position.

Question: How do you assess the position?

Answer: White is probably a little better, but it is not a great deal, and in practice, most Winawer players should be happy enough with such a familiar structure. Of course, if Black could play the move ...g6-g7, he would be in clover, but alas, the rules do not permit this!

15 dxc5

Question: Slightly surprising!

Answer: Well, we have seen similar ideas before in this book. White wins a pawn, at least temporarily, and hopes that, even if Black regains it, the opening of the position will favour the white bishop-pair.

15 0-0 is the main alternative. Then after 15...e5 16 ♘xe5 (16 ♘g5 ♖f8 17 c4 is a major alternative, when 17...exd4! 18 cxd5 ♘e5 is unclear, but seemingly satisfactory for Black) 16...♘xe5 17 dxe5 ♕xe5 18 c4 (18 ♖e1 ♕f6 was equal in M.Bluvshtein-A.Barsov, Hastings 2004/05) 18...d4 19 f4 ♕c7 20 ♕f3 White was maybe slightly better in D.Stellwagen-J.Timman, Malmo 2006, but Black held the draw without huge problems, despite being pressed for quite a few moves.

15...e5 16 ♗e2?!

Rather passive. A more critical continuation is 16 ♘g5 ♖f8 17 c4. Now Watson quotes the game Y.Pelletier-S.Kindermann, Biel 2003, which continued 17...e4 18 cxd5 (18 ♗e2 ♕e5 is fine for Black) 18...exd3 19 d6 ♕d7 20 dxe7 ♕xe7+ 21 ♗e3.

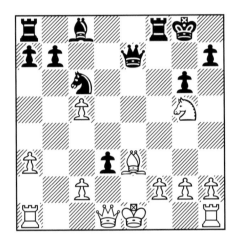

Here Kindermann has suggested 21...♖f5! 22 ♘f3 ♗e6 23 0-0 ♗d5 24 ♘d2 ♖h5 with an unclear position, in which Black seems to have quite good chances.

> **Question:** This is all pretty hairy, compared with the usual blocked Winawer structures after ...c5-c4 by Black.

Answer: That is true. The more fluid plan with ...e6-e5 in this line results in an altogether more dynamic position, but one in which Black seems to be holding his own.

16...♗g4 17 0-0 ♗xf3

> **Question:** Why give up the bishop?

Answer: It is not forced, but Black prefers to eliminate the knight, which can otherwise cause trouble by jumping to g5 at some moment. In the structure resulting from this exchange, Black feels his knights are the equal of White's bishop-pair.

18 ♗xf3 e4 19 ♗g4 ♘f5

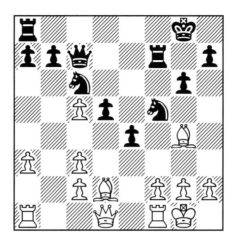

Question: What is your assessment of this position?
White has an extra pawn and the two bishops, after all!

Answer: Yes, but I think chances are still about equal. The extra pawn is not very significant, in view of the trebled c-pawns, and Black's pieces are all active and well placed. It is not so easy to activate the white bishops, as the enemy knights and centre pawns control a lot of squares. Black has to be careful, especially considering his somewhat draughty king, but with accurate play, I think he is fine.

20 ♗e3 ♘xe3 21 fxe3 ♖xf1+ 22 ♕xf1 ♕e7 23 ♕f4 ♘e5 24 ♖f1 ♖e8

Black is comfortably holding here.

25 h4 h5 26 ♗h3?!

This is the start of White's downward spiral. He still harbours ambitions, and wishes to keep his bishop active on the h3-c8 diagonal, but now the black knight gets the wonderful outpost c4, attacking a host of weak white pawns. 26 ♗e2 looks better, dominating the knight.

26...♔g7 27 a4 ♘c4 28 ♖b1 ♕xc5 29 ♖xb7+ ♖e7 30 ♖xe7+ ♕xe7

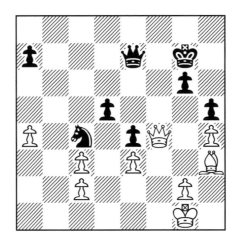

White still has an extra pawn, but it is not felt at all, and the black queen plus knight combination is known to be effective in the endgame. The position should be a draw, but White soon goes wrong.

31 ♔f2 a5 32 ♕g5??

A dreadful misjudgement. White probably thought that, after the queen exchange, his bishop would be better than the knight on an open board, but in actual fact, the bishop has no targets, whilst the white pawns drop like ripe fruit. White should just mark time with 32 ♔e2 and hope that his opponent cannot find a way to strengthen his position.

32...♕xg5 33 hxg5 ♘b6

Now the a4-pawn falls, and the passed black a-pawn will decide the game.

34 ♗e6 ♘xa4 35 ♗xd5 ♘xc3 36 ♗c4 a4

White is losing a piece.

37 ♔e1 a3 38 ♔d2 a2 39 ♗xa2 ♘xa2 40 c3

The knight is trapped, but while White is rounding it up, Black's king sets up a winning pawn ending.

40...♔f7 41 ♔c2 ♔e6 42 ♔b2 ♔d5 43 ♔xa2 ♔c4 44 ♔b2 ♔d3

45 c4

Desperation, but 45 ♔b3 ♔xe3 46 c4 ♔d4 47 ♔b4 e3 sees Black queen with check.

45...♔xc4 46 ♔c2 h4

Zugzwang. Black takes the opposition.

47 ♔d2 ♔b3 0-1

> **Question:** So what is the overall conclusion on the 7...0-0 variation?

Answer: I think Black is objectively okay in these lines. There is no doubt that 7...0-0 is a much calmer and safer way to handle the black position, although it lacks the fireworks of the 7...♕c7 lines. Much depends on the black player's mood and preparation – although I played 7...♕c7 most of the time in my playing days, there were occasions when I just did not fancy the hair-raising struggles that ensue, and preferred to play a quieter, less knife-edge position. On those occasions, I used 7...0-0, which can be played with much less preparation (especially in the main line with 8...f5) and is less stressful on Black's nerves!

Game 19
V.Hort-T.Petrosian
European Team Championship, Kapfenberg 1970

1 e4 e6 2 d4 d5 3 ♘c3 ♗b4 4 e5 c5 5 a3 ♗xc3+ 6 bxc3 ♕c7

We have already seen this variation in Game 14, but this is where we see the real point of the move order.

7 ♕g4

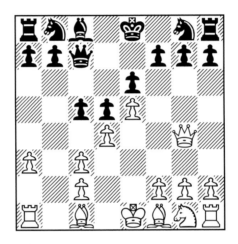

7...f5

This is the point. Having the queen on c7 already allows Black to defend his g7-pawn by advancing the f-pawn, giving him additional possibilities.

> **Question:** Is 7...f6 possible instead?

Answer: This move did indeed become quite popular in the late 1960s, chiefly thanks to the impressive Black win in the game A.Matulovic-R.Byrne, Sousse Interzonal 1967, which continued 8 ♘f3 c4! 9 ♗e2 ♘c6 10 0-0 ♕f7! 11 ♕h3 ♘ge7 12 a4 ♗d7 13 ♗a3 0-0-0 14 a5 h5, and Black stood clearly better, thanks to the poor position of the white queen, which will be a target for the advancing black kingside pawns.

However, nowadays the line is regarded as rather dangerous for Black, thanks to some startling tactical resources, beginning 8 ♗b5+! ♔f8.

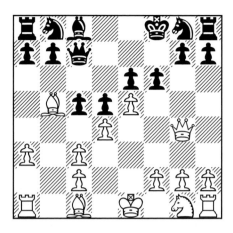

Question: That's a shock!

Answer: For a long time, this move was regarded as a refutation of White's last. The point is that White is now faced with three strong threats: 9...cxd4, attacking c3, 9...♕a5, attacking both c3 and b5, and 9...c4, trapping the bishop on b5. It appears that White has no satisfactory way to meet them all, but later, it became clear that he can simply develop with 9 ♘f3! and then:

a) 9...cxd4? is met simply by 10 0-0 with a large development advantage. This position is extremely dangerous for Black.

b) Likewise, the seemingly devastating 9...♕a5 is answered by the forced but very strong 10 ♖b1!. For example, 10...a6 11 ♗e2 (11 ♗d3 c4 12 ♗e2 ♕xc3+ is less clear) 11...♕xc3+ 12 ♗d2 ♕xc2 13 ♖c1 ♕e4 14 ♕g3 and, once again, White has a huge development lead and a very strong attack.

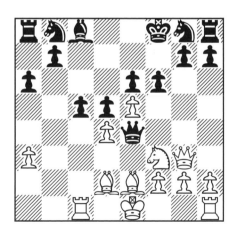

The fact that Black has played ...f6, rather than closing the position with ...f5, makes the development issue that much more serious for him, as the position can open up more after exf6. One recent all-GM encounter saw Black massacred in typical style: 14...♘d7 15 exf6 gxf6 16 ♕d6+ ♘e7 (16...♔f7 is the only hope, but White still has a massive attack after 17 0-0) 17 0-0! ♖g8 (17...♕xe2 18 ♖fe1 ♕d3 19 ♖xe6 is decisive) 18 ♖fe1 ♕g6 19 ♘h4 ♕f7 20 ♗h6+ ♔e8 21 ♗h5! ♕xh5 22 ♖xe6 ♕f7 23 ♘f5 ♔d8 24 ♖xe7 ♕g6 25 ♖xd7+ ♗xd7 26 ♕b6+ 1-0 N.Vitiugov-S.Dyachkov, Russian Team Championship 2008.

c) 9...c4 is the most critical, cutting off the bishop, but now there follows 10 a4! a6 11 ♗a3+ ♘e7.

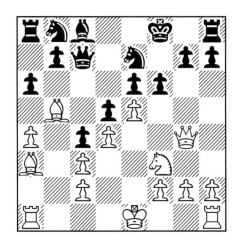

Exercise: Find a strong move for White.

Answer: 12 ♗e8!!. It turns out that the bishop is immune, since after 12...♔xe8 13 ♕xg7 ♖f8 (13...♖g8 14 ♕xh7 is no better) 14 exf6 ♖f7 15 ♕h8+ ♖f8 16 ♕xh7 ♖xf6 17 ♘e5 White has two pawns for the piece, and a clear advantage. Instead, 12...fxe5 13 ♕h5 g6 14 ♗xg6! is again winning for White, which only leaves 12...♕d8. But then there follows 13 ♗h5! ♘bc6 (13...f5 14 ♕h4 g6 still doesn't trap the bishop, because of 15 ♗xg6! – the prelate certainly has a charmed life; 13...g6 14 ♗xg6 hxg6 15 exf6 also wins for White) 14 exf6 gxf6 15 ♘g5! (15 ♘e5! is also good) 15...♕a5 (or 15...fxg5 16 ♕xg5 and Black is helpless against the check on f6) 16 0-0 f5 17 ♕h4 1-0 E.Sutovsky-S.Dyachkov, Moscow 2007. A devastating game, which 'closes' the variation with 7...f6 8 ♗b5+ ♔f8 pretty convincingly.

Returning to the safer 7...f5:

8 ♕g3

This is one of two main lines. 8 ♕h5+ is the other.

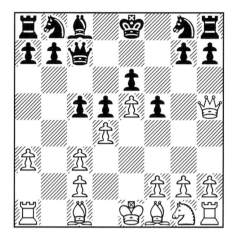

Answer: He can, but White is somewhat better after both 9 ♕xf7+ ♔xf7 10 c4!, and 9 ♗b5+ ♗d7 10 ♕xf7+ ♔xf7 11 ♖b1.

Thus play tends to go 8...g6 9 ♕d1.

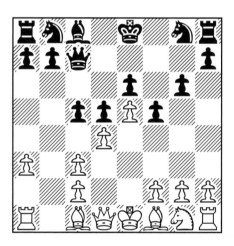

Answer: Yes, this is another of these rather ugly variations, that one sees in the Winawer. However, as usual, the position is nothing like as bad as it first looks. Although his dark squares are a bad accident, Black has his usual compensating factors: the weakened white queenside pawns, in particular, which he can begin to pressure after 9...♗d7!.

> *Question:* Why is this best?

Answer: It is a subtle idea, the point of which we will soon see. The bishop is aiming at the a4-square. Instead, 9...cxd4?! 10 cxd4 ♕c3+ 11 ♗d2 ♕xd4 12 ♘f3 ♕e4+ 13 ♗e2 is a very risky pawn-grab. Black can probably survive with accurate play, but I cannot recommend this for him.

Now White tends to go 10 ♘f3.

> *Question:* Isn't 10 a4 a logical reply, to keep the bishop out?

Answer: It is, but now the pawn grab 10...cxd4 11 cxd4 ♕c3+ 12 ♗d2 ♕xd4 13 ♘f3 ♕e4+ 14 ♗e2 ♘c6 is more justifiable, since Black is a move ahead in development, compared with the analogous line at move 9.

After 10...♗a4 we arrive at a key position.

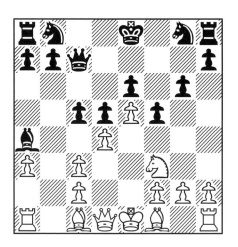

White has several possibilities:

a) 11 ♖b1 is regarded as the most testing of the various alternatives, although 11 dxc5 (see below) looks more dangerous to me. After 11...♘d7 (11...cxd4 12 ♖b4 is one point of White's play) 12 ♗e2 (12 dxc5 is less effective than a move earlier: 12...♘xc5 13 ♗e3 b6 14 ♕d4 ♘e7 15 ♗d3 h6 16 0-0 g5 and Black was fine in T.Wedberg-E.Berg, Malmo 2002) 12...h6 13 dxc5 (13 0-0 ♘e7 is equal – Watson/Lahlum) 13...♘xc5 14 ♖b4 ♗d7 15 0-0 ♘e4 Black had no particular problems in J.Timman-T.Shaked, Merrillville 1997.

b) 11 ♗d3?! is natural, but amounts to a trap of sorts, since it allows 11...cxd4 12 cxd4 ♕c3+ 13 ♗d2 ♕xd3! (one of the points of Black's whole move order) 14 cxd3 ♗xd1 15 ♔xd1.

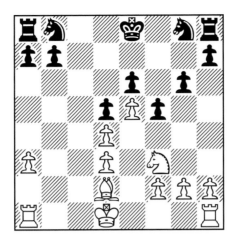

Answer: It is not so terrible, but practice shows that Black has no problems and can even play for the advantage long-term. Play could continue 15...♞c6 16 ♖b1 (16 h4 h6 17 ♔e2 ♞ge7 18 a4 ♔d7 19 a5 ♞d8 20 ♖hb1 ♞ec6 21 ♖b5 ♖b8 22 ♖g1 ♞f7 23 g4 fxg4 24 ♖xg4 ♖hg8 25 ♖b1 h5 26 ♖g2 ♖g7 27 ♖bg1 ♖bg8 28 ♖b1 ♔c7 with an unclear position in J.Egger-L.Johannessen, Istanbul Olympiad 2000, eventually won by Black) 16...b6 17 ♖c1 ♔d7 18 h4 h6 19 ♔e2 ♞ge7 20 ♖c2 ♖ac8 21 ♖hc1 ♞d8 22 ♖xc8 ♞xc8 23 a4 ♞e7 24 ♗e3 ♞f7 25 a5 ♞c6 26 axb6 axb6 and Black eventually won in J.Polgar-I.Morovic Fernandez, Buenos Aires 1992.

c) 11 c4 attempts to open the position, to favour the white bishops: 11...♞e7 12 cxd5 ♞xd5 13 ♗c4 was E.Sutovsky-E.Berg, Internet blitz 2004, and now *Fritz* points out the cute trick 13...cxd4! 14 ♗xd5 ♛a5+ 15 ♛d2 ♛xd5 with equality.

d) 11 ♖a2 deals with the tactical threats on the c-file, but the rook is ugly on a2. Black is fine after 11...♞d7 12 h4 h6 13 ♗f4?! (13 ♗e3 0-0-0 is equal) 13...♞gf6!, as the knight is coming to e4.

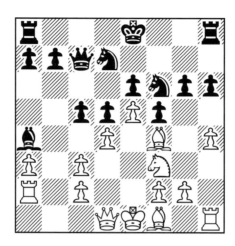

Black rapidly gained the upper hand and won in the following game: 14 ♗xh6 ♖xh6 15 exf6 ♘xf6 16 ♗d3 c4 17 ♕c1 ♕g7 18 ♗e2 ♘e4 19 ♕b2 g5 20 ♕b4 b5 21 ♘e5 a5 22 ♕b2 gxh4 23 ♗f3 ♕g5 24 ♔d1 ♕d2# 0-1 K.Stokke-L.Johannessen, Bergen 2002.

It should be noted that this entire 6...♕c7 system is a major Scandinavian speciality. A really excellent and thorough coverage of the whole line can be found in the 3rd edition of John Watson's *Play the French*, the chapter being guest-written by Norwegian player and organiser, Hans Olaf Lahlum.

e) 11 ♗d2.

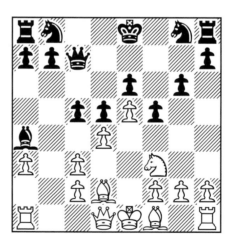

Question: What is the point of this?

Answer: It stops the check on c3, and thus rules out the Polgar-Morovic line. It also sets a nice trap: 11...♘c6 (11...cxd4? 12 cxd4 ♕xc2?? 13 ♗b5+! is the trap; however, 11...♘d7 is also playable: for example, 12 ♗d3 ♘e7 13 0-0 h6 – a typical move in this variation, covering the dark squares h6 and g5, and hoping to expand with ...g6-g5 – 14 h4 ♔f7 15 ♖b1 ♖ac8 16 ♖b2 ♘b6 with decent play for Black in F.Andersson-A.Olssen, Hallstahammer, 2002, as quoted by Lahlum) 12 ♗d3 h6 13 h4 ♘ge7 14 ♕c1 0-0-0 15 ♖h3 ♖h7 16 ♔f1 ♖dh8 17 ♔g1 c4 18 ♗e2 ♘d8 19 g3 ♘ec6 20 ♘h2 g5! with good play for Black, who went on to win in Z.Zhao-E.Berg, Athens 2001.

f) 11 dxc5.

Question: White wrecks his pawn structure again!

Answer: We have seen the idea quite a lot. White wants to open the position and expose the enemy's weakened dark squares. He is prepared to sacrifice his structure to do so. 11...♕xc5 (11...♘d7 12 ♕d4 ♘xc5 13 ♗d3 h6 14 h4 b6 15 0-0 0-0-0 was fairly solid for Black in J.Dworakowska-M.Socko, Ostrow 2002, but here 14 0-0 is possibly a sterner test: 14...♘e7 15 ♗e3 b6 16 ♕h4 and White was better in M.Chandler-A.Kinsman, British League 1998) 12 ♗d2 (12 ♗d3?! allows another Polgar-Morovic trick: 12...♕xc3+ 13 ♗d2 ♕xd3 14 cxd3 ♗xd1 15 ♖xd1 ♘c6 and Black was fine in D.De Vreugt-B.Socko, Ohrid 2001) 12...♘c6 13 ♗d3 0-0-0 14 0-0 h6 "looks solid" according to Lahlum.

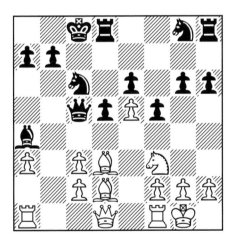

However, 15 ♖b1 ♘ge7 16 ♕c1 g5 17 ♘d4 appears rather dangerous to me.

Overall, 11 dxc5 looks like a critical line for this whole variation.

We now return to 8 ♕g3:

8...cxd4

8...♘e7 has been under a cloud ever since the first game of the Tal-Botvinnik World Championship match of 1960, which continued 9 ♕xg7 ♖g8 10 ♕xh7 cxd4 11 ♔d1, and White won in 32 moves. John Watson attempted to revive the move, with some analysis in the second edition of his *Play the French* series, but did not manage to convince himself of its viability. Readers armed with 21st century analysis engines may wish to make another attempt.

9 cxd4 ♘e7

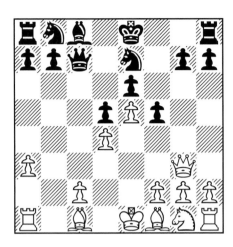

Question: So what is happening here?

Answer: By exchanging on d4 first, Black has prevented White from meeting this by taking on g7. He will follow up with ...0-0, and then ...b6 and ...♗a6, exchanging off his bad bishop.

Question: That looks pretty solid. Isn't Black doing well?

Answer: It is a solid line, but White's chances should also not be underestimated. His doubled pawns have been dissolved, and he has hopes of activating his dark-squared bishop. He still has serious weaknesses on the c-file, it is true, but these can be defended adequately, while he builds up his attack on the other wing. Overall, chances are approximately equal, with a long positional battle in prospect.

10 ♗d2

Covering c3 and so attacking g7.

10...0-0 11 ♗d3 b6 12 ♘e2

This is the usual development plan. The knight heads for f4, from where it will attack the weakened e6-pawn, and also have the possibility of jumping to h5.

12 ♘f3?! seems less effective. One practical example saw White use the plan of taking with the pawn on d3, which we will discuss later, but it brought him no great dividends here: 12...♗a6 13 0-0 ♗xd3 14 cxd3 ♘bc6 15 h4 ♕d7 16 ♕g5 h6 17 ♕g3 ♔h7 18 ♕h2 ♖f7 19 g3 ♖c8 20 ♔g2 ♖ff8 with equal chances in M.Menacher-P.Haba, Leinfelden 2000. Black eventually won, but he outrated his opponent by some 200 points.

12...♗a6

Another Petrosian classic is worth a closer look, for the middlegame strategy: 12...♖f7 13

0-0 ♗a6 14 h4 ♗xd3 15 cxd3.

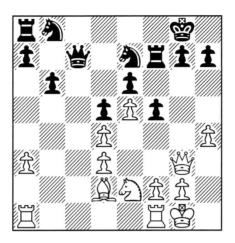

Again this recapture.

Question: What is the point?

Answer: White removes his backward pawn from the c-file and also covers the c4-square, which otherwise represents an outpost for the black knight. However, the downside is that the d4-pawn becomes more vulnerable (it can no longer be defended by c2-c3),and Black has a queenside pawn majority. 15...♘bc6 16 ♗e3 ♕d7 17 ♘f4 ♘g6! 18 ♘xg6 hxg6 19 ♕f4 (19 ♕xg6 is met by 19...f4 20 ♗d2 ♘xd4 with a good game for Black) 19...♕e8 20 g3 ♖c7 21 ♔g2 ♕f7 22 ♖h1 and now Petrosian commenced a Long March with his king:

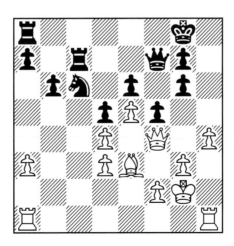

22...♔f8! (evacuating the danger zone) 23 ♕g5 ♔e8 24 ♖ac1 ♔d7 25 h5 gxh5 26 ♖xh5 ♖g8 27 ♖h7 ♔c8 28 ♕h4 ♕g6 29 ♖h8 ♖xh8 30 ♕xh8+ ♔b7, J.Diez del Corral-T.Petrosian,

Palma de Mallorca 1969. The king is extremely safe on the queenside, and such long strategical manoeuvres are typical of this variation. Chances are still objectively equal, although Petrosian went on to win.

13 ♘f4

After 13 ♗xa6 ♘xa6 we have another typical position.

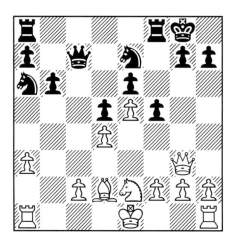

Question: What is the assessment?

Answer: Chances are about equal. White can bring his knight to f4, tying Black down to the defence of e6, and then push his h-pawn, trying to create kingside chances. Black, for his part, has play on the c-file: 14 ♕d3?! ♕c4! (Black is happy to exchange queens, because although he plugs the c-file, he also gets the d5-square, and secures his king from attack) 15 ♕xc4 dxc4 16 ♗b4 ♘xb4 17 axb4 ♘d5 18 c3 a5 19 bxa5 ♖xa5 20 ♖xa5 bxa5 (now Black has a passed a-pawn, and he soon establishes a winning position) 21 ♔d2 f4 22 f3 ♖b8 23 ♖a1 ♖b2+ 24 ♔e1 a4 25 ♖a3 g5 26 g3 ♖b1+ 27 ♔f2 ♖b2 28 ♔e1 ♘e3 29 ♖xa4 ♖b1+ 0-1 K.Goh-P.Haba, Internet (blitz) 2005.

13 ♗b4 is another option for White. A nice demonstration of the virtues of the black position was provided by a well-known Winawer expert, in the following game: 13...♗xd3 14 cxd3 ♖f7 (a typical prophylactic idea; the rook unpins the knight on e7, defends g7 – anticipating ♘f4-h5 – and can later swing across to c7, if occasion permits, to double on the c-file) 15 0-0 ♘bc6 16 ♗d6 ♕d7 17 a4

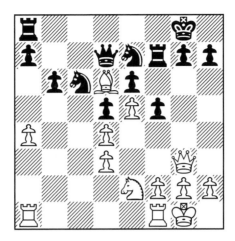

17...f4! (this tactical blow is a thematic idea in such positions) 18 ♕g4 (18 ♘xf4 ♘xd4 is clearly better for Black) 18...f3! 19 gxf3 ♘f5 20 ♗a3 h5! (winning the d4-pawn, after which White's position soon collapses) 21 ♕xh5 ♘fxd4 22 ♘xd4 ♘xd4 and Black was winning in V.Vehi Bach-L.Psakhis, Manresa 1996.

Finally, 13 0-0 ♗xd3 14 ♕xd3 ♖c8 15 ♖fc1 ♕c4 16 ♕xc4 ♖xc4 reaches a typical endgame for this variation. Black has easy play on the queenside, although White's position is hard to break down. Such endings typically arise with the stronger player as Black, and he usually scores quite heavily. A characteristic example was E.Gullaksen-R.Djurhuus, Norwegian Championship 1996: 17 a4 ♘bc6 18 c3 ♘a5 19 ♖cb1 ♔f7 20 h4 ♖g8 21 g3 ♖c7 22 ♔g2 ♘c4 23 ♖a2 ♖b8 24 ♔f3

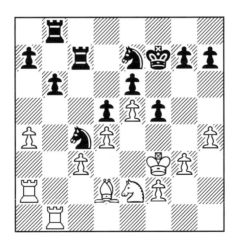

24...a5 25 ♗c1 b5 (Black's last two moves are worth noting, as a typical way to create a passed a-pawn in such positions) 26 ♗a3?! b4! 27 cxb4 ♘xa3 28 ♖xa3 axb4 29 ♖aa1 ♘c6 30 ♔e3 ♘a5 31 ♔d3 b3 32 ♘c3 b2 33 ♖a3 ♘c4 34 ♖a2 ♖b3 35 ♔c2 ♘a5 0-1.

13...♛d7 14 ♝b4

14 h4 is another typical move. After 14...♝xd3 15 ♛xd3...

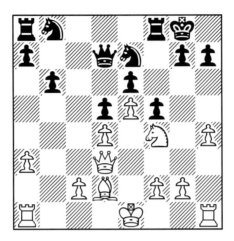

...Black's best is 15...♜c8!.

Question: Why does this deserve an exclamation mark?

Answer: This move of Kaidanov's is generally regarded as the most accurate. Black's idea is to play ...♜c4 and only then bring his knight to c6. The older line was 15...♞bc6, which is probably less precise, though by no means bad. Two famous examples are worth seeing after 16 ♜h3 ♜ac8 17 ♜g3:

a) 17...♚h8 18 h5 ♜f7 19 h6 g6 20 ♜c1 ♜ff8 21 ♞e2 ♞b8 22 ♚f1 ♜c4 23 ♚g1 ♞bc6 (Black's last three moves explain the point of Kaidanov's 15...♜c8; here, Black has lost a couple of tempi with his knight, in order to reach the desired ...♜c4 and ...♞c6 set-up) 24 ♝g5 ♞g8 was S.Reshevsky-M.Botvinnik, The Hague/Moscow 1948. White ought to be better here, but even though he seems to have achieved quite a bit of progress on the kingside, he found it impossible to break through, and Black eventually won.

b) 17...♜f7 18 h5 ♞d8 19 c3 was G.Kasparov-N.Short, Novgorod 1997.

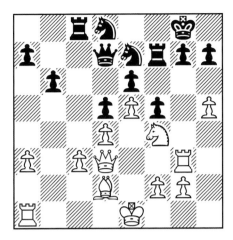

Now Kasparov gives 19...♕a4 as slightly better for Black. Even so, Short subsequently switched to 15...♖c8, which suggests he thinks it better.

After the rook move and then 16 ♖h3 ♖c4 17 ♖g3 ♘bc6 18 c3 ♖f8 (the other rook comes over to defend g7) White has tried:

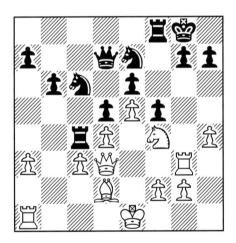

a) 19 ♔f1 ♖f7 20 ♔g1 ♘a5 21 a4 ♕c6 22 ♖a3 ♔f8 23 ♕b1 ♘b7 was agreed drawn in I.Teran Alvarez-N.Short, Spanish Team Championship 2003.

b) So was 19 h5 ♘a5 20 h6 g6 21 ♘h5 ♔h8 22 ♘f6 ♕c8 23 ♗g5 ♖f7 24 ♖f3 ♘ac6 25 ♔f1 ♘b8 in R.Castellanos-L.Psakhis, Andorra 2003.

c) 19 ♘h5 ♘g6 20 ♘xg7? f4! (once again, this typical tactical blow) 21 ♖g5 ♕xg7 and Black was winning in M.Hoffmann-A.Rustemov, German League 2004.

Before we return to 14 ♗b4, 14 ♗xa6 ♘xa6 15 h4 reaches another typical position: for example, 15...♖f7 16 h5 ♖c8 17 c3 ♘b8 18 h6 g6 19 0-0 ♖c4 20 ♘h5 ♕c8 21 ♘f6+ ♔h8.

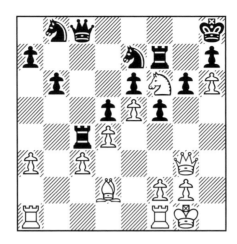

Once again, White looks to have made great progress, but how does he break through? 22 ♕h4 ♘g8 23 ♖fe1 ♕f8 24 g4? (24 a4 is *Fritz*'s preference, but it is not clear what it is doing next after 24...♘c6) 24...fxg4 25 ♕xg4 ♕c8 and Black was fine in I.Almasi-L.Psakhis, Vienna 1996. White's game subsequently collapsed with surprising speed: 26 ♘xg8 ♔xg8 27 ♖ac1 ♘c6 28 ♗g5 ♖f5 29 ♗f6 ♕f8 30 ♔g2 ♕xh6 31 ♖h1 ♕f4 32 ♕xf4 ♖xf4 33 ♖h6 ♘xd4 34 ♖ch1 ♖xc3 0-1.

14...♖f7 15 h4 ♗xd3 16 ♕xd3 ♘bc6

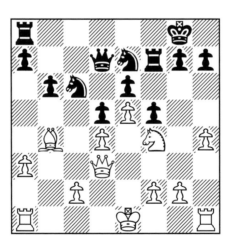

Question: This is all starting to look very familiar!

Answer: Yes, the pattern of the game is much as usual. Black will bring his rook to c4 and pressurise the d4-pawn, whilst White attempts to break through on the other wing. Chances are about equal. The rest of the game is worth seeing, though, as we get a classic

Petrosian exchange sacrifice.

17 ♖h3 ♖c8 18 ♖g3 ♘d8 19 h5 ♖c4 20 h6

We have seen this scenario several times already. It appears that White is making decisive progress on the kingside dark squares, but appearances are deceptive.

20...♘ec6 21 ♘h5 g6

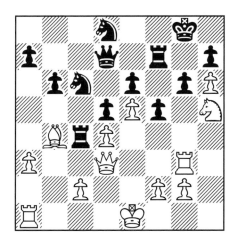

22 ♘f6+ ♖xf6

Forced, of course, but all part of the plan. Black's knights and central pawns will dominate the position, while the white rooks prove ineffective, because of the lack of open files. We have seen several similar examples in this book already, and it is a major positional theme of the Winawer (and indeed, the French more generally).

23 exf6 ♘f7 24 ♕d2 ♖xd4 25 ♖d3 ♖h4 26 ♖h3 ♖g4 27 ♔f1 ♘d6 28 ♖e1

28 f3 is possibly better, but White was presumably reluctant to cut his rook off on h3.

28...♔f7 29 ♗c3 ♘e4 30 ♕d3 ♘c5 31 ♕d1 ♖c4 32 ♗b2 b5 33 ♕e2 ♕d6 34 ♔g1 ♘e4 35 ♖d3 ♕c5 36 ♖c1 e5

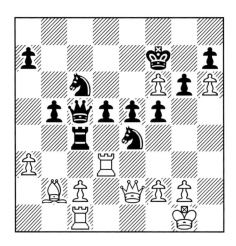

The centralized black force is overwhelming and makes a striking visual impression.
37 ♕e3 d4 38 ♕e2 ♘xf6 39 ♖dd1 ♘d5 40 ♕d2 e4

White is slowly pushed off the board.

41 ♕g5 ♘c7 42 ♖d2 ♘e6 43 ♕h4 a5 44 ♖cd1 ♖xc2 45 ♖xc2 ♕xc2 46 ♖c1 ♕xb2 47 ♖xc6 d3 48 ♖a6 ♕d4 0–1

> **Question:** So do you recommend the 6...♕c7 move order?

Answer: It depends on one's taste. As the examples above show, it generally leads to a more strategical battle than the 6...♘e7 lines. Visually, the positions arising after 7 ♕g4 f5 8 ♕h5+ g6 looks rather ugly, because of the weak dark squares, but once one shakes off the visual impression and looks at the detail of the variations, one finds that Black can usually cover the weak squares with ...h6, and he has good play on the queenside. I think 6...♕c7 is perfectly viable, as an alternative to the main lines with 6...♘e7 or the Portisch-Hook line with 6...♕a5.

Game 20
E.Najer-A.Korobov
Czech League 2011

1 e4 e6 2 d4 d5 3 ♘c3 ♝b4 4 e5 c5 5 a3 ♝a5

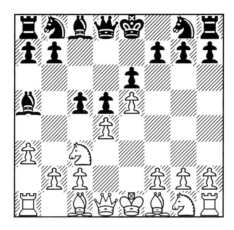

A rather different interpretation of the Winawer than we have seen so far. Black retains his dark-squared bishop and maintains the pin on the knight at c3. This move was invented by Botvinnik in the 1940s, and has been especially associated in more recent years with the Armenian Grandmasters, Vaganian and Lputian.

Black does actually have one other viable move here, namely 5...cxd4. This was actually how he used to play in the very early days of the Winawer, in the late 1920s, but the line quickly went out of fashion after the discovery of 6 axb4 dxc3 7 ♘f3! (7 bxc3 ♛c7 is satisfactory for Black).

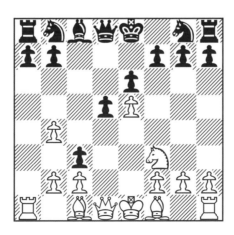

Answer: White's idea is to sacrifice a pawn, to accelerate his development. This proved so dangerous that 5...cxd4 has been virtually banished from master practice ever since, but in the 1990s, the Ukrainian GM, Vereslav Eingorn, revived it (Eingorn is a specialist in offbeat French lines). The only thing most books quote is a game J.Nunn-V.Eingorn, Reykjavik 1990, where Black was whupped, but John Watson gave the whole 5...cxd4 system a closer look in his *Dangerous Weapons: The French* volume, and suggests that improvements may be possible. Interested readers should consult that volume, but briefly, the critical position arises after 7...♘e7 8 ♗d3 ♘d7 9 0-0 ♘c6 10 ♖e1 ♘xb4 11 bxc3 ♘xd3 12 cxd3 0-0 13 ♖a4 f6 14 ♖g4 and now, instead of Eingorn's 14...♘xe5!?, Black should investigate Watson's suggested improvement 14...♕c7!.

6 b4

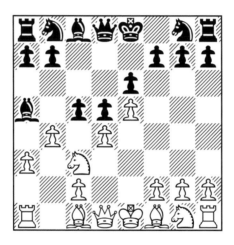

Answer: This dynamic response was suggested by Alekhine, I believe, and is overwhelmingly the most popular line of play for White. With the aid of a pawn sacrifice, he breaks the pin at once.

White does have a few alternatives:

a) 6 ♕g4 mainly transposes to other lines: for example, 6...♘e7 7 ♕xg7 (7 dxc5 ♗xc3+ 8 bxc3 reaches variation 'c') 7...♖g8 8 ♕xh7 cxd4 9 b4 dxc3 10 bxa5 transposes to our main game.

b) 6 ♗d2 is similar to 5 ♗d2, but here, a simple equalizing line is 6...♘c6 7 ♘b5 ♘xd4! 8 ♘xd4 (8 ♗xa5 ♕xa5+ 9 b4 ♕b6 10 ♘xd4 cxd4 11 ♘f3 ♘e7 12 ♕xd4 ♕xd4 13 ♘xd4 ♘g6 is equal) 8...cxd4 9 ♗b5+ ♗d7 10 ♗xd7+ ♔xd7! 11 ♘f3 ♗b6 with equality.

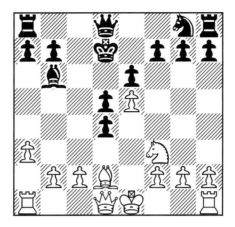

The king looks strange on d7, but White cannot really get at it.

c) 6 dxc5 looks like 5 dxc5, but here, the threat of 7 b4 limits Black's options by forcing him to take on c3 at once. 6...♗xc3+ 7 bxc3 ♘e7 (7...♕c7 8 ♘f3 ♘d7 9 ♗d3 ♘xc5 10 0-0 ♗d7 was also satisfactory for Black in M.Chandler-S.Lputian, Hastings 1986/87) 8 ♕g4 and now Psakhis gave as simplest 8...♘d7 9 ♘f3 (9 ♕xg7 ♖g8 10 ♕xh7 ♘xe5 was fine for Black in S.Reshevsky-M.Botvinnik, Radio match 1946) 9...♕c7 10 ♕xg7 ♖g8 11 ♕xh7 ♘xe5 12 ♕h5 ♘xf3+ 13 ♕xf3 ♗d7 14 ♗f4 ♕xc5 "with a promising position".

6...cxd4

> *Question:* But why not take the other way?

Answer: After 6...cxb4 7 ♘b5 White has a very strong attack: for example, 7...♘c6 8 axb4 ♗xb4+ 9 c3 ♗e7 10 ♗d3 a6 11 ♕g4 ♔f8 12 ♗a3 (Psakhis), and White has tremendous compensation for the pawn.

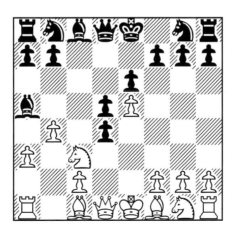

7 ♕g4

The parting of the ways. The text is the sharpest, and currently poses the 5...♗a5 variation its sternest theoretical challenge.

> **Question:** It all looks pretty odd – with an enemy piece
> attacked and his own piece en prise, White ignores both!

Answer: It is a very sharp approach, but of course, we are already familiar with the general idea from other Winawer lines. Black must always reckon with this queen raid, attacking his vulnerable spot on g7. The alternative is 7 ♘b5, which leads to a rather less frantic game. Play continues 7...♗c7 8 f4 and now the main line is 8...♗d7.

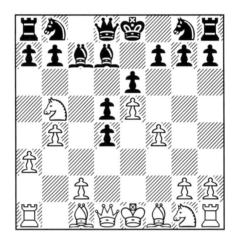

> **Question:** That is a little surprising. What about "knights before bishops"?

Answer: Well, of course, the entire Winawer is a rebuke to that particular opening shibboleth! But the text is a very logical move in the circumstances. Black wants to eliminate the annoying knight on b5, which hangs over his head in rather Damocletian fashion, and at the same time, Black would also get rid of his traditionally bad French bishop.

White usually replies 9 ♘f3.

> **Question:** Doesn't it make more sense to take the other bishop?

Answer: *Prima facie*, one would think so, yet in practice, 9 ♘xc7+ is less popular here, and seems to pose Black fewer problems. After 9...♕xc7 we reach an important position.

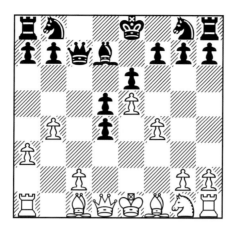

Question: What is going on?

Answer: We have another typical Winawer battle, albeit with some differences caused by the position of the white b-pawn. Black has lost his dark-squared bishop, and has the usual issues on the dark squares, whilst his extra pawn is clearly only a temporary thing, as White will soon recapture on d4. However, Black is ahead in development, and, most obviously, the advance of the white b-pawn has left him with weaknesses down the c-file. Black's remaining bishop is going to come to a4, attacking the backward c2-pawn, and generally exercising unpleasant pressure on the white queenside. Then Black will develop his remaining pieces, castle short, and bring a rook to the c-file. Practice suggests he has a decent game:

a) 10 ♗b2 ♗a4 11 ♗d3 ♘c6 12 ♘f3 ♕b6 13 ♘xd4 ♘ge7 14 ♕d2 a5! (an unpleasant blow to the white queenside, which reveals another dark side to the advance b2-b4) 15 ♗c3 with a further divide:

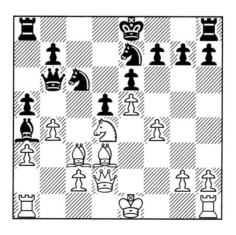

a1) 15...0-0 16 b5 ♘b8 17 ♘e2 ♘f5

> **Question:** What is the assessment?

Answer: Black is fine here. He needs to ensure his bishop on a4 does not get trapped or shut completely out of play, and he also need to fight for the d4-square, to keep the white dark-squared bishop under control, but if he does these things, he should have no problems. The game remained balanced after 18 h4 h5 19 ♖h3 ♘d7 20 ♖b1 ♕c7 21 ♗xf5 exf5 22 ♗d4 ♖fc8 23 ♖g3 ♘f8 until White lost his head completely and lost in just two more moves: 24 e6?! ♘xe6 25 ♗e3? ♕xc2 0-1, J.Friedel-V.Belov, Moscow 2008.

a2) 15...axb4 16 axb4 ♔d7! was the highly creative course of the game M.Bluvshtein-S.Lputian, Mallorca Olympiad 2004.

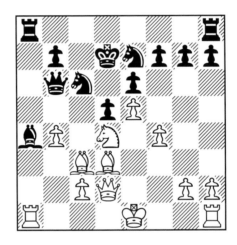

> **Question:** What is Black playing at?

Answer: Lputian decides that his king is actually safer on d7 than it would be on the king-side. In French positions, with the centre pawns locked together in the traditional fashion, this is frequently the case. After 17 ♘xc6 ♕xc6 18 0-0 ♗b5 (once again this exchange of bishops) 19 ♗d4 ♘f5 20 ♗c5 b6 21 ♗xb5 ♕xb5 22 c4 ♕xc4 23 ♗xb6 ♖hc8 Black was fine, and eventually went on to win.

b) Another high-level encounter went 10 ♘f3 ♗a4 11 ♗d3 ♘e7 12 ♗b2 ♘bc6 13 ♕e2 a6 14 0-0 ♕b6 15 ♕f2 ♗b5 (this manoeuvre is worth noting; Black exchanges off White's impor-tant light-squared bishop, after which the black king will feel much more secure on the kingside) 16 ♘xd4 ♗xd3 17 cxd3 ♖c8 18 ♖fc1 0-0 19 ♘xc6 was agreed drawn in P.Svidler-R.Vaganian, Moscow 2004.

Returning to 9 ♘f3 and after 9...♗xb5 10 ♗xb5+ ♘c6 (10...♘d7 has also been played, aiming to keep the c-file open for the black rooks; however, the text is more common, since

Black can defend the d4-pawn and make it more difficult for his opponent to recover that pawn) 11 ♗b2 (11 0-0 ♘ge7 12 ♗d3 ♘f5 13 ♗xf5 exf5 14 ♗b2 ♕d7 15 ♔h1 0-0 16 ♘xd4 ♘xd4 17 ♗xd4 ♖fd8 was also perfectly satisfactory for Black in Ni Hua-S.Lputian, Internet 2004, although he eventually lost a long game) 11...♘ge7 12 ♗d3 ♗b6 13 0-0 a6 14 ♔h1, as in E.Schmittdiel-R.Vaganian, German League 2004, 14...♖c8 looks fine for Black.

All in all, it is clear that 7 ♘b5 does not pose him any serious problems.

Now back to the position after 7 ♕g4:

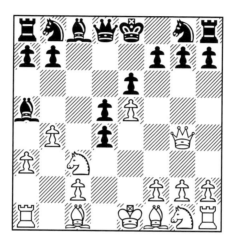

7...♘e7

Question: Is 7...♔f8 possible here?

Answer: It has not been played much at GM level, but both Botvinnik and Lputian have ventured it, if very occasionally (only once in each case, as far as I can see). The move looks as playable as the similar move in other lines, such as the Portisch-Hook Variation. For example, 8 ♘b5 (8 bxa5 dxc3 9 ♘f3 ♘e7 10 ♗d3 ♘d7!? 11 ♕b4 was a bit better for White in W.Unzicker-M.Botvinnik, Amsterdam 1954, but here 10...♘bc6 11 0-0 ♕xa5 looks more natural) 8...♗b6 9 ♘f3 ♘c6 10 ♗b2

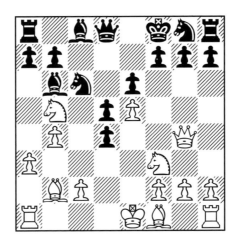

10...f6 (pugnacious, but simply 10...♘ge7 11 ♘bxd4 ♘xd4 12 ♘xd4 ♛c7 looks reasonable for Black) 11 ♘bxd4 ♘xe5 12 ♘xe5 fxe5 13 ♘xe6+ ♗xe6 14 ♛xe6 ♛f6 15 ♛xf6+ ♘xf6 was equal in N.Firman-S.Lputian, Sochi 2005.

All things considered, 7...♔f8 looks as though it may be worth a closer look, especially if Black's theoretical problems in the main line persist.

8 bxa5 dxc3 9 ♛xg7 ♖g8 10 ♛xh7

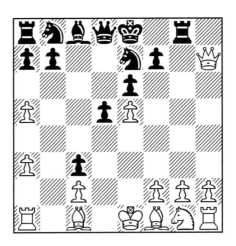

> *Question:* So what is going on here? It looks as though we are heading for another total mess!

Answer: That is absolutely right. We reach another position similar to the main line seen in Games 16 and 17. The main difference is that Black's pawn has already arrived on c3, somewhat earlier than in the other line. The effect of this is that Black is not threatening a queen check on c3 in some lines, which allows White to develop his knight more actively on f3.

10...♞bc6 11 ♞f3

The alternative is 11 f4, which leads to positions quite similar to the main line Winawer. For example, 11...♛xa5 12 ♞f3. Here we see the difference referred to in the previous note. In the main line Winawer, the threats of a check on c3 force this knight to develop to e2, where it is less active and does not threaten to raid Black's position with ♞g5.

> **Question:** Yes, but on the other hand, Black is usually a pawn
> down in many of those normal Winawer lines, because his
> c3-pawn drops off. Here, he has material equality.

Answer: Well spotted – glad to see you are paying attention!
Play may go 12...♝d7 13 ♜b1.

> **Question:** What about 13 ♞g5 in this position? Isn't that rather dangerous?

Answer: It is critical, but then Black has the interesting idea 13...0-0-0!? 14 ♞xf7 ♞f5.

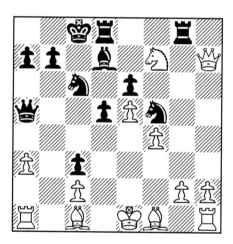

> **Question:** What's this? Isn't he just losing the exchange?

Answer: He is sacrificing it, yes. After 15 ♞xd8 ♛xd8 he has a large development lead, in exchange for his material investment.

I once sat next to an extraordinary game between the English IM, Andrew Kinsman, who was an expert on the 5...♝a5 Winawer, and Swedish GM and theoretician, Thomas 'The Hitman' Ernst. Both players rattled out their moves to this point, and continued playing at express speed: 16 ♛h3 ♞cd4 (in poker terms, Black is 'all in') 17 ♛xc3+ ♚b8. Ernst now rattled out the move 18 a4 (18 g3 ♕b6 is unclear), at which point Kinsman thought for the first time in the game. He eventually played 18...♕h4+ and the game continued 19 g3 ♖xg3 20 hxg3 ♕xh1

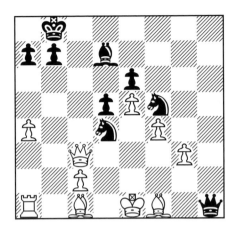

21 ♔f2? (21 ♖a3 is equal, according to *Fritz*) 21...♕h2+ 22 ♗g2 ♘e2! 23 ♕f3? (by now even the relatively best 23 ♕a3 ♘exg3 is much better for Black) 23...♘fd4 and Ernst resigned in T.Ernst-A.Kinsman, Gausdal 1995. The whole game lasted about 45 minutes!

Going back to the position after 15...♕d8, it is interesting to look at things with the computer. It starts off by assessing the position as winning for White, but the longer you leave it, the lower its evaluation sinks. White's 16th and 17th moves are its first choice, yet once one reaches the position after 17...♔b8, the assessment drops to zero! All in all, this is a fascinating variation, and one which is typical of many lines of the 5...♗a5 Winawer. Black frequently invests an exchange for dynamic counterplay, relying on his active minor pieces and the exposed white king.

Returning to 13 ♖b1. Black goes 13...0-0-0 14 ♕d3 d4.

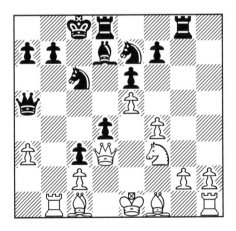

Question: It is very similar to the lines seen in Game 17.

Question: It is very similar to the lines seen in Game 17.

Answer: Yes, and the general remarks made there apply here too. I think chances are balanced. For example, 15 g3 ♔b8 (another Vaganian game went 15...♕d5 16 ♗g2 ♕a2 17 ♖b5 a6?! 18 ♖c5 ♔b8 19 0-0 ♘a7?! 20 ♘xd4 and White was much better in A.Grischuk-R.Vaganian, Izmir 2004, but 17...b6 looks a better choice) 16 ♗g2 ♗c8 (we have seen this manoeuvre in the main line Winawer too; Black plans ...b6 and ...♗b7) 17 ♘g5?! (17 ♖b5 ♕a4 is unclear) 17...b6! 18 ♗xc6 (a huge concession, but 18 ♘xf7 ♗a6 19 ♕e4 ♖d5 is tremendous for Black) 18...♘xc6 19 ♘xf7 ♗a6! (once again, a black exchange sacrifice) 20 ♘xd8 ♖xd8 21 ♕e4 d3! 22 ♗e3 (22 ♕xc6 d2+ 23 ♔f2 ♗b7 wins) 22...dxc2 23 ♖c1 ♕b5 24 ♖xc2 ♗b7 25 ♔f2 ♘d4 0-1 K.Kulaots-R.Vaganian, Mallorca Olympiad 2004.

We now return to Najer's 11 ♘f3:

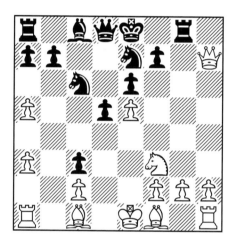

11...♕c7

Question: Why doesn't Black take the a5-pawn?

Question: Why doesn't Black take the a5-pawn?

Answer: The trouble with 11...♕xa5?! is that it expends a vital tempo, and allows White to develop his forces aggressively with 12 ♗d3 ♗d7 (12...♖xg2 is bad after 13 ♘g5) 13 0-0 0-0-0 14 ♗g5 (Psakhis) and Black's game is difficult. We see the key problem here – if Black does not pressurize the e5-pawn sufficiently, the enemy dark-squared bishop is free to develop great activity from g5.

12 ♗f4

Here again, we see White exploiting the fact that he has been able to develop his knight to f3. Thanks to this, he can defend the e5-pawn with pieces, avoiding the need to shut his important dark-squared bishop in with f2-f4.

12...♗d7 13 a6!

This move had been known since the 1960s, but it was Volokitin's revival of it that has placed the whole 5...♗a5 Winawer under something of a theoretical cloud in recent years. Previous practice had gone 13 ♗d3 0-0-0 14 ♗g3 ♕xa5 (now Black is able to take on a5, even though he has lost a tempo in so doing) 15 0-0 ♖h8 (this led to two outstanding victories for Khalifman, but Vaganian has also played 15...♘f5 which also seems adequate: for example, 16 ♗xf5 exf5 17 ♕xf7 ♖df8 18 ♕h7 f4 19 ♗xf4 ♗f5 20 ♕h4 ♖h8 21 ♕g3 ♖hg8 22 ♕h4 ♖h8 23 ♕g3 ♖hg8 24 ♕h4 ½-½ A.Grischuk-R.Vaganian, Mallorca Olympiad 2004), with a divide:

a) 16 ♕g7 d4 17 ♕g4 ♘f5 18 ♖fb1 ♘xg3 19 ♕xg3 ♕c7.

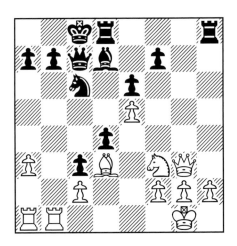

White has achieved nothing at all, and is now outplayed in impressive style: 20 ♔f1 ♖hg8 21 ♕f4 f5 22 h3 ♔b8 23 ♖e1 ♗c8 24 ♘g5 ♖d5 25 ♘f3 ♘e7 26 ♖ab1 ♘g6 27 ♕h2 ♕h7 28 ♖b4 ♘h4 29 ♘xd4? (29 ♘xh4 ♕xh4 was necessary, although here too, Black is for choice) 29...♘xg2 30 ♖eb1 ♕d7 31 ♘e2 ♖xd3! (it just had to happen! this exchange sacrifice is more immediately decisive) 32 cxd3 ♕xd3 33 ♖c1 c2 34 ♖d4 ♕f3 35 ♘f4 b6! 36 ♘xg2 ♗a6+ 37 ♔g1 ♗b7 0-1 J.Polgar-A.Khalifman, Hoogeveen 2000.

b) In the same event, another Khalifman game went 16 ♕xf7 ♖df8 17 ♕g7 ♖hg8 18 ♕h6.

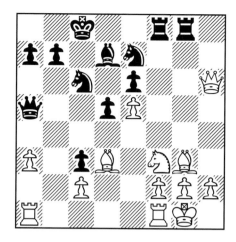

A.Galkin-A.Khalifman, Hoogeveen 2004, continued 18...♖xf3!.

Question: Another long-term exchange sacrifice?

Answer: Indeed. They are a feature of such positions. Play went on 19 gxf3 ♘d4 20 ♕f4 ♘ef5.

Question: What has Black got?

Answer: Despite being an exchange and a pawn down, Black has decent practical chances, because his knights are just so much more active than the enemy rooks. It is the same phenomenon we have seen many times in this book – the lack of open files reduces the effectiveness of the rooks.

21 ♔h1 ♗b5 22 ♖fd1 ♗xd3 23 ♖xd3 ♕c5 24 ♕c1 ♔b8 25 ♕d1 ♖c8 (Black is extremely calm, not thrashing about in the search for an immediate tactical solution, but just playing normal moves, on the basis that the formal material count is irrelevant – his knights are at least the equivalent of the white rooks; in addition, the white bishop on g3 is actually a very poor piece, having no mobility at all) 26 ♗f4 ♘c6 27 ♕e1 ♕c4 28 ♗g5 ♘cd4 29 ♕d1 ♕a4 30 ♖a2 ♕c4 31 ♖a1 ♕a4 32 ♖a2 ♘b5 (refusing the draw by repetition) 33 f4 ♕e4+ 34 f3 ♕a4 35 ♕e1 d4 36 h4 ♘c7.

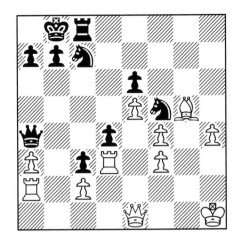

Black just strengthens his position methodically, and now stands better. White now blundered with 37 ♕e4?? and resigned without waiting for the reply, but he was already in trouble. It is again noteworthy how the computer spends almost the whole game claiming a clear advantage for White, and approving of almost all of his moves, yet at some point, it becomes clear that White has nothing.

These two great wins by Khalifman are well worth studying carefully, as they illustrate so many of the themes of the 5...♗a5 Winawer.

Returning to the critical 13 a6:

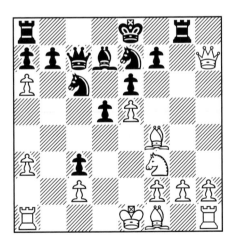

13...0-0-0

Question: Why not just 13...b6 keeping the queenside closed?

Answer: The trouble with that is that, by comparison with the lines examined in the previous note, White has just secured his extra pawn, and turned it into a thorn in Black's side. Having the moves a6 and ...b6 included must be a significant benefit to White. Having said that, though, even then the position is not so clear, especially in practice. The English IM, Thomas Rendle, for example, scored a notable win against a GM opponent, after 14 ♗g3 0-0-0 15 ♗d3 ♖h8 16 ♕xf7 ♖df8 17 ♕g7 ♖hg8 18 ♕h6 ♖xf3 (all just as in the Khalifman textbook!) 19 gxf3 ♘d4 20 ♕f6 ♘ef5 21 ♔f1 ♕c5 and, once again, the silicon monster claims a white advantage, but in reality, it is all just totally unclear.

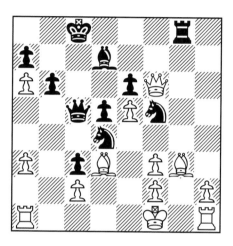

Black went on to win in S.Del Rio Angelis-T.Rendle, Gibraltar 2005.

14 ♕d3

A strange choice. The logical follow-up is 14 axb7+ ♔b8 (14...♕xb7?! leaves the black king exposed after 15 ♕d3; Volokitin claims a decisive advantage, but even if that is a touch exaggerated, Black is not to be envied: for example, 15...♕b2 16 ♕d1!, as in D.Bryson-D.Wagener, Leon 2001) 15 ♕d3.

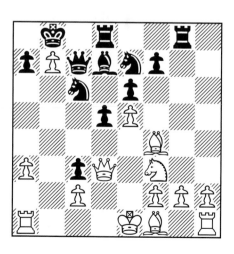

Now the key Volokitin game continued 15...♖g4 16 g3 ♘g6 17 ♕xc3 ♘xf4 18 h3 ♘xh3 19 ♖xh3 ♘xe5 20 ♕xc7+ ♔xc7 21 ♘xe5 ♖e4+ 22 ♔d2 ♖xe5 23 ♗d3 and White was just clearly better in A.Volokitin-S.Lputian, Mallorca Olympiad 2004.

Volokitin himself suggested Black players should look into 15...d4, with the point that 16 ♘xd4? ♘xd4 17 ♕xd4 ♗b5 18 ♕e4 ♗xf1 19 ♔xf1 ♘f5 leaves Black with some initiative, although even here, three pawns is a lot. However, practice has suggested Black still has problems: for instance, 16 ♗g3 (Psakhis gives 16 ♖b1 ♖g4 17 ♗g3 ♘f5 18 ♗e2 as "also looks great for White") 16...♘f5 17 ♕c4 ♘ce7 18 ♖b1 and White was better in J.Moreno Carnero-A.Jerez Perez, Sanxenxo 2004.

All in all, Black is in some trouble in this entire variation. 13...b6 looks relatively best, but it is a significant concession to leave the a-pawn alive. It is easy to see why the 5...♗a5 system is experiencing a theoretical crisis at present.

14...♖g4 15 ♗g3?!

White could still transpose into Volokitin-Lputian, by means of 15 axb7+ ♔b8 16 g3.

15...♖e4+ 16 ♔d1 ♘a5 17 axb7+ ♔b8

Now the position is much less clear. The poor position of the white king gives Black full compensation for his material deficit.

18 ♗e2 ♘f5 19 ♖e1 ♕c5 20 ♖b1 ♗a4

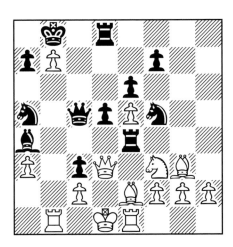

White is already defenceless against the various threats, notably 21...♘d4.

> **Question:** It seems amazing that his position should collapse so quickly!

Answer: Maybe, but this is in the nature of the whole variation. White does not develop normally in this line, and with his king in the centre, accidents can always happen. We saw the same thing repeatedly in the context of Games 16 and 17 – even when White is objectively better in such positions, it only takes one error to bring the house crashing down around him.

21 ♕a6 ♕xa3 22 ♗b5 ♕a2 23 ♖c1 ♗xc2+! 24 ♖xc2 ♕b1+ 25 ♖c1 c2+ 0-1

> *Question:* So what is your verdict on the 5...♗a5 system?

Answer: It is very interesting. One merit is that positional lines, such as 7 ♘b5, give White very little, so he has to enter the extremely sharp main line with 7 ♕g4, if he wants to play for an advantage. Such wild lines offer great practical chances for the black player, whatever their objective theoretical problems, and many white players are not comfortable in such positions.

> *Question:* But is it any good for Black?

Answer: That is a harder question to answer. At the time of writing, Black is in some trouble in this main line with 13 a6, and he desperately needs an improvement. As noted above, his best practical chance is probably 13...b6, and just play as in Del Rio Angelis-Rendle, but it is not pleasant to have to allow White to keep his pawn on a6. If this does not hold water, maybe Black could look into the rare 7...♔f8, especially as a surprise weapon.

Game 21
A.Karpov-J.Nogueiras
Rotterdam 1989

1 e4 e6 2 d4 d5 3 ♘c3 ♗b4 4 e5 c5 5 ♗d2

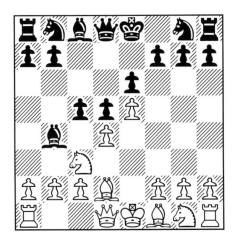

Question: We have not seen this before! White
wants to prevent his pawns being doubled?

Answer: Yes. This is a move first popularized by Bogoljubow. It is not terribly ambitious, but is one of White's most solid responses to the Winawer.

White's other major alternative here is 5 dxc5.

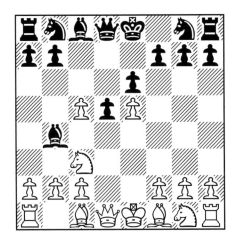

This was brought to prominence after Reuben Fine used it to administer a severe hiding to Botvinnik at AVRO 1938.

Question: What is the idea?

Answer: White abandons any attempt to establish a pawn centre and instead places his faith in rapid development. It is more dangerous than it looks at first sight, and over the past 25 years, English GMs Joe Gallagher and Julian Hodgson have both used it with considerable success. After 5...♘c6 (the main line, but among other options, Psakhis likes the solid set-up 5...♛c7 6 ♘f3 ♘d7 7 ♗f4 ♘e7 8 ♗d3 ♘xc5 9 0-0 ♗xc3 10 bxc3 ♘xd3 11 ♛xd3 ♗d7, which was an old game J.Gallagher-L.Hansen, London 1987; this looks like a good choice, especially if Black wishes to keep more play in the position than in the "Knott endgame" below) 6 ♘f3 Black has:

a) The main line is 6...♘ge7 7 ♗d3 d4 8 a3 ♗a5 9 b4 ♘xb4 10 axb4 ♗xb4 11 0-0 ♗xc3 12 ♖b1.

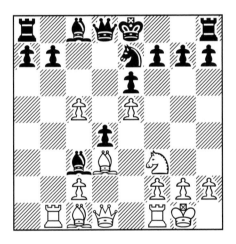

Question: What is happening here? It looks very messy.

Answer: It is. Black has an extra pawn, but White's attacking chances should not be underestimated. More to the point, theory runs very deep here (Watson's main line includes a suggested black improvement on move 19, for example), which may not be to every black player's taste, given that this is a sideline.

b) 6...d4 is a move barely covered in the books, but which has been played several times by English FM and French aficionado, Simon Knott. It results in early simplification and an endgame, where Black seems to be holding his own without undue problems: 7 a3 ♗a5 8 b4 dxc3 (the point; White cannot avoid the exchange of queens) 9 bxa5 ♛xd1+ 10 ♔xd1.

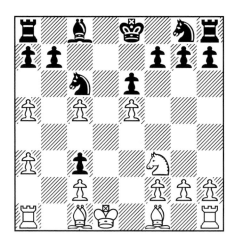

Question: What do you make of this position?

Answer: White is temporarily a pawn ahead, but a5 is dropping, of course. White has the two bishops and the usual potential pressure on the dark squares, but his pawns are less secure than Black's. All in all, a typical Winawer position. To my knowledge, Knott has reached this position three times in rated games, and never lost, including one game against Joe Gallagher, the principal expert on the 5 dxc5 line: 10...♘xa5 (10...♘ge7 was twice chosen by Knott in later games, but looks less good after 11 ♗b5) 11 ♘d4 ♗d7 12 ♘e2 ♖c8 13 ♗e3 ♘e7 14 ♘xc3 ♘f5 15 ♗d2? (15 ♗f4 ♖xc5 16 ♘e4 is equal) 15...♖xc5 16 ♘e4 ♖xe5 17 ♗d3 b6 18 g4 ♗c6 19 f3 was J.Gallagher-S.Knott, London 1986, and now 19...♘d4 is much better for Black.

5 ♕g4 is also possible and was a favourite in his youth of English GM Mark Hebden.

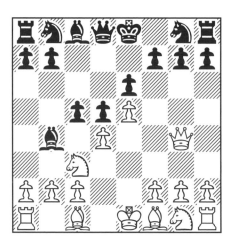

After 5...♘e7 White has two main options: 6 dxc5 (6 a3?! is well met by 6...♕a5!) and now Simon Williams' forcing suggestion 6...♗xc3+ (instead, 6...♘bc6 allows considerable complications after 7 ♕xg7) 7 bxc3 ♕a5 8 ♗d2 ♘g6 looks like a simple and economical way for Black to play; 6 ♘f3 was Hebden's favourite, but then the simple sequence 6...cxd4 7 ♘xd4 ♘g6 8 ♗d3 0-0 9 ♗xg6 fxg6! once served me well against the man himself.

Returning to Karpov's 5 ♗d2:

5...♘e7 6 ♘b5

The alternative is 6 a3 ♗xc3 7 ♗xc3, insisting on the bishop-pair.

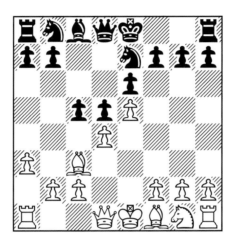

Question: This looks like a success for White. He has the two bishops, without having incurred the usual mangled queenside pawns. Isn't he better here?

Answer: No, not really. His centre cannot be maintained, and Black has easy development. The only problem for Black is that his best and simplest path to equality is also rather drawish, so if he wants to play for a win, he must take slightly more risks. 7...♘bc6 8 ♘f3 cxd4 9 ♘xd4 (9 ♗xd4 avoids the simplification, but offers nothing after, for example, 9...♘f5 10 c3 ♗d7 11 ♗e2 ♖c8 12 0-0 0-0, V.Savon-V.Hort, Skopje 1968) 9...♘xe5 10 ♘xe6 ♗xe6 11 ♗xe5 0-0 12 ♗d3 ♘c6 13 ♗g3 ♕f6 has been played a great deal, and is really very equal.

7...b6 is the usual way to try to keep some play in the position. A recent example by a top player was 8 ♗b5+ (the typical device to avoid a bishop exchange after ...♗a6) 8...♗d7 9 ♗d3 ♘bc6 10 ♘f3 ♘g6 11 0-0 0-0 and Black had no problems in D.Mastrovasilis-A.Shirov, Porto Carras 2011. Instead, 8 b4 ♕c7 9 ♘f3 was played in the famous game R.Nezhmetdinov-M.Tal, USSR Championship 1957, and now, instead of Tal's 9...♘d7, a clean solution is 9...cxb4 10 ♗xb4 a5 (Uhlmann's 10...♗a6 is also fine) 11 ♗d2 0-0 12 ♗d3 ♗a6 with equality, as in J.Friedman-B.Gulko, Philadelphia 1993.

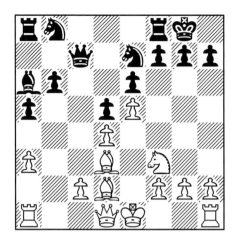

That game ended in short order, after White had a rush of blood: 13 ♗xh7+?? ♔xh7 14 ♘g5+ ♔g8 15 ♕h5 ♕xc2. Oops! White had obviously missed this. He resigned after 16 g4 ♕d3.

6...♗xd2+ 7 ♕xd2 0-0

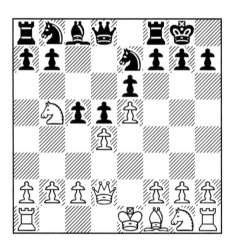

8 dxc5

This is a major crossroads. White has two main approaches – either exchange off the central pawns, as in the game, relying on piece occupation of d4, or else aim to build a pawn centre, starting with 8 c3. The intention is to follow up with f4.

> **Question:** Is this good?

Answer: Practice suggests that neither plan poses Black any great problems. Building the pawn centre with c3 and f4 involves delaying White's development, and Black is able to attack the centre with all means at his disposal, such as ...f6, ...♞c6, ...♛b6, ...♞f5, etc. He should always secure adequate counterplay.

Question: But what about the knight on b5? That is going to entrench itself on d6, where it looks very strong.

Answer: Actually, it is no real threat. The knight can easily be challenged by ...♞c8 or ...♞f5, whereupon it will usually have little choice but to exchange itself off.

Black has various sensible replies to 8 c3. Watson quotes an effective treatment from a recent game: 8...♗d7!.

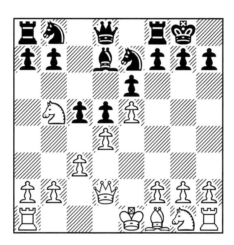

Question: Can't White win a pawn with 9 dxc5 followed by a later b4, to defend the pawn?

Answer: He can, but after 9...♗xb5 10 ♗xb5 ♞d7 he must first surrender his bishop by 11 ♗xd7 ♛xd7 and then after 12 ♞f3 ♛c7 13 b4 Black has the effective (and thematic) pawn sacrifice 13...b6!. After 14 cxb6 axb6 he has excellent play on the queenside, against the backward a- and c-pawns. Such pawn sacrifices often occur after dxc5 in this line, and practice shows that Black generally has good compensation.

The alternative is 9 ♞d6 cxd4 10 cxd4 ♛b6 11 f4 ♞bc6 12 ♞f3 ♞c8 (just as outlined above; the proud knight on d6 is exchanged off almost immediately) 13 ♞xc8 ♖axc8.

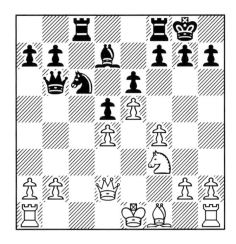

Question: How do you assess this position?

Answer: Black is just better. He is ahead in development and has serious counterplay against d4 and down the c-file. White's pawn centre is more of a liability than a strength. Play continued 14 ♗d3 g6 (eliminating ♗xh7+, and so threatening to take on d4) 15 ♗b1 ♖c7 16 0-0 ♖fc8 17 ♖d1 ♘b4 with a comfortable advantage in B.Yildiz-N.Zhukova, Tbilisi 2011.

8...♘d7

8...♘bc6 is also possible, with the same pawn sacrifice idea of ...b6 that was seen in the last note. However, the text seems simplest. Two pawns are attacked, so Black gets his pawn back at once, and the Sicilian structure gives him typical queenside play, plus the possibility of breaking against the centre with f6.

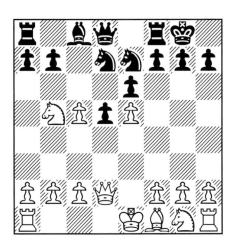

9 f4?!

This is dubious, and a rather optimistic choice by Karpov, who was usually so careful about creating weaknesses in his own position. Now e4 is weakened irretrievably, and Black's knight will immediately take aim at this juicy outpost.

9 ♘f3 is more cautious, but gives Black good play after 9...♘xc5 10 ♗d3 ♕b6 11 ♖b1 ♗d7 12 ♘bd4 ♘xd3+ 13 cxd3 ♖fc8 14 0-0 ♖c7 15 ♖fc1 ♖ac8 16 ♖xc7 ♕xc7, with easy equality in H.Spangenberg-O.Panno, Pena City 1996.

9 ♕c3 is probably the best move.

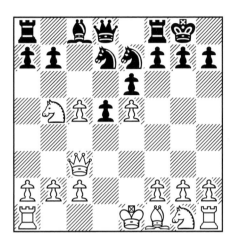

Question: Doesn't that make it hard for Black to regain his pawn?

Answer: Not really. He has easy equality after 9...a6 10 ♘d6 ♕c7 11 ♘f3 (11 b4? a5 undermines the white queenside structure) 11...♕xc5 12 ♕xc5 ♘xc5, as in P.Garbett-I.Ibragimov, Turin 2006, the only drawback being that the position is rather dull. If Black is seeking a more dynamic game, he can try, among others, 9...f6 10 exf6 ♘xf6 which also offers comfortable equality, whilst retaining more play in the position. For example, 11 ♗d3 ♘c6 12 f3 e5 13 0-0-0 ♗e6 14 ♘e2 and now the thematic 14...b6 ensured him good play in C.Peptan-D.Poldauf, Groningen 1995.

9...♘xc5 10 ♘d4

10 ♗d3 ♘xd3+ 11 ♕xd3 ♘g6 12 g3 ♕a5+ 13 c3 ♗d7 14 ♘d4 f6 15 ♘gf3 fxe5 6 fxe5 b5 gave easy equality in J.Meister-A.Yusupov, Osterburg 2006.

10...♕b6 11 0-0-0 ♗d7 12 ♘gf3 ♖fc8

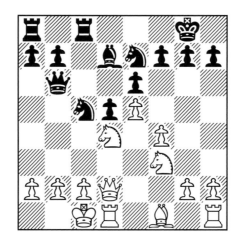

Answer: Black is very comfortable. He has a typical Sicilian pawn structure, with counter-play on the open c-file, whilst White has not really got going on the other flank. In addition, White always has to worry about a possible enemy knight penetration on e4.

13 ♕e3 ♖c7 14 ♔b1 ♖ac8 15 ♖c1 a6 16 g4 ♘c6 17 h4 ♘e4 18 ♖h2 ♘a5

Both sides are playing very logically, but it is clear that Black is dictating. White's king-side pawn advance is as much about clearing the second rank, so his rook can defend laterally, as it is about attacking the black king.

19 ♗d3 ♘c5 20 c3 ♘a4 21 ♔a1 ♗b5 22 ♗b1!?

22 h5 is more aggressive.

22...♘c4 23 ♕e1

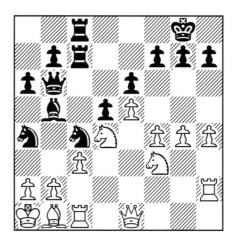

23...♘cxb2!

Black exchanges two pieces for rook and pawn, but exposes the white king. Materially, the balance is about even, but positionally, the exposed white king gives Black the advantage.

24 ♖xb2 ♘xb2 25 ♔xb2 ♗e2+ 26 ♔a1 ♗xf3 27 ♘xf3 ♕a5 28 ♘d4 ♕a3 29 ♘b3?

29 ♘e2 was essential. Now Black establishes a winning advantage.

29...b5

The pin on the c-file means that the c3-pawn is doomed.

30 f5 b4 31 ♖c2 ♖xc3?!

31...bxc3 was more convincing.

32 ♖b2 a5 33 ♕d2 a4 34 ♘d4 ♖3c4

34...♖c1 35 ♖xb4 ♖1c4 was safer.

35 fxe6 fxe6?

And now 35...♕c3 was essential.

36 ♘xe6

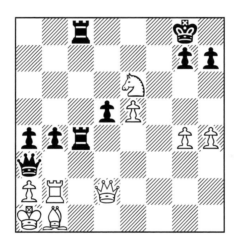

Suddenly, the tables have turned completely, and the black king comes under a decisive attack.

36...♕c3 37 ♕xd5 ♔h8 38 ♘g5 ♖f4 39 ♘e4 ♕c1 40 ♖xb4

40 ♖c2! would have ended the game at once, but Karpov's move is still winning.

40...a3 41 ♖b3 1-0

A narrow escape for Karpov and a tragedy for his opponent. However, it is clear that the opening was a success for Black, and he has nothing really to fear from this 5 ♗d2 system.

Game 22
A.Chistiakov-T.Petrosian
Moscow Championship 1956

1 e4 e6 2 d4 d5 3 ♘c3 ♝b4 4 e5 b6

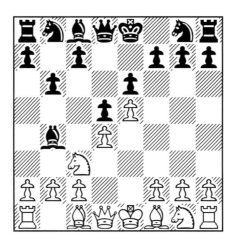

Question: I thought Black always played 4...c5 here?

Answer: This move initiates an altogether different interpretation of the Winawer. Rather than counterattack in the centre with ...c5, Black adopts a much slower, more strategical plan – he intends to keep the position closed and develop within his own three back ranks. The move 4...b6 has two ideas: either to exchange the bad bishop with ...♝a6, or else to fi- anchetto it with ...♝b7. Either way, Black usually holds back his c-pawn for a considerable time.

Question: It looks rather passive.

Answer: There is indeed a danger that Black will find himself too cramped and passive in such lines. They are certainly not everyone's cup of tea. These lines had a vogue in the 1960s and early 1970s, with Petrosian being the past master. Bronstein and the young Ulf Andersson also won many impressive games with such lines. This inspired others to take up the system, but in many cases, disappointment awaited these new converts – they found that the resulting positions did not seem anything like as easy to play as Petrosian and others made them look! Lev Psakhis, for example, is one of the world's greatest French experts, but he comments, a propos the 4...b6 lines, in his book *The Complete French* that "if this system were judged purely on the results of my games, it would have to be prohibited by law, so low is my score with it".

    4...♕d7 is another way to introduce the same sort of approach.

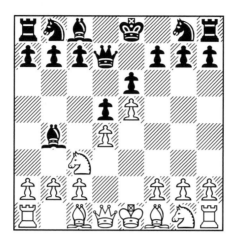

Question: Wow! That looks a very strange move!

Answer: The idea is similar to the 6...♕c7 Winawer we have already seen. Black wants to be able to meet 5 ♕g4 (other white moves may well transpose to 4...b6, since the black queen usually goes to d7 in such lines anyway, so as to facilitate long castling; with the pawn still on c7, the queen lacks another good square on the second rank: for example, 5 ♗d2 b6, etc) with 5...f5 when his queen defends the g7-square.

Another classic Petrosian victory, over a very powerful opponent, is worth seeing, as it shows how helpless even world-class players can sometimes look in these positions: 6 ♕g3 b6 7 h4 ♗b7!? (rather than exchanging bishops, Black just fianchettoes and prepares long castling) 8 ♗d3!? (8 ♗d2 ♘c6 9 ♘f3 0-0-0 10 0-0-0 followed by ♘e2-f4, was suggested by Petrosian biographer, P.H. Clarke) 8...♘c6 9 ♘ge2 0-0-0 10 ♗d2 ♘h6 11 a3?! (Petrosian clearly did not fear 11 ♗xh6, but that is what Keres nonetheless recommended, to be followed by 11...gxh6 12 ♕e3, g3 and ♘f4) 11...♗e7 12 ♗b5 (12 ♕xg7? ♘g4 leaves the white queen in trouble) 12...♖dg8 13 ♕d3 ♘f7 14 0-0-0 ♔b8 15 ♘f4 ♕c8!.

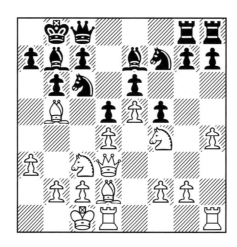

Answer: It is typically deep Petrosian manoeuvring. He just unpins his knight on c6 and prevents ♗a6, exchanging off the bishop that defends his king.

Play continued 16 ♘ce2 ♘cd8 17 ♕b3?. A world-class player (double Candidate in 1959 and 1962!) is so bamboozled by Petrosian's in-depth manoeuvring that he just drops a pawn. Even so, after 17 c3 c5 18 ♔b1 (Clarke), Black simply stands better on both flanks.

Answer: It is hard to pinpoint a clear error. Rather, White has just made a series of superficially natural moves, ones which do not fit together terribly well, whereas Black's byzantine-looking moves turn out to harmonise perfectly. Such was often the experience of Petrosian's opponents in these positions! However, the thing to ask yourself, before you rush to take up these ...b6 systems, is "Can I play like Petrosian?".

F.Olafsson-T.Petrosian, Bled 1961, concluded 17...c6! 18 ♗d3 c5 19 dxc5 ♗xc5 (two pawns are hanging, and Petrosian goes on to win at a canter) 20 ♘h3 ♘xe5 21 ♗f4 ♘df7 22 ♗b5 ♔a8 23 ♘d4 ♘g6

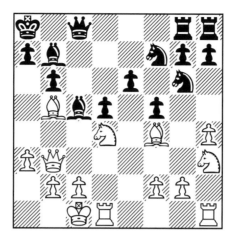

24 ♕a4 ♗xd4 25 ♗d7 ♕f8 26 ♖xd4 e5! 27 ♖b4 exf4 28 ♖xb6 ♘fe5 29 ♖xb7 ♔xb7 30 h5 ♕d6 31 hxg6 ♕xd7 32 ♕xf4 ♘xg6 0-1. An incredibly impressive advert for these ...b6 lines, but as the note to move 17 emphasises, it is a case of *caveat emptor*!

Returning to the immediate 4...b6:

5 ♕g4

As usual, this is the most direct response, attacking g7, but here, it may not be best. Another standard anti-Winawer option is 5 a3. The game G.Kasparov-V.Ivanchuk, Horgen 1995, a classic black victory which we cannot ignore, then continued 5...♗f8.

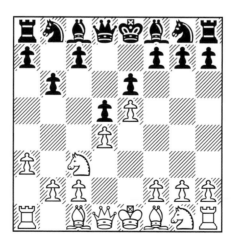

Question: Uh? Why not take on c3?

Answer: Black could take on c3, but the retreat to f8 is a typical idea in such lines. Black is playing very slowly and solidly. He keeps his dark-squared bishop, defends g7, and prepares to develop the rest of his pieces with moves such as ...♗b7 (or ...♗a6), ...♘c6, ...♕d7, ...♘e7 and ...0-0-0.

Kasparov played to seize kingside space, 6 ♘f3 ♘e7 7 h4, and now Black has:

a) 7...h5 fights for space, but concedes White an outpost on g5: 8 ♗g5 ♗a6 9 ♗xa6 ♘xa6 10 0-0 ♕d7 11 ♕d3 ♘b8 12 ♘e2.

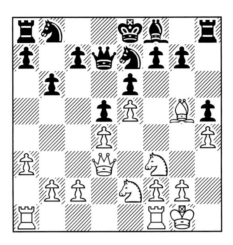

Question: What is the idea?

Answer: White gets ready to advance c4. This is a typical plan in such positions. White has more space, but Black has got rid of his bad bishop and has no real weaknesses. White needs to open some lines, in order to get at Black's position.

Following 12...♘bc6 13 c4 dxc4 14 ♕xc4 ♘d5 (the cost of White's c4 advance has been to give Black an outpost on d5 and a potential target on d4) 15 ♖ac1 ♘ce7 16 ♗xe7 ♗xe7 17 ♘c3 0-0-0?! (17...c6 was better, although White is still slightly better after 18 ♘xd5 cxd5 19 ♕c7) 18 ♘xd5 exd5 19 ♕a6+ ♔b8 20 e6! ♕c8 (20...♕xe6? 21 ♖xc7! ♔xc7 22 ♕xa7+ ♔d6 23 ♕xb6+ ♔d7 24 ♕b5+ ♔d6 25 ♘e5 wins, and if 20...fxe6 21 ♘e5) 21 ♕xc8+ ♔xc8 22 exf7 and White was clearly better in A.Sokolov-L.Portisch, Moscow 1990.

b) Thus Ivanchuk preferred 7...h6 8 h5 a5.

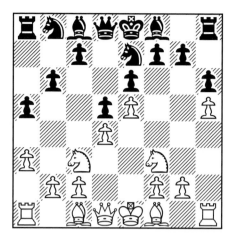

Answer: This type of strategy is typical of the whole variation. Because the position is closed, rapid development is less of a priority than normal, and more consideration can be given to longer-term strategical manoeuvring. The text is a typical move. Black intends ...♗a6, exchanging bishops, and both sides are trying to out-tempo each other – Black wants to delay ...♗a6 until White has moved his king's bishop, whilst White is trying to avoid moving the bishop, hoping that any exchange of bishops will occur without him having wasted a tempo on a move such as ♗d3. Black's 8...a5 is a waiting move, as part of this process, which also gains queenside space.

Kasparov continued 9 ♗b5+.

Answer: I did and he was, but he now recognizes that he lacks any other really useful waiting moves, so he switches his plan. He initiates a manoeuvre, similar to what we saw in the lines with ...♕c7 and ...b6 – White gives a check on b5, hoping to upset the coordination of the black pieces.

9...c6 10 ♗a4

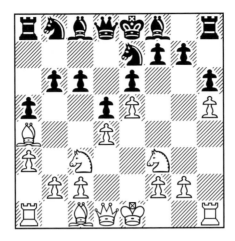

This is the key. Now the exchange of bishops is avoided.

Question: Yes, but surely the white bishop is miserably passive where it stands now?

Answer: True, but White intends in the medium term to move his knight from c3, advance c2-c3 and then drop the bishop back to c2. That way, his bishop finally reaches its desired diagonal, whilst avoiding the bishop exchange. The downside, however, is that the black bishop also gets rather a nice diagonal, cutting through the white position.

10...♘d7 11 ♘e2 b5 12 ♗b3 c5

At last, Black makes the standard central pawn break. This is frequently delayed much longer even than this.

Question: Why?

Answer: Well, as explained above, all the slow manoeuvring and delayed piece development in this line is often justified all the while the position remains closed, but if it opens up, the lack of development can prove fatal. Black therefore usually has to be very careful not to allow the game to open up too quickly, and ...c7-c5 tends to do that; hence, this central pawn break has to be delayed.

Question: So why does Ivanchuk play it here?

Answer: He judges that, in this position, his development lag is not so great, and so he can afford to commence pressure against the white centre. It is the need for such careful and precise judgements that makes these slow ...b6/♕d7 systems so hard to handle as Black.

13 c3 ♘c6 14 0-0 ♕c7

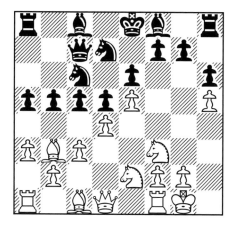

Question: How is this position?

Answer: I think White is objectively somewhat better. As usual in this line, he has more space, and I see nothing special on the black side to compensate for this. However, in the further course of the game, Kasparov is outplayed completely, and loses one of his worst-ever white games.

15 ♖e1

15 ♘h2, intending f4-f5, was Tischbierek's suggestion, but the following line shows that this plan is not so easy to carry out: 15...♗a6 16 f4?! b4 (threatening 17...♗xe2, winning the d4-pawn) 17 ♗e3 bxc3 18 bxc3 ♖b8 19 ♗c2 ♗e7 20 f5 cxd4 21 cxd4 ♗g5! and White has some problems. This is a typical example of how difficult it can be to exploit White's space advantage in these lines.

15...c4 16 ♗c2 ♘b6 17 ♗f4 ♗e7 18 ♗g3 ♖b8

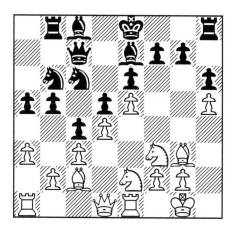

Question: This is all a bit obscure!

Answer: Black is scratching around for something to do. Castling short is clearly out of the question (just ♗b1 and ♕c2 would then be very strong), and it is just not clear what he should do. He therefore manoeuvres around, waiting for White to reveal his plans.

19 ♘h2 ♕d8 20 ♘g4

20 ♘f4 intending ♕g4, looks better.

20...b4 21 axb4 axb4 22 cxb4?!

This looks strange. 22 f4 seems more logical.

22...♘xb4 23 ♗b1 ♗d7 24 b3?

Scratching a spot usually makes things worse. He should leave the queenside alone.

24...♖a8 25 ♖xa8 ♕xa8 26 bxc4 ♘xc4

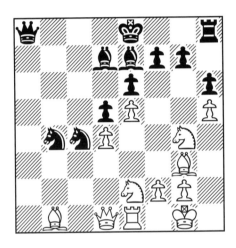

27 ♘c1?

Completing a miserable collapse. 27 ♗f4 is better, but by now Black has an obvious advantage anyway.

27...♗a4 28 ♕e2 ♕a7!

Amazingly, White simply cannot defend the d4-pawn.

29 ♘e3 ♕xd4 30 ♘xc4 dxc4 31 ♕f1 0-0 0-1

Kasparov had had enough. A shockingly bad game by the 13th World Champion, but one which points up some of the characteristics of this line. Although objectively White reaches a middlegame where he must be better (he just has more space for no compensation), it can be extremely hard to get to grips with the rather slippery black position. Some white players seem to find such positions very hard to play.

Thus far, we have seen Black having all the fun, but lest you get the feeling that it is "Black to play and win" in these lines, here is a more impressive treatment by White: 5 ♗d2. This modest move is probably one of White's best choices.

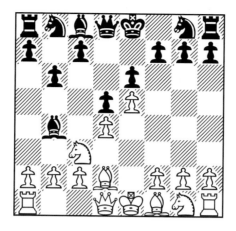

Question: It looks innocuous. What is the point?

Answer: The move does several things. Firstly, it prevents the pawns being doubled after a subsequent ...♗xc3+. Secondly, it sets up the possibility of ♘ce2, offering the exchange of dark-squared bishops. In general, in this line, White's queen's bishop is his inferior bishop, since the white centre pawns are fixed on dark squares, so an exchange of these bishops should suit him. Once Black has played ...♘e7, for example, the reply ♘ce2 may well force the exchange. Finally, 5 ♗d2 avoids a premature commitment of the white queen on the kingside, and waits for Black to commit himself.

Play may continue: 5...b6 6 ♗b5! (we saw this idea in Kasparov-Ivanchuk, White avoids the exchange of light-squared bishops) 6...c6 7 ♗a4 a5 8 a3 ♗f8 9 ♘ce2 ♗a6 10 c3 ♘e7 11 ♘f3 ♘f5 12 0-0 ♗e7 13 ♖e1 ♗xe2 (else the knight will come to f4, leaving the enemy queen's bishop patrolling an empty diagonal) 14 ♕xe2 ♘a6 15 ♗c2 ♘c7.

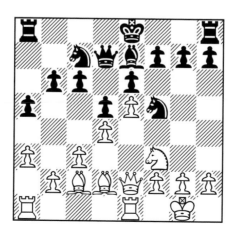

Thus far, we have been following the game J.Nunn-R.Hübner, Brussels 1986.

Question: And what is the assessment? Black looks to be fine.

Answer: In fact, Nunn assesses the position as "extremely unpleasant for Black". He may appear okay on the surface, but he has no real counterplay, and his king has no safe place to hide. Black's only active piece is the knight on f5, and this can always be driven away by g4. Nunn quickly built up a winning advantage, although a blunder eventually cost him half a point.

Finally we return to Chistiakov-Petrosian, and 5 ♕g4:

5...♗f8

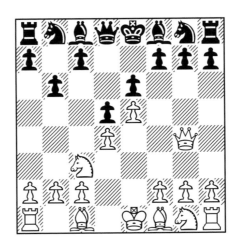

Once again, this undeveloping move. As we have already said, Black takes the view that the bishop has done its job on b4, by provoking the white e-pawn to advance to e5, and now he retains the bishop, covering his dark squares. In this position, he also asks the white queen what she is now doing on g4 – as we will see, the queen often proves a target here, for the onrushing black pawns.

6 ♘f3 ♕d7 7 a3 ♘c6

Once again, there was nothing particularly wrong with 7...♗a6, to exchange off the bad bishop, but as in the game against Olafsson, Petrosian prefers a more complicated approach, keeping pieces on. As we will see, a glorious future awaits the supposedly 'bad bishop'.

8 ♗e3 ♗b7 9 ♗b5?!

Question: Why do you mark this as dubious?
I thought this was a standard idea in this line?

Answer: It is a standard idea if Black is trying to exchange bishops by ...♗a6, but here, Black has already committed himself against that plan. As Clarke notes, White has no way of reinforcing the pin, so 9 ♗d3 would be simpler.

9...0-0-0 10 0-0 ♘ge7

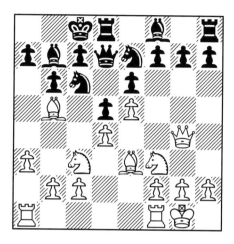

11 b4?!

Question: This looks sensible, trying to attack on
the queenside. What is wrong with it?

Answer: The problem is that, as Steinitz and Lasker pointed out, one should only attack when one has an advantage that justifies doing so. Here, despite his extra space, White actually has to be careful, because his queen is misplaced and will soon come under attack from the black forces on the kingside. Clarke recommends 11 ♘d2 ♘f5 12 ♕e2.

11...f6!

Black starts his attack on the enemy centre. Now the knight on f3 is tied to defending e5, so White cannot get his queen back from the kingside.

12 ♖fe1

12 exf6 looks crackers, and I am not surprised that Chistiakov did not play it, but it may be the best try. After 12...gxf6 13 ♗d3 *Fritz* actually assesses the position as slightly better for White, but I do not believe this. One thing readers should note about these ...b6 systems is that computer programs (much like many human players of the white pieces!) tend to overrate the white position, because of the space advantage. In this instance, the open g-file will surely come back to haunt White, in the medium term.

12...♘f5 13 ♕h3 h5 14 g3

14 g4? fails to 14...hxg4 15 ♕xh8 ♗xb4 winning.

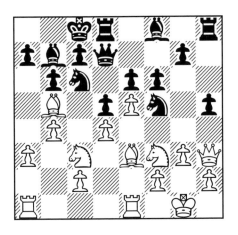

14...a6 15 ♗a4?

The bishop has no future on b3. Both 15 ♗d3 ♘xe3 (15...g5 is also good) 16 fxe3 (16 ♖xe3 g5!) 16...fxe5, and 15 ♗xc6 ♕xc6 16 ♗d2, as given by Clarke, are somewhat better, but still pretty awful for White.

15...g5! 16 g4

Forced, else 16...g4 will win the d4-pawn and demolish the white position, but now the white monarch's residence suffers serious structural damage.

16...hxg4! 17 ♕xh8 gxf3! 18 ♕h5

18...♗xb4 is a big threat, of course, and 18 ♗xc6 ♕xc6 19 ♕xf6 ♗e7 20 ♕g6 and now the simple prophylactic move 20...♔b8! (Clarke) ensures that e6 will not fall with check, and so 21 ♘d1 ♕xc2 is curtains: 22 ♕xe6 ♕e4.

18...b5 19 ♘xb5

Desperation, since the bishop is dead wood on b3.

19...axb5 20 ♗xb5 fxe5 21 ♔h1 ♕g7

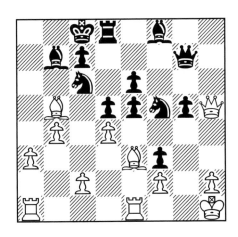

22 ♗xc6

The only way to hold his centre together, but now the 'bad' bishop will rule the light squares.

22...♗xc6 23 dxe5 ♗e7

23...d4 24 ♗xg5 ♗e7 is also winning easily, but Petrosian does not even give White the g5-pawn!

24 b5 ♗b7!

The b5-pawn, on the hand, he scorns – the queen's bishop belongs on the long diagonal.

25 ♕g4 ♖h8

The rest is a horror show.

26 ♕g1 d4 27 ♗d2 g4 28 ♗f4

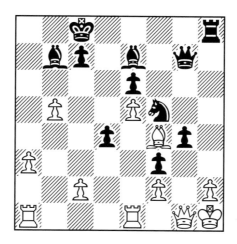

28...g3!

Forcing mate.

29 ♗xg3 ♘xg3+ 0-1

30 ♕xg3 ♕xg3 31 fxg3 f2+ is a finish to warm the heart of any French Defence player.

> **Question:** That was wonderfully impressive!
> These ...b6 systems look highly attractive.

Answer: Well, as I hope I have made clear, I would urge caution on the part of Black. When the systems go well, they look fantastically impressive – one gets the idea that Black can just shut his eyes, play all these moves like ...b6, ...♕d7, ...♗b7/a6, ...♘c6, ...0-0-0, etc, and practically win by force. Needless to say, it is not so easy. At the start of this section, I quoted Lev Psakhis' words about his own terrible results in these lines. Another grandmaster who has written of a similar experience is Hans Ree. He tells of how he was blown away by games such as the above, and took up the ...b6 systems himself as Black, yet found them incredibly hard to handle, and scored badly. There is a very fine line between solidity and passivity, and it often takes a Petrosian to tell the difference. There really are not many Petrosians around, believe me!

Question: So are you saying "don't touch these lines as Black?"

Answer: No, I am not saying that. If you like the positions, then give them a try, by all means. As we have seen, many white players also find them difficult to play against, and you may achieve good results. If you play them and like them, that is great, but I would urge you not to assume they are as good as Petrosian made them look. The Nunn-Hübner game, quoted in the notes above, is much more typical of the negative side.

Question: Any final advice?

Answer: Yes. If you do decide to investigate these lines further, then get hold of a copy of the book *French Winawer: Modern and Auxiliary Lines*, by Moles and Wicker. It is a wonderful treatment of these systems, and the only decent one I know of. Although published in 1979, which makes it positively prehistoric for an opening book, that matters little in this case, because the nature of these ...b6 systems means that concrete theory plays a small role – it is ideas, rather than forcing lines, which dominate.

R.Fischer-V.Kovacevic
Rovinj/Zagreb 1970

1 e4 e6 2 d4 d5 3 ♘c3 ♗b4 4 a3

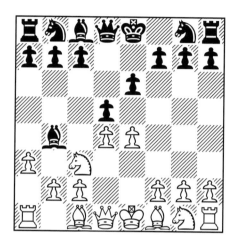

Question: What is this? White is sacrificing a pawn?

Answer: Well, yes and no. In fact, as we will see, White can regain the pawn by force. What he is doing is trying to bring about a more open game than usually occurs after 4 e5. He forces the exchange of bishop for knight, thereby gaining his traditional Winawer birth-right of the bishop-pair and unopposed dark-square bishop, but without closing the centre. He thereby hopes that he will be able to make more effective use of the bishops.

Question: Does this get played much nowadays?

Answer: No. In recent years, it has lost popularity, but in the past, it was played regularly by Alekhine, Smyslov and Fischer, so it must be respected. It is one of the sharpest replies to the Winawer, and the black player needs to be well armed against it.

4...♗xc3+ 5 bxc3

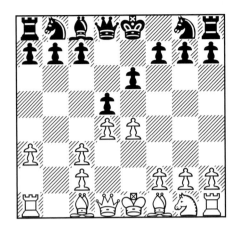

5...dxe4

Answer: Not forced exactly, but no other move really makes much sense, in my opinion. 5...♘e7, for example, hopes to transpose into the main line, if White plays a rapid e4-e5, but he has no reason to do so. After 6 ♗d3 c5 7 exd5 exd5 8 dxc5, Psakhis claims that Black is not really equalizing, and I agree. The two bishops are likely to be strong in such an open position.

6 ♕g4

This is the point of White's fourth move., With the aid of this typical anti-Winawer queen raid, White regains his sacrificed pawn.

In recent years, especially at amateur level, the move 6 f3 has achieved a degree of popularity.

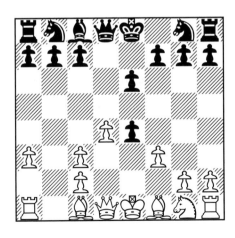

White makes it a real gambit, along the lines of the Blackmar-Diemer Gambit (1 d4 d5 2 e4 dxe4 3 ♘c3 ♘f6 4 f3).

Question: What do you think of the line?

Answer: To be brutally honest, I think it is what is sometimes euphemistically called "a consignment of geriatric shoemakers"! Unlike the Blackmar-Diemer, here White is not even threatening to capture on e4 (because of the reply ...♕h4+), so Black has a wide choice. 6...c5 looks the most logical, but John Watson's 6...♘d7 is also good. White has nothing for his pawn, in my opinion.

6...♘f6 7 ♕xg7 ♖g8 8 ♕h6

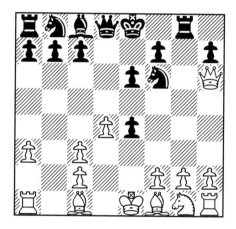

This is the *tabiya* for the variation.

Question: So what is going on?

Answer: White has regained material equality, and has his two bishops, with the dark-squared bishop potentially being quite strong. However, he has poor development, and it is also not entirely clear where his king will go. It is unlikely to be safe on the queenside, whilst kingside castling takes a little time, in view of the need to keep the g2-pawn defended. Black has three main moves here, all of which are equally respectable.

8...♘bd7

This is probably the most solid option. Black plans to develop with ...b6, ...♗b7, ...♕e7 and ...0-0-0.

8...♖g6 immediately forces the white queen to determine her position, and prevents the pin on the knight after ♗g5. However, in view of the fact that the queen often finds herself somewhat stranded on h6, it is arguably not so logical to force her back to a central post so early. 9 ♕e3 (9 ♕d2 is a major alternative: for example, 9...b6 10 ♗b2 ♗b7 11 0-0-0 ♕e7 12 c4 ♘bd7 13 ♘e2 0-0-0 J.Dukhin-M.Ustinov, Rybinsk 2001, as quoted by Watson; Black is fully developed and stands well) 9...♘c6 10 ♗b2 ♕d6?! (10...b6) 11 f3 exf3 12 ♘xf3 was another Fischer game, played just two rounds before the main game, in the same tournament. It is worth seeing, as it shows how dangerous White's dark-squared play can be in this line, if he gets going: 12...♗d7 13 0-0-0 0-0-0 14 c4 ♘g4?! 15 ♕d2 f5?.

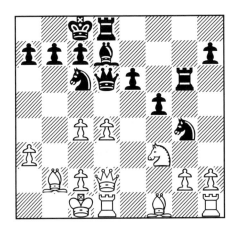

This weakens the dark squares even further. R.Fischer-W.Uhlmann, Zagreb 1970, concluded: 16 d5! ♘b8 17 h3 ♘f6 18 ♘e5 ♘e4 19 ♕d4 ♖g3 20 ♘f7 ♕f4+ 21 ♔b1 c5 22 ♕e5 ♕xe5 23 ♗xe5 ♖dg8 24 ♗d3 (Fischer begrudges giving his wonderful dark-squared bishop for the rook!) 24...♖xg2 25 ♗xe4 fxe4 26 ♘d6+ ♔c7 27 ♘xe4+ ♔b6 28 ♘f6 ♗a4 29 ♘xg8 ♗xc2+ 30 ♔c1 ♘d7 31 ♖dg1 1-0. A powerful display by Fischer, and an example of what Black must be wary of in this variation.

Instead, 8...c5 9 ♘e2 ♗d7 (9...♘bd7 transposes to the note to Black's 9th, below) is an interesting line, recommended by John Watson in his latest French volume. Funnily enough, I saw it recommended by Andrew Martin in a small pamphlet on the Winawer some 25 years ago (!), and once used it to good effect myself: 10 ♗g5 ♖g6 11 ♕h4 ♗c6

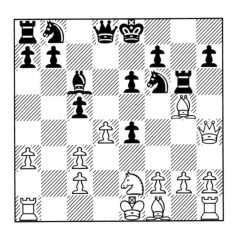

12 ♘f4? (naive, to say the least; critical is 12 d5! exd5 13 ♘f4 ♖xg5 – 13...♕a5? 14 ♗xf6 defends c3, which is the point of White's 12th – 14 ♕xg5 ♘bd7 15 ♗e2 ♕a5 when Black has a pawn for the exchange, and a powerful pawn centre, with chances about equal) 12...♕a5! (refuting White's last; the game continued in amusing fashion) 13 0-0-0? ♕xa3+ 14 ♔b1 ♘d5! (the move White had missed) 15 ♘xd5 ♗xd5 16 c4 e5! and White did not last very long in J.Hickman-S.Giddins, Bradford 1988.

9 ♘e2

Ljubojevic once surprised Korchnoi with 9 ♘h3 and scored a striking victory.

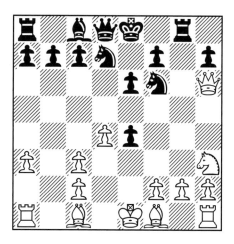

Question: What is the point?

Answer: The move has a couple of points. Firstly, it defends g5, so the bishop will be defended additionally if it comes to that square. Secondly, f2 is defended, which may be important if Black later plays ...♘g4 (a recurring theme in this line, as we will see). Korchnoi's rather bad defeat resulted in the move becoming quite popular for a while, but it seems that objectively, Black is fine:

a) Korchnoi chose 9...c5 10 ♗e2 ♕a5 11 ♗d2! ♖xg2? (Ftacnik's 11...cxd4 12 cxd4 ♕f5 is probably still fine for Black, who follows up with ...b6 and ...♗b7) but after 12 ♘g5! (revealing another point of 9 ♘h3 – sometimes, the knight can jump to this square, rather than the bishop; the rook on g2 is now in trouble) 12...cxd4 13 ♕g7! ♖xg5 14 ♕xg5 ♕xg5 15 ♗xg5 he was just worse and went on to lose in L.Ljubojevic-V.Korchnoi, Tilburg 1986.

b) 9...b6 (sticking to the standard plan) 10 ♗e2 (10 ♘g5 is more active: for example, 10...♖g6 11 ♕h4 ♗b7 12 ♘xh7 ♘xh7 13 ♕xh7 ♕f6 with an unclear position; White has won a pawn, but still lags in development, and will have to lose further time with his queen) 10...♗b7 11 0-0 ♕e7 led to an impressive black win in G.Lane-J.Tisdall, Gausdal 1987: 12 a4 0-0-0 13 ♗a3 c5 14 ♕h4 ♕d6 15 ♖fd1 e3 16 f3

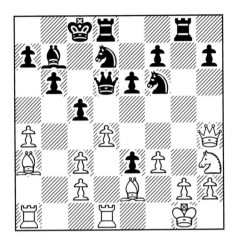

16...♖xg2+! 17 ♔xg2 ♖g8+ 18 ♘g5 (18 ♔h1 ♘g4 wins) 18...h6 19 ♖g1? (19 dxc5 was essential, when 19...hxg5 20 cxd6 gxh4+ 21 ♔f1 ♘e5 is unclear, according to the computer) 19...hxg5 20 ♕g3 ♕d5 21 ♔f1 ♘h5 22 ♕g2 ♘f4 23 ♕g3 ♘xe2 24 ♔xe2 ♕c4+ 0-1.

9...b6

9...c5 is also worth considering, and has been the choice of several very strong GMs in recent years.

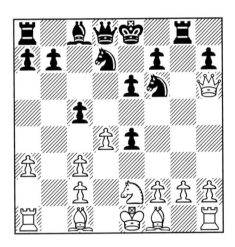

Now:

a) 10 a4 ♕c7 (10...b6 11 a5 ♗b7 12 dxc5 bxc5 13 ♘g3 ♘g4 14 ♕f4 ♕f6 with equality, was an old game M.Basman-R.Vaganian, Hastings 1974/75, but it seems a little odd to give the white a-pawn a target like this) 11 dxc5!? ♕xc5 12 ♕d2 ♘b6 13 a5?! (13 ♕d4 ♕xd4 14 cxd4 ♗d7 is equal) 13...♘bd5 with an unclear position, where Black's active pieces and superior pawn structure at least compensate for his dark-square weaknesses, D.Andreikin-N.Vitiugov, Saratov 2011.

b) 10 h3 is an important option.

Question: What is the point?

Answer: White stops the knight raid ...♘g4, and also prepares an extended fianchetto of his king's bishop with g4 and ♗g2. 10...♕a5 11 ♗d2 b6 (11...♕a4 was a later Ponomariov choice: 12 ♘g3 b6 13 dxc5?! bxc5 – 13...♖g6 14 ♕h4 ♘xc5 looks strong – 14 ♗e2 ♗a6 15 0-0 ♖g6 16 ♕h4 ♗xe2 17 ♘xe2 ♕xc2 and Black was doing very well in I.Nepomniachtchi-R.Ponomariov, Moscow (blitz) 2010) 12 c4 ♕a4 13 ♘c3 ♕xc2 14 ♘b5 cxd4 15 ♗b4 was B.Jobava-R.Ponomariov, Warsaw (blitz) 2010.

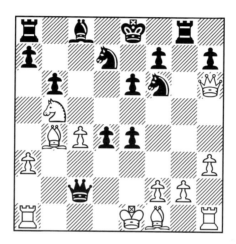

Now the computer's 15...a5! looks better for Black, the point being 16 ♘d6+? ♔e7! 17 ♘xc8+ ♔d8 when Black has a winning advantage.

c) Psakhis quotes one of his own games, K.Georgiev-L.Psakhis, Sarajevo 1986, which continued 10 g3 b6 11 ♗g2 ♗b7 12 0-0 ♕e7 13 a4 ♘g4! 14 ♕f4 f5, and concludes that "the opening has ended quite pleasantly for Black".

10 ♗g5 ♕e7

This move conceals several points. As well as preparing ...♗b7 and ...0-0-0, it also prevents White from castling long, and sets a tactical trap.

11 ♕h4

11 ♘g3? would walk into the trap: 11...♘g4! 12 ♗xe7 ♘xh6 and the bishop on e7 is trapped: 13 ♗h4 (or 13 ♗b4 a5) 13...♖g4.

11...♗b7

Black develops according to the now familiar plan. He intends long castling.

12 ♘g3

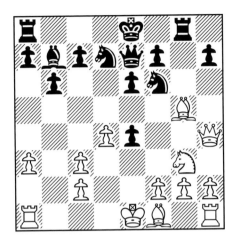

12...h6!

White was threatening 13 ♘h5.

13 ♗d2

Answer: Taking with the queen is impossible, because of 13 ♕xh6?? ♘g4! (this tactic is a recurring theme in this line) 14 ♗xe7 ♘xh6 and the white bishop on e7 is again trapped: 15 ♗h4 (if 15 ♗b4 a5) 15...♖g4. He can take the other way, but after 13 ♗xh6 ♖g4 14 ♕h3 0-0-0, his queen is rather awkwardly placed. Fischer tries to avoid this, but his move also fails to pose Black any serious problems.

13...0-0-0

Answer: Black has a fine game. He has completed his development, his pawn on e4 is securely defended, and the white queen is somewhat vulnerable on h4. Objectively, the game is no more than equal, as White has certain trumps too (the dark-squared bishop, most notably), but in practice, White's position is probably the more difficult to play.

14 ♗e2 ♘f8!

Underlining the slight vulnerability of the white queen.

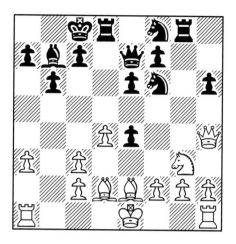

15 0-0!?

15 ♘h5 was suggested by Suetin, and is probably better, although not with Suetin's suggested follow-up: 15...♘8h7?! (15...♘8d7 16 ♘g3 is probably best play) 16 ♗f4 (White should capture on h6) 16...♖xg2 17 ♗e5 ♘d5 (17...♖g5! 18 ♘xf6 ♘xf6 19 ♕xh6 ♖g6 20 ♕h4 ♖dg8 also gives Black a decisive advantage) 18 ♕xe7 ♘xe7 19 ♗g3, which he described as "enlivening White's pieces". However, 19...e3 is just winning for Black: for example, 20 ♖f1 ♘g5 21 fxe3 ♘f5 22 ♗f4 ♘e4.

15...♘g6 16 ♕xh6 ♖h8 17 ♕g5

17 ♕e3 looks more sensible. After 17...♘d5 18 ♕g5 ♘xc3 19 ♗h5 ♕xg5 20 ♗xg5 ♖dg8 the position is unclear/equal. Of course, one must bear in mind that, with the white pieces against a much weaker player, 'equals' was not what Fischer was looking for. It is also alleged that the Soviet players in the tournament (Smyslov, Korchnoi, and Petrosian) had prepared Kovacevic before the game, and even went so far as to feed him moves during it, so Fischer's defeat is perhaps not as shocking as at first it might seem.

17...♖dg8 18 f3!

Setting a nice trap.

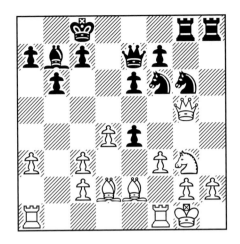

18...e3!!

A brilliant riposte. 18...♘h4 looks strong, but then there follows 19 fxe4!! ♖xg5 20 ♗xg5 and White is at least equal.

19 ♗xe3

19 ♕xe3 is no better after 19...♘d5 20 ♕f2 ♕h4.

19...♘f8 20 ♕b5 ♘d5 21 ♔f2

21 ♗d2 a6! 22 ♕d3 ♕h4 wins.

21...a6 22 ♕d3 ♖xh2

The attack is overwhelming.

23 ♖h1 ♕h4 24 ♖xh2 ♕xh2 25 ♘f1 ♖xg2+ 26 ♔e1 ♕h4+ 27 ♔d2 ♘g6!

The Yugoslav master continues to conduct the attack with great verve.

28 ♖e1 ♘gf4 29 ♗xf4 ♘xf4 30 ♕e3 ♖f2 0-1

Precise to the very end. There is no defence to the threat of 31...♘xe2.

Game 24
A.Stripunsky-Y.Shulman
US Championship 2010

1 e4 e6 2 d4 d5 3 ♘c3 ♗b4 4 ♘ge2

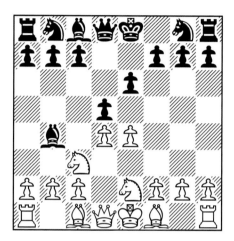

Another of the more popular fourth move alternatives.

Question: It looks a bit clumsy! What is the idea?

Answer: White simply wishes to prevent his pawns being doubled. Given the chance, he will follow up with 5 a3, and force the enemy bishop either to retreat, or to take on c3, in which latter case, White will recapture with the knight. However, it is true that the move is rather clumsy, and clogs up White's development. For that reason, although it has always enjoyed a degree of popularity, especially at amateur level, it does not pose Black any serious problems.

4...dxe4

This is the most natural move, of course, but it could be argued that, to some extent, it plays into White's hands. An alternative approach is to argue that the knight is poorly placed on e2, and that Black should therefore just carry on developing, rather than assisting White in unravelling. After 4...♘f6 (even 4...♘c6 has been tried, with a similar philosophy in mind, but this seems a little extravagant) White has:

a) 5 ♗g5 transposes into a line of the McCutcheon, which is considered harmless, after 5...dxe4 6 a3 ♗e7 7 ♗xf6 ♗xf6 (7...gxf6 is also possible) 8 ♘xe4 0-0, etc.

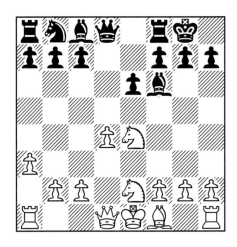

Answer: Indeed, it is quite similar to the line 3 ♘c3 ♘f6 4 ♗g5 dxe4 5 ♘xe4 ♗e7 6 ♗xf6 ♗xf6. In fact, White has gained a tempo over the Burn, since he has played both ♘e2 and a3, whilst Black has only played ...0-0.

Question: Does that mean White has an improved version?

Answer: Not really, because both of White's moves are sub-optimal. His king's knight would much rather be on f3, and the pawn being on a3 rather than a2 is of no real value. Indeed, if White were to castle long, as he usually does against the Burn, it could even be argued that a3 is a weakness, which may make it easier for Black to open lines on the queenside.

b) 5 e5 ♘fd7 has not been played that much over the years, but in recent times, it has been used by GM French experts such as Moskalenko and Rustemov. For example, 6 ♕d3 (6 a3 ♗e7 7 f4 0-0 8 g3 c5 9 ♗e3 ♘c6 10 ♗g2 b6 11 0-0 ♗a6 was comfortable for Black in H.Asis-V.Moskalenko, Montcada 2006) 6...0-0 7 a3 ♗e7 8 ♕g3 ♔h8 9 ♗e3 c5 10 0-0-0 ♘c6 11 f4

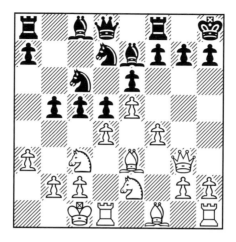

11...b5! 12 ♘xb5 (12 dxc5 b4 13 axb4 ♘xb4 also gave Black a nice initiative in J.De la Riva Aguado-V.Moskalenko, Sitges 2006) 12...♖b8 13 ♘ec3 c4 gave Black very dangerous play in R.Perez-A.Rustemov, Spain 2002.

All in all, 4...♘f6 looks like a perfectly respectable way for Black to play, and also has the merit of avoiding the quite heavily-analysed main lines. Given that 4 ♘e2 is often played by weaker players, this may be an attraction for the higher-rated black player, looking to get his opponent 'out of book'.

5 a3 ♗xc3+

A major crossroads. The text is the critical move, aiming to hang on to the gambit pawn.

5...♗e7 is a safer way to play. Black returns the pawn, but retains the bishop-pair, and again reaches a type of Burn French structure, where the white knight on e2 is less than optimally placed. After 6 ♘xe4 ♘f6 the main line is 7 ♕d3.

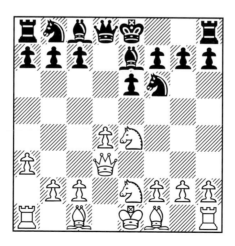

> *Question:* That looks a little strange. What is the point?

Answer: White brings his queen to an aggressive position and prepares long castling. Even so, Black is rock solid, and has no great problems: for example, 7...♘bd7 (7...0-0 8 ♗f4 ♘d5 9 ♗g3 ♘c6 10 c4 f5 11 ♘d2 ♘f6 12 0-0-0 e5 13 d5 f4 14 ♗h4 ♘g4 was unclear and satisfactory for Black in D.Campora-B.Gulko, Oropesa del Mar 1996) 8 ♗f4 0-0 9 0-0-0 b6 10 ♘2c3 ♗b7

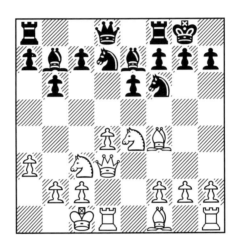

11 ♘xf6+ ♘xf6 12 ♗e2 ♘d5 13 ♘xd5 ♗xd5 14 ♗f3 ♗g5 15 ♕e3 ♗xf4 16 ♕xf4 ♗xf3 ½-½ E.Ghaem Maghami-V.Korchnoi, Port Erin 2004, was another solid treatment by a super-GM. The only issue for Black in this whole 5...♗e7 line is generating winning chances if White does not do anything crazy.

6 ♘xc3 ♘c6

Hanging on to the pawn with the greedy 6...f5? has been discredited ever since the famous miniature A.Alekhine-A.Nimzowitsch, Bled 1931, which saw Black splattered after 7 f3! exf3 8 ♕xf3 ♕xd4? (this is larceny on a grand scale; the computer may claim that Black is objectively okay after 8...♘c6 but it is still hard to recommend this plan to Black in good conscience) 9 ♕g3 ♘f6 10 ♕xg7 ♕e5+ 11 ♗e2 ♖g8 12 ♕h6 ♖g6 13 ♕h4 ♗d7 14 ♗g5 ♗c6

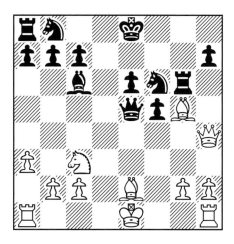

15 0-0-0 ♗xg2 16 ♖he1 ♗e4 17 ♗h5 ♘xh5 18 ♖d8+ ♔f7 19 ♕xh5 1-0.

7 ♗b5

7 ♗e3 is an interesting gambit that was played a number of times by the late Dutch IM, Johan van Mil.

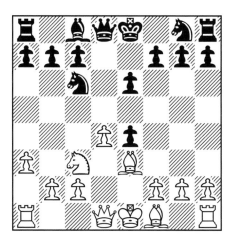

> *Question:* What is the idea?

Answer: White simply develops with ♕d2 and 0-0-0, and keeps his bishop-pair. Johan won some nice games with it, although objectively, 7...♘f6 8 ♕d2 ♘e7! 9 ♗g5 ♘ed5 is fine for Black.

7 d5 is another option. White trades central pawns and regains his sacrificed pawn, with a symmetrical structure, in which he still has the bishop-pair: 7...exd5 8 ♕xd5 ♗e6 9 ♕xe4 (9 ♕xd8+ ♖xd8 is fine for Black, because ...♘d4 will be annoying) 9...♘f6 10 ♕h4.

Even so, he seems to have no objective advantage after 10...♗f5!

7...♘ge7

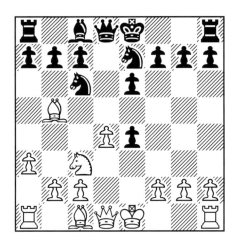

8 ♗e3

Although in the present game, it makes no difference, White usually flicks in 8 ♗g5 here, and only after 8...f6 does he play 9 ♗e3.

> *Question:* Why is that?

Answer: His argument is that Black's position is slightly weakened by the inclusion of the move ...f7-f6. If Black follows up with ...f6-f5, it transposes anyway and makes no difference, but if Black prefers the plan with ...e6-e5 (see the next note), then White hopes the presence of the pawn on f6 will harm Black slightly.

> *Question:* Why doesn't White simply recapture his pawn on e4?

Answer: There is nothing wrong with the move, but it offers no advantage: 8 ♘xe4 0-0 9 c3 e5 and Black is comfortable. The text is more ambitious.

8...0-0 9 ♕d2 f5

9...e5 is a perfectly good, if less ambitious, alternative.

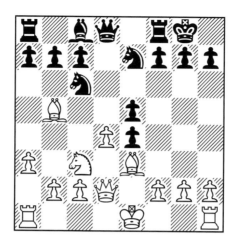

White has:

a) 10 d5 ♘d4! 11 ♗c4 (11 ♗xd4? exd4 12 ♕xd4 c6 13 ♗c4 ♘f5 is better for Black and 14 ♕d2? e3! 15 fxe3 ♕h4+ even wins) 11...♘ef5 12 0-0-0?! (12 ♘xe4 b5 13 ♗a2 ♗b7 is comfortable for Black) 12...♘d6 13 ♗a2 ♘4f5 14 h3 ♘xe3 15 ♕xe3 f5 and Black was simply much better in S.Garcia Martinez-W.Uhlmann, Leipzig 1983.

b) 10 dxe5 ♕xd2+ 11 ♗xd2 ♘xe5 12 ♘xe4 ♗f5 is just equal, despite the white bishop-pair, as he cannot avoid a weakness on e4: 13 f3 (not 13 ♘g3? ♗xc2 14 ♖c1 ♗d3) 13...♗xe4 14 fxe4 a6 15 ♗e2 ♘7c6 with equality, K.Mokry-R.Knaak, Bratislava 1983.

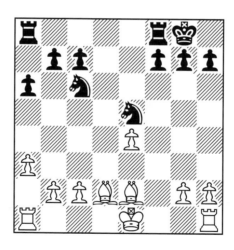

Question: But why doesn't the bishop pair give White the better ending?

Answer: Not only is the e4-pawn weak, but, more importantly still, the black knights have such a great, secure central outpost on e5. Usually, when the bishop-pair outplays knights in the endgame, it is because the knights lack a secure central outpost. When they have one, as here, the knight is not inferior to the bishop.

Even with the move ...f7-f6 included (8 ♗g5 f6 9 ♗e3 0-0 10 ♕d2), 10...e5 is still perfectly good here, and, indeed, it is Watson's first choice for Black in his latest French volume.

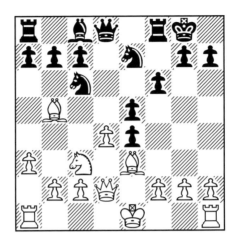

After 11 ♗c4+ (other moves do not really try to exploit the move ...f7-f6 – compare the note to 9...f5 in the main game) 11...♔h8 12 d5 ♘d4 13 0-0-0 ♗g4! 14 ♖de1 c5 15 dxc6 ♘exc6 16 h3 (16 ♘xe4 ♖c8 17 ♔b1 ♘a5 is equal, as given by Watson) 16...♗f5 17 g4 ♗g6 18 ♖d1 ♖c8 White has nothing for the pawn, A.Tukhaev-M.Rodshtein, Herceg Novi 2005.

Going back to the position after 9...f5:

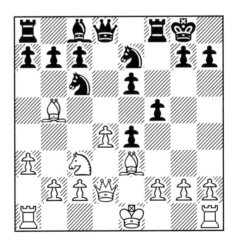

Black decides to keep the gambit pawn, which is the most ambitious continuation.

Question: So isn't Black just a pawn up here?

Answer: White is not entirely without compensation. He has the bishop-pair, with the dark-squared bishop being especially valuable here, given the way the black central pawns are all on light squares. Of course, as Winawer players, we should be used to seeing this as Black, but here, the position is more open than usual (there is no fixed e5-d4-c3 vs. e6-d5 pawn chain). White will play f3, trying to open the g-file. With accurate play, Black is fine, but he needs to be careful – one inaccuracy and things can go very wrong for him, as I found to my cost a couple of times when playing the black side.

10 0-0-0

The immediate 10 f3 is also possible. Then 10...exf3 (10...f4 11 ♗xf4 ♕xd4 12 fxe4 e5 13 ♗e3 ♕xd2+ 14 ♗xd2 ♘d4 is a comfortable equalizer, Y.Solodovnichenko-M.Feygin, German League 2003) 11 0-0-0?! is a speculative gambit, which Black can accept or decline: 11...e5 (*Fritz* is having none of it, and assesses 11...fxg2 12 ♕xg2 f4 as "winning for Black" – a little optimistic, perhaps, but he should be much better, even so) 12 ♗c4+ ♔h8 13 d5 ♘d4 is equal, Y.Solodovnichenko-C.Marzolo, Illkirch-Graffenstaden 2004.

10...a6

Widely regarded as best, although 10...♘d5 is also possible, and conceals a very nasty trap.

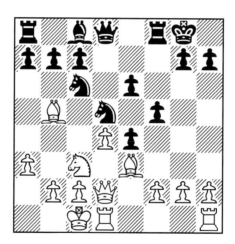

11 ♗g5?? e3 12 ♗xe3 f4 13 ♘xd5 ♕xd5 and Black wins a piece, M.Pavlov-W.Uhlmann, Halle 1981.

> **Question:** That looks great! So why is 10...♘d5 not the main line?

Answer: The trouble is that, after 11 ♘xd5! exd5 12 ♗xc6 bxc6 13 ♗f4 we reach a position, about which Psakhis writes: "although Black may not have much chance of losing, he has absolutely no chance of winning; the difference in strength of the bishops is too great".

11 ♗xc6 ♘xc6

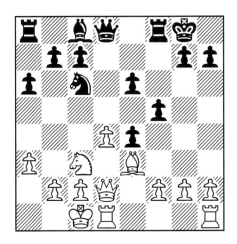

12 f3

12 ♗g5 is the alternative: 12...♕d7 13 d5 ♘e7 (13...exd5 14 ♘xd5 ♕f7 15 ♗f4 ♖d8 16 ♗xc7 ♖d7 was equal in J.Hector-C.Matamoros Franco, Copenhagen 2002; 13...♘e5 also looks perfectly okay for Black) 14 dxe6 ♕xe6 15 f3 h6 16 ♗xe7 ♕xe7 17 fxe4 fxe4 with equality, H.Westerinen-I.Thompson, Gausdal 2006.

12...e5

12...exf3 13 gxf3 e5 is the alternative equalizer: e.g., 14 d5 ♘a5 15 ♕e2 b5 16 f4 exf4 17 ♗xf4 ♗d7 18 ♖hg1 ♖f7 with equality in N.Neelakantan-P.Harikrishna, Kolkata 2000.

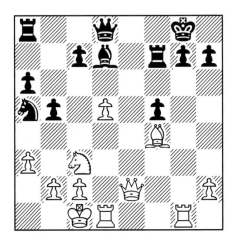

However, it is worth running this on a few moves, to show some of the dangers that can befall Black in these lines, if he is guilty of even a moment's inattention: 19 ♖g3 ♕f6 20 ♖dg1 ♘c4 (20...♖e8!) 21 ♕h5 ♘e5?? 22 ♘e4! (suddenly Black is lost) 22...♘d3+ 23 cxd3 fxe4 24 ♗e5 ♕f5 25 ♕xf7+ ♔xf7 26 ♖xg7+ ♔e8 27 ♖g8+ ♕f8 28 dxe4 and White won.

13 d5

13 dxe5 ♕xd2+ 14 ♗xd2 (14 ♖xd2? f4 15 ♗c5 e3 is much better for Black) 14...exf3 15 gxf3 ♗e6 is a well-known equality, seen many times in practice.

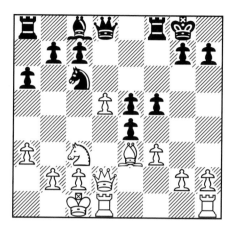

13...♘a5

Another possibility is 13...♘e7 14 ♗g5 h6 15 ♗xe7 ♕xe7 16 fxe4 fxe4 17 ♘xe4 ♗f5, again with equality.

> *Question:* An awful lot of these variations end in equality!

Answer: That is true. This is one drawback of the whole 4...dxe4 and 5...♗xc3+ variation. It is deeply analysed, and many variations fizzle out to a fairly dead equality.

14 ♕e2

14 ♗c5 ♘c4 15 ♕e2 ♘d6 16 fxe4 ♕g5+ 17 ♔b1 f4 also gave Black no problems in G.Hartmann-G.Hertneck, German League 1989.

14...b6 15 fxe4 f4

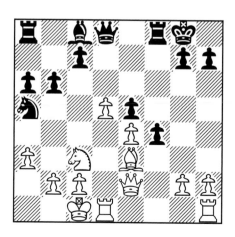

> **Question:** So how should we assess this position?

Answer: It is just balanced. White has regained his pawn, and we have opposite-coloured bishops. However, the fact that so many other pieces are on the board, and the kings are castled on opposite sides, means that, although equal, the position is far from drawn.

16 ♗d2 ♘b7

The knight heads to the natural blockading square d6.

17 ♖df1?!

The start of a plan of breaking up the black kingside pawn chain with g3, but White had obviously missed his opponent's surprise 19th move.

17...♘d6 18 g3 ♗h3 19 ♖f2?

Objectively, the exchange sacrifice 19 gxf4 was better, but White perhaps can be forgiven for missing the next move.

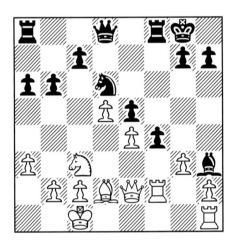

19...♗g2!

Very imaginative! Now Black secures his pawn on f3 and has a clear advantage.

20 ♖e1 f3 21 ♕e3 h6 22 ♘e2 ♕e8 23 ♘g1 ♕h5 24 h3 ♗xh3?!

A strange decision, which squanders most of Black's superiority. He would still have a clear plus after 24...♘c4 25 ♕c3 ♘xd2 26 ♕xd2 ♖f7.

25 ♖xf3?!

25 ♘xh3 ♕xh3 26 ♖xf3 is better.

25...♗g2 26 ♖xf8+ ♖xf8 27 ♗b4 ♕g4 28 ♗xd6 cxd6

Following the mutual lapses at moves 24-25, Black retains a nice advantage. White's pieces are passive and the e4-pawn weak.

29 ♔b1

This loses a pawn, but 29 ♕xb6 ♕xg3 is even worse.

29...♕xe4! 30 ♕xe4 ♗xe4 31 ♖xe4 ♖f1+ 32 ♔a2 ♖xg1 33 ♖b4

Passive play is no better.

33...b5 34 a4 ♖xg3 35 axb5 axb5 36 ♖xb5 h5

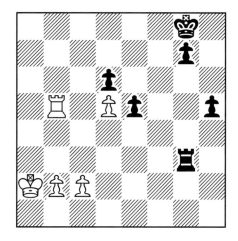

Now Black is winning. His kingside pawns are too many and too fast.

37 ♖b8+ ♔h7 38 b4 h4 39 ♖f8 h3 40 ♖f1 e4 41 b5 ♖f3 42 ♖g1 e3 43 b6 e2 44 ♖e1 h2 45 ♖h1 ♔g6 0-1

1 e4 e6 2 d4 d5 3 ♘c3 ♗b4 4 ♗d2

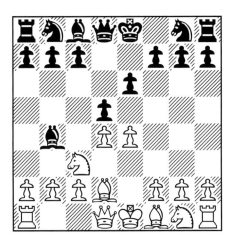

Question: Doesn't this lose a pawn?

Answer: Well, once again, it is a sharp attempt by White to obtain a more open position than would arise after 4 e5. The move involves a pawn sacrifice that is at least temporary, and may become permanent.

Question: Is the move any good?

Answer: Objectively, probably not. It has never achieved the level of popularity amongst GMs that 4 a3 has enjoyed, for example. The main problem here is that White ends up losing his d-pawn.

This is probably a convenient place to round up White's other fourth moves, that we have not already covered:

a) 4 ♕g4 is the most direct way to implement the traditional ♕g4 idea. However, without any preliminary supporting of the white centre, it comes up short after 4...♘f6 5 ♕xg7 ♖g8 6 ♕h6 ♖g6 (Watson suggests that the immediate 6...c5! is even better: for example, 7 e5 cxd4 8 a3 ♗f8 9 ♕xf6 ♕xf6 10 exf6 dxc3 11 bxc3 ♘d7 and Black has the superior structure, with no attendant compensation for White) 7 ♕e3 c5!.

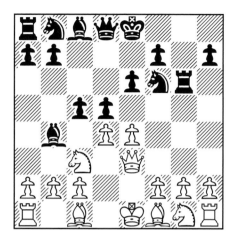

This vigorous attack on the centre is best, and highlights the fact that White's house is built on sand, rather than rock. 8 ♗d2 ♘g4 9 ♕d3 ♘c6 with enormous pressure against the white centre.

b) Even 4 ♕d3 has been played here!

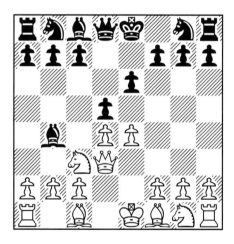

> *Question:* That looks pretty beginner-like!

Answer: It is a rather odd move, to say the least. The main idea is that 4...dxe4 5 ♕xe4 ♘f6 6 ♕h4 may see the white queen in an aggressive position. Even here, Black should have no real problems, but it seems illogical to play into White's hands like this. Instead, 4...♘e7 is a simple developing move, which asks White how he intends to develop his pieces. Typical play then is 5 ♗d2 b6, when a top-level encounter V.Anand-N.Short, Wijk aan Zee 1990 saw Black with no problems after 6 ♗e2 (6 ♕g3!? is proposed by Psakhis) 6...0-0 7 a3 ♗xc3 8

♗xc3 a5 9 ♘f3 ♘d7 10 exd5 exd5.

   c) 4 exd5 exd5 is a sub-line of the Exchange Variation.

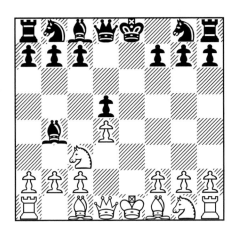

Question: Isn't this just very drawish?

Answer: That is its reputation, but it is not entirely deserved. Plenty of practice has shown that both sides can make something of the position, if they are determined to do so. Indeed, Magnus Carlsen recently used the line successfully as White, and commented afterwards that he believes it should be possible to fight for a small advantage, even here.

   White has:

   c1) Larsen's old move 5 ♕f3 has long been known to be well met by 5...♕e7+!.

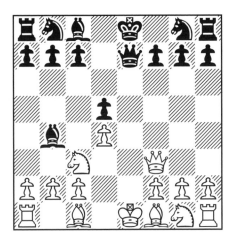

Question: Why is this good? It looks a bit odd.

Answer: The problem for White is that he has no good way to parry the check. Whichever minor piece he puts on e2 will block in the other minor piece, whilst 6 ♗e3 also has its problems, as we will see: 6 ♘ge2 (6 ♗e3?! leads to problems after 6...♘f6 7 ♗d3 c5!) 6...♘c6 7 ♗e3 ♘f6 and White's pieces are awkwardly placed and vulnerable to moves such as ...♗g4, and ...♘g4.

c2) 5 ♗d3 with a further divide:

c21) 5...♘c6 (Black of course has a very wide choice of how to develop here, but the text is probably the main line) 6 a3 is the nearest thing to a critical line in this variation. White keeps open a path for his queen to emerge on the kingside. It should not be underestimated by the black player, as White can often create a dangerous initiative, in the face of inaccurate black play. By contrast, the old 6 ♘ge2 offers less than nothing: 6...♘ge7 7 0-0 ♗g4 (it is useful to provoke the weakening f3, before exchanging bishops) 8 f3 ♗f5 with equality.

After 6...♗xc3+ (6...♗e7 is a solid treatment, but the text is more normal) 7 bxc3...

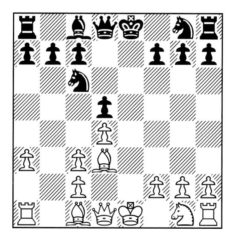

...now 7...♘ge7 is the most common, but Black has several alternatives:

c211) 7...♕f6 anticipates the white queen's emergence, as well as preparing ...♗f5, to exchange light-squared bishops: 8 ♘e2 (8 ♖b1 ♘ge7 9 ♕f3 ♕xf3 10 ♘xf3 f6 11 0-0 b6 12 ♖e1 ♔d8 13 ♖e2 ♗f5 was equal in A.Domont-M.Ulibin, Biel 2007) 8...♗g4 9 h3 ♗h5 10 0-0 ♘ge7 11 ♕d2 ♗g6 12 ♘f4 ♗xd3 13 ♘xd3 0-0-0 14 a4 ♘a5 and Black again had no real problems, eventually winning a long game, A.Vuilleumier-M.Apicella, Lausanne 2006.

c212) 7...♘ce7 is a favourite of the veteran Hungarian GM and French expert, Ivan Farago.

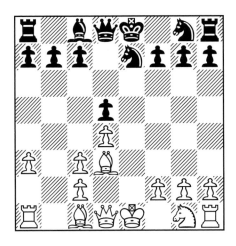

Question: What is the idea?

Answer: Black admits that his queen's knight is not ideal on c6, and re-routes it to the king-side. He intends ...♘f6 and ...♗f5. Another point is that, by keeping the king's knight ready to jump to f6, he deprives White of the move ♕h5. Play may go 8 ♕f3 (8 ♘f3 ♗g4 9 ♖b1 b6 10 0-0 ♘f6 11 ♖e1 0-0 12 ♗g5 ♕d6 with a small edge for White was C.Varga-I.Farago, Zala-karos 2008) 8...♘f6 9 ♗g5 ♘e4.

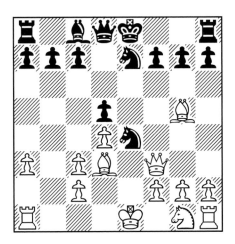

Question: Eh? Doesn't this lose a pawn?

Answer: It sacrifices one, yes. In compensation, Black exchanges off White's good bishop and reaches a position with opposite-coloured bishops, and the better pawn structure.

Farago has played this several times, so he clearly believes in it: 10 ♗xe4 dxe4 11 ♕xe4 f6 12 ♗f4 (12 ♗e3 0-0 13 ♘e2 c6 14 ♕d3 ♗f5 15 ♕d2 ♗e6 16 0-0 ♗c4 offered similar compensation in I.Jakic-I.Farago, Bibinje 2006, where Black eventually won) 12...0-0 13 ♘e2 ♖e8 14 ♗e3 ♘d5 15 ♕d3 ♕e7 16 0-0 ♘xe3 17 fxe3 ♕xe3+ 18 ♕xe3 ♖xe3 with equality, but again, Black went on to win against a lower-rated opponent in M.Pacher-I.Farago, Austrian League 2008.

c213) 7...♘ge7 8 ♕h5!? reveals the main point of White's play here. He takes advantage of the fact that Black has committed his knight to e7, to occupy a strong square with his queen, and prevent the exchanging manoeuvre ...♗f5. Black has to be a little careful here, although he can equalize if he is: 8...♗e6 9 ♘f3 ♕d7 10 ♘g5 0-0-0 11 ♘xe6 (11 ♘xf7?? ♕e8) 11...♕xe6+ 12 ♗e3 g6 13 ♕f3 ♘f5 is equal.

c22) There is nothing at all wrong with 5...♘f6: for example, 6 ♘ge2 ♗g4 7 0-0 0-0 8 f3 ♗h5 9 ♘f4 ♗g6 10 ♘xg6 hxg6 11 ♘e2 ♖e8 12 ♗g5 ♗e7 13 ♘g3 ♘bd7 14 f4 ♘h7 15 ♕f3 c6 with equality, M.Carlsen-F.Vallejo Pons, Bilbao 2012.

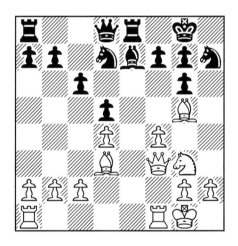

Now Magnus got a bit ambitious with 16 h4?! and would have been struggling after 16...♕b6!.

c23) 5...c6 is another solid option: for instance, 6 ♕f3 and now 6...♕f6 (6...♘f6 keeps more tension) is a rock-solid approach, which been played twice by Ivanchuk: 7 ♗f4 (7 ♕xf6 ♘xf6 8 ♘ge2 ♘bd7 9 a3 ♗e7 10 f3 h5 11 h4 ♘f8 12 ♘f4 ♗d7 13 ♔f2 0-0-0 led to a quick draw in E.Alekseev-V.Ivanchuk, Biel 2009) 7...♘e7 8 ♕g3 ♘d7 9 ♘ge2 0-0 10 0-0-0 ♘g6 11 ♗g5 ♕d6 12 ♕xd6 ♗xd6 with dead equality in J.Moreno Carnero-V.Ivanchuk, Calvia Olympiad 2004.

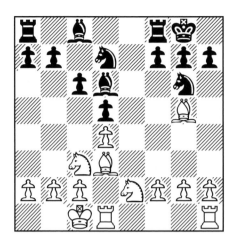

> ***Question:*** But how does Black win such a position?

Answer: By playing on! Ivanchuk went on to win this game, for example, despite playing an opponent rated over 2500. Even such symmetrical positions can be won, if the player is sufficiently determined and does not just give his opponent a draw.

Returning to 4 ♗d2:

4...dxe4

This is probably the best move, but it is quite heavily analysed, and players seeking fresher pastures might like to look at 4...♘c6.

> ***Question:*** What is the point?

Answer: Black continues developing, and also attacks the white d-pawn, which is quite hard to defend, with the bishop stuck on d2:

a) My only experience of this line was a highly enjoyable one, albeit against some rather feeble white play: 5 ♗b5?! ♘ge7 6 e5 ♗d7 7 ♕g4?! ♘f5 8 ♗xc6 ♗xc6 9 ♘f3 ♗e7! 10 0-0? h5 11 ♕f4 ♖g8 12 h3 g5 13 ♕h2 g4 14 hxg4 hxg4 15 ♕h7

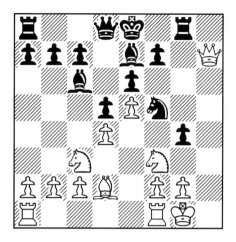

and now 15...♗d7! and White did not last much longer.

b) 5 ♕g4 has also been tried: 5...♘f6 6 ♕xg7 ♖g8 7 ♕h6 ♖g6 8 ♕e3 and now 8...♘g4! (Watson) looks fine (at least) for Black.

c) 5 a3 ♗xc3 6 ♗xc3 ♘f6 7 e5 ♘e4 8 ♗d3 ♘xc3 9 bxc3 ♕e7 and Black went queenside, with a perfectly good position in L.Ljubojevic-U.Andersson, Palma de Mallorca 1971.

5 ♕g4

This standard queen raid on the black kingside is the point of White's play. 5 ♘xe4? basically just loses a pawn after 5...♕xd4. Admittedly, Alekhine did go on to beat no less a player than Salo Flohr from this position, after 6 ♗d3 ♗xd2+ 7 ♕xd2 ♕d8 (A.Alekhine-S.Flohr, Nottingham 1936), but in his tournament book, he admitted that his fifth move had been a *"lapsus manus"* and that he had intended 5 ♕g4.

5...♘f6 6 ♕xg7 ♖g8 7 ♕h6

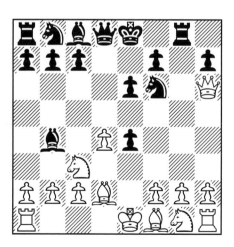

7...♕xd4

Grabbing the second pawn is the most logical, and probably objectively best.

Answer: Yes, 7...♖g6 being the principal one. John Watson analyses this in some detail in *Play the French 3*, and it is a valid way to play, but taking on d4 strikes me as a simpler and stronger solution.

8 0-0-0

Answer: Neither your eyes nor your arithmetic can be faulted!

Answer: Just as with the 4 a3 lines, he has broken up the black kingside by taking on g7, and he also has hopes that the black queen will prove exposed on d4. However, there are two crucial differences from the 4 a3 line. Firstly, White does not have any central pawn structure on c3 and d4. Secondly, and even more importantly, he has not actually forced the exchange of Black's Winawer bishop, and so his usual hopes of developing serious dark-square compensation are much less realistic here. Furthermore, Black now has a highly unpleasant retort:

8...♗f8!

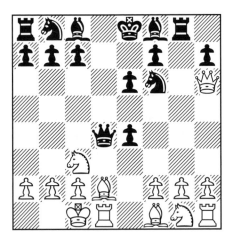

Answer: "*Reculer pour mieux sauter*", as they say down my local. The bishop retreats from an exposed position (avoiding ideas such as ♘b5, for example), and, most importantly, drives the white queen into a rather poor position. With the black queen on d4, her white opposite number is unable to retreat to the centre on e3, and so has to retreat down the h-file, where she is much less well placed. I believe this move was first played by the great David Bronstein, back in 1950.

9 ♕h3?!

This is actually not the best move. The critical line is 9 ♕h4 when play continues 9...♖g4 10 ♕h3.

> **Question:** Why is this better than the game?

Answer: White has lured the black rook to g4, where he hopes it will prove exposed. Now play usually continues 10...♕xf2, nicking another pawn, and also threatening to embarrass the white queen.

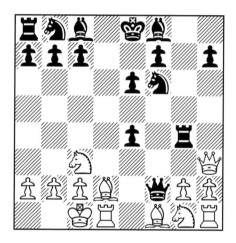

11 ♗e2 (in the stem game, White tried 11 ♘b5?!, but after 11...♘a6 12 ♔b1 ♗d7 13 ♗e3 ♕f5 14 ♘d4 ♕g6 15 ♘b3 ♘b4 Black had two extra pawns and the initiative, I.Boleslasky-D.Bronstein, 14th matchgame, Moscow 1950) 11...♖h4 (11...♖g6 12 g4 ♕c5 is a suggestion of Psakhis, which has only been tried in one or two amateur games, as far as I can see, whilst Watson analyses 11...♕xg2 12 ♗xg4 ♕xg4 13 ♕xg4 ♘xg4 14 ♘xe4 as equal).

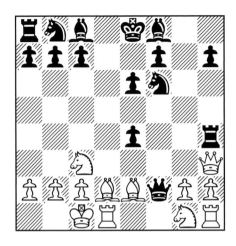

Answer: In this case, appearances are deceptive! White has the clever trick 12 ♕xh4! ♕xh4 13 g3 and, lo and behold, the black queen is trapped!

Answer: Alas, no. His ingenuity only brings him an ending which is at best unclear, and probably a bit worse for him after 13...♕h6! 14 ♗xh6 ♗xh6+ 15 ♔b1.

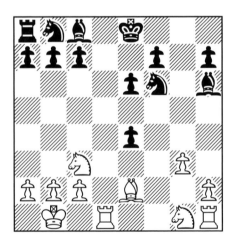

Answer: White has an extra exchange, but Black has two extra pawns and the bishop-pair. His e-pawn(s) are passed, although the e4-pawn may be a tad vulnerable. There have been a lot of practical tests of this position, which suggest that Black probably has the edge, although an assessment of 'unclear' is perhaps the fairest. A recent game, quoted by Watson, continued 15...♘c6 (15...♗d7 is equal) 16 ♘h3 (16 ♘b5 ♔e7 17 ♘xc7 ♖b8 is presumably the idea, when *Fritz* prefers Black after 18 ♘b5 e5) 16...e5 17 ♘f2 ♘d4 and Black was just better in Z.Ivekovic-S.Martinovic, Zagreb 2011.

9...♕xf2

Now Black is simply better, because without the rook on g4, White has far fewer tactical tricks, and cannot develop his kingside rationally.

10 ♘ge2 ♗d7

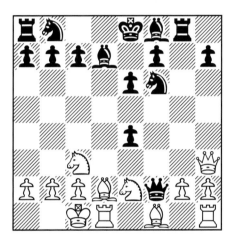

11 g4?!

Question: Wow! That looks a bit crazy!

Answer: It is a sign of desperation. Normal moves are not much better: for example, 11 ♘g3? e3 (11...e5 looks good, but is less convincing after 12 ♘cxe4 ♘xe4 13 ♘xe4 ♗xh3 14 ♘xf2 ♗e6 although even here, Black is just a pawn up) 12 ♗e1 ♕f4 13 ♗d3 (13 ♔b1 e5 traps the queen) 13...♕h6 and after the queens come off, White is two pawns down.

11 ♗e3 is probably objectively best, but White's position is cheerless after 11...♕f5.

11...♖xg4 12 ♘g3 e3 13 ♗e1 ♕f4 14 ♗g2

14 ♗e2 ♖h4 15 ♕f1 ♗c6 is just hopeless, so White tries to fish in troubled tactical waters.

14...♕h6

Fritz's 14...e2+ 15 ♖d2 ♗c6 16 ♗xc6+ ♘xc6 17 ♘gxe2 ♕h6 looks even more convincing.

15 ♕xh6 ♗xh6 16 ♗xb7 ♗c6 17 ♗xa8 ♗xa8

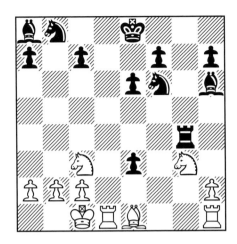

Question: What is happening here?

Answer: The point of Black's play is that he will regain the exchange, thanks to the dual threats of ...♗xh1 and ...e2+. At worst, he will emerge with an extra pawn and what should be a technically winning ending.

18 ♖g1 e2+ 19 ♖d2 ♗e3 20 ♘cxe2 ♘bd7 21 ♖f1 ♗g2 22 ♖f2 ♗d5

Rather an amusing picture! I suspect Black was enjoying himself at this point!

23 ♘c3 c6 24 ♖fe2 ♗xd2+ 25 ♔xd2 h5

After having his bit of fun, Black has finally taken back the exchange, and is a pawn up. The remainder is a technical task, which Black carries out without undue difficulty, and which is not of great interest to our theme, so we will pass through it fairly briefly.

26 b3 ♔f8 27 ♘f1 ♖g1 28 ♘e3 ♗f3 29 ♖f2 ♘e5 30 ♖f1 ♖xf1 31 ♘xf1 ♗g2 32 ♘e3 ♘e4+

It seems rather odd to head for opposite-coloured bishops. 32...♘f3+ 33 ♔e2 ♘xe1 34 ♔xe1 ♗h3 looks simpler.

33 ♘xe4 ♗xe4 34 ♗g3 ♘f3+ 35 ♔e2

35 ♔c3 offers better defensive chances.

35...e5 36 ♘c4 f6 37 ♔e3 ♗d5 38 ♘d6 ♘d4 39 c4 ♗e6

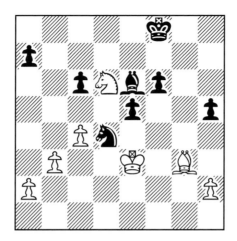

40 ♗f2 ♘f5+ 41 ♘xf5 ♗xf5 42 b4 a6 43 a4 ♗d7

Black's connected passed pawns in the centre should decide things, providing he is careful not to get them blockaded on the wrong colour squares.

44 ♔e4 ♔f7 45 b5 cxb5 46 cxb5 axb5 47 axb5 ♔e6

47...♗xb5 was good enough, but Black prefers to avoid letting the white king in after 48 ♔d5.

48 b6 ♗c6+ 49 ♔e3 f5 50 ♔d3 ♔d5 51 ♗h4 f4 52 ♗d8 e4+ 53 ♔c3 e3 54 ♔d3 ♗b5+ 55 ♔c3 ♗a6 0-1

Index of Variations

Note: Figures refer to page numbers of relevant games.